TEACHING WRITING FOR ACADEMIC PURPOSES TO MULTILINGUAL STUDENTS

Examining what is involved in learning to write for academic purposes from a variety of perspectives, this book focuses in particular on issues related to academic writing instruction in diverse contexts, both geographical and disciplinary. Informed by current theory and research, leading experts in the field explain and illustrate instructional programs, tasks, and activities that help L2/multilingual writers develop knowledge of different genres, disciplinary expectations, and expertise in applying what they have learned in both educational and professional contexts.

John Bitchener is Professor of Applied Linguistics at the Auckland University of Technology, New Zealand.

Neomy Storch is Associate Professor in ESL and Applied Linguistics at the University of Melbourne, Australia.

Rosemary Wette is a senior lecturer in Applied Language Studies at the University of Auckland, New Zealand.

ESL & Applied Linguistics Professional Series

Eli Hinkel, Series Editor

Mann/Walsh	*Reflective Practice in English Language Teaching: Research-Based Principles and Practices*
Pawan/Fan/Miao, Eds.	*Teacher Training and Professional Development of Chinese English Language Teachers: Changing From Fish to Dragon*
Nassaji/Kartchava, Eds.	*Corrective Feedback in Second Language Teaching and Learning: Research, Theory, Applications, Implications*
Bitchener/Storch/Wette, Eds.	*Teaching Writing for Academic Purposes to Multilingual Students: Instructional Approaches*
Macalister/Mirvahedi, Eds.	*Family Language Policies in a Multilingual World: Opportunities, Challenges, and Consequences*
Ortmeier-Hooper/Ruecker	*Linguistically Diverse Immigrant and Resident Writers: Transitions from High School to College*
Johnson/Golombek	*Mindful L2 Teacher Education: A Sociocultural Perspective on Cultivating Teachers' Professional Development*
Hinkel	*Teaching English Grammar to Speakers of Other Languages*
McKay/Brown	*Teaching and Assessing EIL in Local Contexts Around the World*
Dörnyei/Henry/Muir	*Motivational Currents in Language Learning: Frameworks for Focused Interventions*
Jones/Richards, Eds.	*Creativity in Language Teaching: Perspectives from Research and Practice*
Evans/Anderson/Eggington, Eds.	*ESL Readers and Writers in Higher Education: Understanding Challenges, Providing Support*
Hinkel	*Effective Curriculum for Teaching L2 Writing: Principles and Techniques*
Farrell	*Promoting Teacher Reflection in Second-Language Education: A Framework for TESOL Professionals*

Visit **www.routledge.com/education** for additional information on titles in the ESL & Applied Linguistics Professional Series

TEACHING WRITING FOR ACADEMIC PURPOSES TO MULTILINGUAL STUDENTS

Instructional Approaches

Edited by
John Bitchener,
Neomy Storch, and
Rosemary Wette

Routledge
Taylor & Francis Group
NEW YORK AND LONDON

First published 2017
by Routledge
711 Third Avenue, New York, NY 10017

and by Routledge
2 Park Square, Milton Park, Abingdon, Oxon, OX14 4RN

Routledge is an imprint of the Taylor & Francis Group, an informa business

Library of Congress Cataloguing in Publication Data
A catalog record has been requested

ISBN: 978-1-138-28421-0 (hbk)
ISBN: 978-1-138-28423-4 (pbk)
ISBN: 978-1-315-26966-5 (ebk)

Typeset in Bembo
by diacriTech, Chennai

CONTENTS

PART II
Instruction in Specific EAP Knowledge and Skills: Academic Genre-Based Instruction 67

Instructional Tasks and Activities

Approaches to Academic Language Development

CONTRIBUTORS

Dr John Bitchener is a Professor of Applied Linguistics at Auckland University of Technology, Auckland, New Zealand, where he is supervising 12 doctoral candidates and teaching thesis/dissertation writing. His primary research interest is the potential of written corrective feedback for L2 development and he has co-authored books on the subject with Ferris (Routledge, 2012) and with Storch (Multilingual Matters, 2016). He is also well known for his *Writing an Applied Linguistics Thesis or Dissertation: A Guide to Presenting Empirical Research* (Palgrave Macmillan, 2010) and, in July 2017, a new book entitled *A Guide to Supervising Non-Native English Writers of Theses and Dissertations: Focusing on the Writing Process* will be available.

Dr Neomy Storch is an Associate Professor at the School of Languages & Linguistics, the University of Melbourne. She teaches a range of ESL and Applied Linguistics subjects and convenes the ESL program. Her research focuses predominantly on topics related to second language writing, including collaborative writing, feedback on L2 writing, and assessing writing development. She has published extensively on these topics, including a book on collaborative writing (2013) and a co-authored book on corrective feedback with Professor Bitchener (2016). She is a member of the editorial board of the *Journal of Second Language Writing* and *Language Teaching Research*.

Rosemary Wette is a senior lecturer in Applied Language Studies at the University of Auckland. She is involved in courses and supervisions related to the teaching and learning of L2 academic writing, and in second language teacher education. She has published research studies on aspects of academic writing development in the *Journal of Second Language Writing*, *System*, and *ELT Journal*.

Christine Pearson Casanave worked in Japan for 14 years, teaching English content courses to undergraduates at a Japanese university, and issues in L2 writing and qualitative inquiry to MATESOL and doctoral students at two American universities. Now in California, she works online with doctoral students, and writes, publishes, and presents on topics in L2 teacher preparation and dissertation writing, with a special focus on writers and their experiences. She is on the editorial boards of several journals, and is currently the book review co-editor (with Yongyan Li) for *Journal of Second Language Writing*. Her primary work currently consists of advising doctoral students at Temple University's Japan campus who are working on qualitative dissertation projects.

Dana Ferris is a Professor and Associate Director for Second Language Writing in the University Writing Program at the University of California at Davis. An applied linguist by training, she directs a large program for second language readers and writers and teaches courses in writing, grammar, and pedagogy, as well as doctoral seminars on L2 writing and response to student writing. She is the author or co-author of eight books and over 60 journal articles and book chapters, published in both applied linguistics/TESOL and composition/writing venues. Her research has focused on second language writing and writers and on a range of questions related to response to student writing. She was the founding editor-in-chief of the *Journal of Response to Writing* and currently is an associate editor of the *Journal of Second Language Writing.*

Dr Jennifer Hammond is an Honorary Associate Professor in the Faculty of Arts and Social Sciences, University of Technology Sydney. She has taught for many years in the fields of language and literacy education, EAL education, and research design. Her research interests are in literacy development, classroom interaction, and the implications of socio-cultural and systemic theories of language and learning in EAL education. With colleagues, she has completed research into the nature of high challenge, high support pedagogies designed to meet the needs of EAL students, including students of refugee background, in mainstream classes. She has published widely in these areas.

Ken Hyland is a Professor of Applied Linguistics and Director of the Centre for Applied English Studies at the University of Hong Kong. He is best known for his research into writing and academic discourse, having published over 220 articles and 26 books on these topics and received 28,000 citations on Google Scholar. His most recent books are *Teaching and Researching Writing* (Routledge, 2016) and *The Routledge Handbook of EAP* (co-edited with Philip Shaw, 2016). A collection of his work is due soon (*The Essential Hyland*, Bloomsbury, 2017). He is founding co-editor of the *Journal of English for Academic Purposes* and was co-editor of *Applied Linguistics.*

Icy Lee is a professor in the Faculty of Education at The Chinese University of Hong Kong, where she is currently serving as Chairperson of the Department of Curriculum and Instruction. Her main research interests are second language writing and second language teacher education. She has served on the editorial board of a number of international journals, including *TESOL Quarterly* and *ELT Journal*. Currently she is co-editor of the *Journal of Second Language Writing*. Her publications have appeared in numerous international journals such as *TESOL Quarterly, Language Teaching, System,* and the *Journal of Second Language Writing.*

Rosa M. Manchón is Professor of Applied Linguistics at the University of Murcia, Spain. She has published extensively on L2 writing in the form of articles and guest edited issues in top applied linguistics journals, chapters in collective works, and edited books, including *Writing in Foreign Language Contexts: Learning, Teaching and Research* (Multilingual Matters, 2009), *Learning-to-Write and Writing-to-Learn in an Additional Language* (John Benjamins, 2011), *L2 Writing Development: Multiple Perspectives* (De Gruyter Mouton, 2012), *Task-based L2 Language Learning: Insights from and for L2 Writing* (with H. Byrnes. John Benjamins, 2014), and *The Handbook of Second and Foreign Language Writing* (with P. Matsuda, De Gruyter Mouton, 2017). She was a past editor of the *Journal of Second Language Writing.*

Brian Paltridge is a Professor of TESOL at the University of Sydney. His most recent publications are *Ethnographic Perspectives on Academic Writing* (with Sue Starfield and Christine Tardy, Oxford University Press, 2016), *Getting Published in Academic Journals* (with Sue Starfield, University of Michigan Press, 2016) and *The Discourse of Peer Review* (Palgrave Macmillan, 2017). He is currently writing a book titled *Writing for Research Purposes* to be published by Shanghai Foreign Language Education Press. He is co-editor of *TESOL Quarterly* and an editor emeritus of *English for Specific Purposes.*

Tony Silva directs the Graduate Program in Second Language Studies/ESL in the Department of English at Purdue University, where he teaches graduate courses for PhD, MA, and Certificate students and writing support courses for graduate and undergraduate international students. With Ilona Leki, he founded and edited the *Journal of Second Language Writing from 1992–2007*, and with Paul Kei Matsuda he founded and hosted the (now annual and international) Symposium on Second Language Writing from 1998 to 2013. He has co-edited or co-authored eight books and has published articles in numerous journals. He is an active member of the TESOL International Association, where he has served as a member of the Board of Directors; he has also served the Conference on College Composition and Communication as a member of their Executive Board.

Christine M. Tardy is an Associate Professor of English Applied Linguistics at University of Arizona, where she also directs undergraduate second language writing courses. Her research focuses on academic writing, genre theory and pedagogy, and policies and politics of English. She has published numerous journal articles and book chapters; her recent book, *Beyond Convention: Genre Innovation in Academic Writing*, was published with University of Michigan Press in 2016.

ACKNOWLEDGEMENTS

This book would not have been possible without the commitment and hard work of all the contributing authors. Given the caliber of the contributors, our task, as editors, was that much easier than it might have been with less experienced authors.

We are grateful too for the wonderfully efficient work of our administrative assistant, Samira Kakh. Without her keyboard expertise, the task of coordinating and checking submissions would have been so much more difficult and time-consuming.

Finally, we are extremely grateful for the support and guidance of Naomi Silverman and the whole editorial and production team at Routledge. We would also like to acknowledge the thoughtful comments from two anonymous reviewers of the initial proposal.

1

INTRODUCTION

John Bitchener, Neomy Storch and Rosemary Wette

Teaching multilingual students how to write for academic purposes is an area of interest to both teachers and researchers across the globe as, increasingly, students are studying in universities where their mother tongue is not the language of instruction or communication. As a result, a large number of students are now studying in English-speaking contexts where the academic writing expectations are different to those in contexts where they have previously studied, and English for academic purposes (EAP) teachers and instructors/advisers are needed to help them to cope with the challenges of this situation. Teacher training, both pre-service qualifications and in-service courses, is essential so that teachers can make informed decisions about the best instructional approaches to employ in their classes. These qualifications and courses draw on the findings of research and best pedagogical practice as reported in journal articles and book chapters.

In view of the current and growing importance of EAP writing instruction, it is perhaps surprising that relatively few edited collections explore the variety of institutional and socio-cultural contexts in which EAP writing instruction is currently offered. These range from primary to tertiary education in public and private institutions, and from contexts where English is embedded, to those where it is widely used, to contexts where English is not usually spoken outside the classroom. English is taught by a variety of teachers who are both native and non-native speakers of the language with different qualifications, experience and levels of proficiency to classes of different sizes, and to learners whose age, proficiency levels, disciplinary interests and type or strength of motivation also differ. The volume addresses this diversity by providing overviews of writing in three different geographic contexts, discussion of issues associated with genre-based approaches, and task options for specific learners and classroom contexts, as well as issues in academic language development, including written corrective feedback.

This book is of potential interest to a diverse group of readers. These readers include students undertaking graduate courses in applied linguistics and teacher education, course administrators, experienced teachers of EAP writing in different educational contexts, supervisors and established scholars in the field. For all these readers, the book has many attractive features: the breadth of topics covered, the practice-based issues that are discussed, and the accessibility of its writing style. For graduate students in Applied Linguistics and Education courses, this book would be an invaluable supplementary text. The chapters provide not only concrete examples of applied research but also identify topics related to EAP writing that require additional investigation. For experienced teachers, supervisors and administrators, the book would be a useful source book, providing examples of the kind of challenges in the design and implementation of EAP instruction for specific cohorts of L2 writers, and suggestions on how these challenges can be overcome.

A key strength of the field of EAP writing is that, by and large, research is strongly oriented to practice, and the chapters in this volume provide evidence of this close connection. Contributing authors are all highly experienced teachers as well as researchers, and are therefore able to bridge the theory-practice divide as they draw on current scholarship and research findings to identify issues of current importance in the field, and make practical suggestions for teaching and learning strategies to meet the needs of particular groups of learners.

Between the Introduction and the Epilogue, the chapters are grouped into three parts, each one exploring an important theme in learning to write for academic purposes. They are ordered to progress from EAP courses in university degree programs, to instruction in specific EAP knowledge and skills, and then to future research and scholarship.

In Part I, *EAP Courses in University Degree Programs* (Chapters 2, 3 and 4 by Paltridge, Hyland and Silva), the development of multidisciplinary and discipline-specific EAP courses at undergraduate and postgraduate levels in Australia, Hong Kong and the United States is described, and curriculum and methodological choices are explained. In Part II, *Instruction in Specific EAP Knowledge and Skills*, the seven chapters are organized in three sub-sections: issues in academic genre-based instruction (Chapters 5, 6 and 7 by Tardy, Bitchener and Wette); particular instructional tasks and activities (Chapters 8 and 9 by Hammond and Storch); and proactive and reactive approaches to academic language development (Chapters 10 and 11 by Ferris and Lee). In Part III, *Future Research in EAP*, the single chapter (Chapter 12, by Manchón) provides an overview of pedagogically oriented research agendas for the years ahead. The book concludes with an Epilogue (Chapter 13, by Casanave). What follows is a summary of each chapter providing a more detailed outline of the content and organization of the book.

In Chapter 2, Paltridge draws on the work of EAP and academic literacies to argue that writing in the academy requires a deep awareness of the complex relationship between language and the social and cultural context in which a text resides. This context shapes, for example, the values attached to a text as well as to readers' expectations. Thus, academic writing classes need to focus on both text and context, on the language and discourse features of a text as well as on the literacy expectations of the academy. Paltridge then describes three courses taught at his university: for undergraduate, postgraduate (MA) and doctoral students. The overriding aim of the courses is to bring together the theory and practice of writing in an academic context. He provides a detailed description of the courses in terms of the topics covered and the kind of activities that students are required to complete. Thus, the chapter provides invaluable advice to course designers and teachers of EAP writing.

In Chapter 3, Hyland gives an account of the introduction of disciplinary-specific EAP courses at the University of Hong Kong, where, in 2012, a radical restructuring of tuition resulted in a 3-year degree being replaced with a 4-year Bachelor degree. Students' final year of schooling therefore became their first year of university study. The need for academic writing instruction at university was acknowledged, and a decision was made to require all incoming students to complete a Core University English (CUE) course, with an additional requirement to complete a discipline-specific course before graduation. The Year 1 CUE course draws students' attention to the importance of accuracy, clarity, coherence, cautious claiming and the establishment of a clear line of thought or argument. English in the Discipline (ED) courses are taken in either Year 2, 3 or 4, and Hyland describes how ED courses were developed across a range of subject areas. He also presents research findings that show clear disciplinary differences in particular genre features: in the way authorial identity is constructed, in the text types students need to produce, and in the way feedback responses are delivered. The chapter ends by reiterating the value of academic writing instruction that is embedded in particular disciplinary contexts and communities.

In Chapter 4, Silva traces the long-term development of a multi-disciplinary EAP writing program at Purdue University in the United States. He begins with a description of this institutional context and the L2 writing provision it offers, as well as his long-standing involvement with the program. He then profiles the graduate students who teach undergraduate writing courses, and the specialized training they are required to complete before taking on ESL Writing courses. In line with its main aim of documenting this course as an example of effective practice, the chapter outlines its syllabus and the five written assignments that students are required to produce: an autobiographical account, and a topic of personal interest that will be the focus of the four remaining assignments (proposal, synthesis paper, interview report and argument essay). Each assignment is drafted in three stages, with feedback from peers and the instructor at each stage. Classroom methodologies include explicit instruction, individual as well as small group conferencing and individual writing tasks. Silva ends by conceding that this program is privileged in that it is very securely established and well-resourced, but hopes, nevertheless, that readers will find information in the chapter useful in their own teaching contexts.

In Chapter 5, Tardy considers challenges of genre instruction in the academic writing classroom that will be of interest to a wide readership, including, of course, those involved in second language writing teacher education. She explains that, while attempting to not teach genres as prescriptive formulas or templates, teachers sometimes report how challenging they find it to implement a genre approach that recognizes its dynamic and social characteristics. Tardy adds that, because this can be the case for more experienced teachers, it may be even more of an issue for novice teachers. Thus, the aim of the chapter is to explore teachers' perspectives on implementing genre approaches in their academic writing classrooms, to identify key challenges and consider how teacher education might minimize or address the challenges. Based on an in-progress study of US writing teachers in early undergraduate writing classes, Tardy identifies some of the key obstacles they face in teaching with genre before presenting a number of implications for supporting not only this cohort but also those in other contexts.

In Chapter 6, Bitchener focuses on the creation of argument in the literature review of a doctoral dissertation as one example of an academic part-genre that L2 writers can sometimes struggle with. He begins with a discussion of the knowledge and skills that writers need in order to create an argument, the reasons L2 writers may encounter issues with argument creation and some of the pedagogical approaches that have been recommended to help students overcome the difficulties they may experience. Then, in the second part of the chapter, he describes a seven-stage scaffolded approach that can assist L2 writers develop a focused and coherent argument for one theoretical unit or section of a literature review. Bitchener explains that this approach can also be applied to other part-genres of a doctoral dissertation and to other academic genres that draw upon a wide range of literature. The chapter concludes with a discussion of the many advantages of using this approach and with suggestions about who, in particular, might benefit from the approach.

In Chapter 7, Wette begins with an outline of research and scholarship on writing using sources to date, and the shift in attention in recent years from issues of legitimacy to instruction and skill development. Writing using sources is a multi-faceted skill that includes analytic and synthetic reading skills, thinking skills to make decisions about what to cite and what type of citation to use and writing skills that draw on the students' knowledge of appropriate grammar and vocabulary. The chapter describes the findings of two studies with novice and post-novice students in order to comment further on skill components that appear to be readily learned, as well as those that are often problematic. It then proposes a trajectory of skill development in order to show the number and variety of abilities that need to be developed, and a possible learning sequence. The final section presents practical information in the form of suggested course content and instructional tasks for learners at different levels of capability. It concludes by stating the need for EAP courses to provide sustained, explicit instruction, a range of practice tasks and constructive feedback to assist students towards proficiency in this essential, complex academic literacy skill.

In Chapter 8, Hammond focuses on effective academic literacy instruction of English as an additional language (EAL) students in mainstream junior high school classes. She argues that more effective literacy instruction for EAL (and indeed all students) requires raising teachers' knowledge about language and literacy and specifically their understanding of the notion of "literate talk." Hammond begins with an explanation of what literate talk means, and why EAL learners need explicit support to be able to engage in such talk. This discussion draws heavily on systemic functional linguistics, but does so in a very accessible way. Hammond then describes a professional development program which involved teachers in applying the notion of literate talk to task analysis. Teachers analyzed tasks used in science classes for the nature of the language they require and mapped these tasks on a continuum from most spoken to most written language. Hammond suggests that the insights teachers gain from such analysis and reflection can be applied to the design of more effective writing class activities across the disciplines.

In Chapter 9, Storch discusses how best to implement collaborative writing activities. She begins by providing a rationale for such activities in EAP classes and argues that collaborative writing tasks can serve twin goals: train learners for the kind of writing they are likely to encounter outside the language classroom and provide opportunities for learners to deliberate about how to express their ideas. The chapter then focuses on three key decisions that EAP teachers need to make in order to implement successful collaborative writing activities, in the face-to-face or computer-mediated environment (e.g., Wikis). These decisions revolve around choice of writing task, the optimal grouping of students and how to assess such activities. Storch recommends that in making these decisions teachers need to consider their learners' L2 proficiency and the goals of the EAP writing class (language learning vs. learning to write for professional and academic purposes). The discussion of these decisions draws not only on a growing body of research, but also on Storch's own experience of implementing collaborative writing with her EAP students.

In Chapter 10, Ferris considers the *what* and *how* of instruction that seeks to facilitate second language writers academic language development. Acknowledging the extensive literature on L2 development from a more reactive perspective, namely, corrective feedback, she argues in this chapter for a more proactive approach as well, especially for helping writers acquire the types of complex language that may enable them to better realize their academic and professional purposes. The aim of the chapter, then, is to provide teachers with practical strategies for addressing language with their EAP students in ways that are authentic and fully integrated with other classroom goals and activities so that students can be prepared to communicate successfully for a range of academic purposes. Thus, Ferris discusses principles that teachers can use to select lexical and syntactic structures for their classes and ways in which they can teach them so as to avoid their being taught as lists or as items in decontextualized grammar lessons. The accessibility of insights provided in this chapter will be welcomed by busy teachers.

In Chapter 11, Lee discusses the perennial question of how teachers can provide effective written corrective feedback (WCF) but at the same time make this task manageable. The chapter deals specifically with two alternative strategies for the provision of WCF: comprehensive versus targeted WCF. Lee begins with defining these two alternative strategies to feedback provision, and then critically reviews the extant body of research to discuss the pedagogical advantages and disadvantages of the two alternatives. She concludes that, since this body of research has not shown conclusively which is the most effective form of WCF, the best approach is for teachers to adopt a strategy that takes into consideration the learners' proficiency level and the nature of the errors, or a middle position that combines both strategies. Lee also provides a comprehensive list of principles that should guide the selection of targeted forms for circumstances where targeted WCF is appropriate. She concludes the chapter by outlining areas that require additional investigation. Thus, the chapter has something valuable to offer to both L2 writing teachers and researchers.

In Chapter 12, Manchón explores several dimensions of the interaction between language and writing in academic settings from both retrospective and forward-looking perspectives. Focusing on the multi-faceted and situated nature of this interaction, she begins her discussion with a consideration of the way in which the linguistic component of L2 academic literacies has featured in recent disciplinary contributions. This leads to an overview of the main strands of research on the role of language in the learning and teaching of a second language in diverse academic contexts where the distinction is made between research focusing on texts and research focusing on the writer. The ensuing detailed analysis of contributions centered on writers dominates the second part of the chapter and leads to a series of pedagogical implications arising from the issues raised and the theoretical and empirical research avenues suggested.

The epilogue by Casanave provides a summary of the key themes covered in this book. In summarizing these themes, she interweaves the advice provided by the contributing authors about how to provide effective EAP instruction. She notes that while the advice offered is broad in its coverage, relating to students across the educational spectrum, it is also very much situated, drawing as it does on the authors' teaching experiences in very specific educational contexts. The epilogue concludes with some thought-provoking topics such as transfer, agency and risk that need further reflection and investigation, and that extend the discussion about EAP teaching and scholarship that has been initiated by the chapters of this book.

PART I

EAP Courses in University Degree Programs

2

CONTEXT AND THE TEACHING OF ACADEMIC WRITING

Bringing Together Theory and Practice

Brian Paltridge

Introduction

Learning to write in the academy involves acquiring a repertoire of linguistic practices that are based on complex sets of discourses, identities and values. These practices, however, vary according to context, disciplinary culture and genre. This chapter discusses and exemplifies ways in which this can be addressed in the teaching and learning of academic writing. Tasks are described that focus on this at the levels of undergraduate, postgraduate and thesis and dissertation writing. In these tasks, students consider the institutional and audience expectations of the texts they are writing and the ways of knowing, doing and writing that are particular to their academic disciplines.

Context and Academic Writing

The relationship between language and context has been discussed by authors such as Malinowski (1923, 1935) and Firth (1964), as well as more recently by Hasan (1995, 1999), Halliday (2007, 2009), Martin (1984) and Martin and Rose (2008). The concepts of *context of situation* and *context of culture* (Halliday, 2007, 2009) have been especially important in systemic functional genre studies (Hood, 2013; Martin & Rose, 2008) and in particular the view that these notions are essential for understanding and interpreting how language is used in particular situational and cultural settings, a view that has special relevance for the teaching of academic writing. The engagement that students have with the texts they write, further, as Forest and Davis (2016, p. 20) point out, are "shaped by the diverse sociocultural and institutional practices that exist in different programs, colleges, universities, and places." The teaching of academic writing, then, needs to be sensitive to contexts of writing as these shape how and what students write in the disciplines (Forest & Davis, 2016). Lillis (2013), equally, argues that writing cannot and should not be viewed as separate from contexts of use and users; that is, texts, uses and users need to be subjects of empirical research, and issues of power, identity, participation and access "are central to writing practices and as such need to be taken account of in exploring what writing is and does" (p. 16).

Context and English for Specific Purposes

Context is especially important in English for specific purposes research (Paltridge, 2013). Swales, for example, as early as 1985, says:

> It is not only texts that we need to understand, but the roles texts have in their environments; the values, congruent and conflictive, placed on them by occupational, professional and disciplinary memberships; and the expectations those memberships have of the patternings of the genres they participate in, be they monographs, textbooks, lectures, examination papers, memos, minutes, testimonials. (Swales, 1985, p. 219)

Swales returns to this in the Foreword to Casanave's (2014) book *Before the Dissertation*, where he looks back to the proposal he made in 1985 saying:

> [The study of texts] should be widened to include more study on the processes by means of which those texts are conceived, generated, and negotiated. (Swales, 2014, p. v)

Students as Researchers

In her book *Text, Role and Context*, Ann Johns (1997) proposes students carry out investigations of the genres they need to acquire and the contexts in which they occur so they can understand why they are written as they are and how they can create a text that both meets their audience's expectations and achieves its goal. This work takes up Swales' (1993) call for greater contextualization of genres where he argued that, when dealing with genres, "we ignore investigating context of situation and contexts of culture at some peril" (Swales, 1993, p. 691), a view that is especially important for the teaching and learning of academic writing.

Within all this, of course, it is important to avoid causative or deterministic views of context (Hasan, 1999). We should not assume, for example, that every text in the same situation will be the same even though there are traces of similarities in each of the texts and the contexts. We should not, further, assume that one (that is, context) will determine the other (that is, the text). The relationship between text and context, rather, as Hasan (1999) argues, is dialogic in that context and text interact with each other in a bi-directional, mutually constitutive way.

It is clear, then, that not all information that is required for understanding academic writing can be derived from the text itself. There is, as Freedman (1999) has pointed out, the need to go "beyond the text" (p. 764) in order to explore the social and cultural context in which texts occur as well as to explore insiders' views on texts in order to make descriptions of academic genres pedagogically most useful. Johns (1997) suggests, in training students to *act as researchers*, that we help them write texts that consider the institutional and audience expectations of their area/s of study and the *ways of knowing, ways of doing* and *ways of writing* that are particular to specific academic disciplines. Students can be trained, she argues, to unpack the knowledge and skills that are necessary for membership of their academic community. We should give students, she argues, the skills to ask questions of the texts they are required to produce, of the context in which the texts are located, and of the people who will be reading and judging the effectiveness of the texts. Students may then decide to produce a text that fits with these expectations, or they may write a text that challenges, or indeed resists, what is expected of them.

Johns (2014, 2015, 2016) develops these ideas further, citing the work of Prior (2004) who points out that "[Writing] is about ways of working—ways of acting—that align readers, texts, and contexts" (p. 167). The question then, as Johns (2015) asks, is:

> How can we entice students to become genre scholars, to be curious about and invested in texts and their contexts of all kinds? … encouraging novice or ESL/EFL students to become deeply invested in genre studies—perhaps for the rest of their lives. (pp. 365–366)

It is crucial, then, in academic writing classes, not just to focus on language and discourse features of texts, but also the socially situated nature of texts, why they are written as they are and the role they are playing in their particular setting (Bowles, 2012). As Flowerdew (1993) has argued, we need to focus on the process of learning about, and acquiring genres, rather than just the end product, or specific variety of genre. We cannot, he argues, always predict the range of genres students will need to be able to participate in. We can, however, give them strategies for learning about genres so they can learn not only what their texts are expected to look like, but also why they are written as they are in the particular academic and disciplinary setting. Students, thus, should be given opportunities to reflect on the genre and the situation in which texts are produced so that when they write their texts they are aware of how the social and cultural context of the text impacts on how they write it and what they will write. This includes a focus on the language of the text but also elements of the situation such as their status as writers, the type of audience and the physical context of the text (Johns, 2016). As Johns (2016) points out, what is prototypical and conventional in a genre is not just in the text itself. It is also in elements of the situation such as the purpose of the text, its structure, its visual appearance and its content—as well as in its language or tone. Gaining an understanding of the complexity of the writing situation and the influence it has on writers and texts, thus, is essential to successful academic writing. This view aligns with the views held by people working in the area of academic literacies (Lea, 2008; Lea & Street, 1998, 1999, 2006; Lillis & Scott, 2007) by asking questions such as: "What is the nature of academic writing? What does it mean to 'do' academic writing? [and] What is involved [in doing academic writing] for different participants in different disciplinary and institutional contexts?" (Lillis, 2006, p. 32).

An Ethnography of Writing

Grabe and Kaplan (1996) provide suggestions for an ethnography of writing which provides a framework for examining the social and cultural context of academic writing. This view considers who writes what to whom, for what purpose, why, when, where and how. That is, it examines the audience of a text, the writer's purpose and the genre required by the task. It also considers the writing in terms of the situation in which it takes place, and the use or uses of the writing. Students can be asked to undertake an analysis of the context in which the text they are writing occurs, and consider how the situation in which they are writing impacts upon what they write and how they write it. For example, they can be asked to consider the setting of the text in the sense of whether it is written for a first year university course, or a postgraduate program of study. They can also be asked to consider the purpose of their text, that is, whether it is to display knowledge and understanding of something, to demonstrate particular skills, to convince the reader, to argue a case, and at more advanced levels, to critique and break new ground. Expected content is another important matter, such as what points of view and claims are accepted in the particular area of study, and what points of view and claims are not (and why).

The intended audience for the text also needs to be considered. This includes the reader's role and purpose in reading the text, and the criteria that will be used to judge the success of the text. Johns (1990) discusses the expert all-powerful reader of students' texts who can either accept or reject students' writing as coherent and consistent with the conventions of the target discourse community, or not. In her view, knowledge of this audience's attitudes, beliefs and expectations is not only possible but essential for students learning to write in academic settings. As Swales and Feak (2012) point out in their book *Academic Writing for Graduate Students*, even before students begin to write, they need to consider their audience. They need to have an understanding of their audience's expectations and prior knowledge of what they are writing about, as these will impact upon the content and form of their piece of writing.

The relationship between the reader and writer of the text is a further consideration as this impacts on what students say in their text and how they say it. This can be one of the most difficult things for students in that they often have to write about something their reader already knows or knows better than they do. General expectations and conventions for the text, as well as particular expectations, conventions and requirements of the student's field of study also need to be considered. This includes how students are expected to refer to other texts in their text, how they should quote, the extent to which they should paraphrase, the level of critical analysis required (or not) of them, the level of originality expected of them and the amount of negotiation that is possible (or not) in terms of all this. Other matters include the background knowledge, values and understandings it is assumed students will share with their readers, including what's important to their readers and what is not. This is especially important as different types of academic writing often involve different approaches to the construction and presentation of knowledge (see the section "Writing and Disciplinarity" below, also Wingate & Tribble, 2012) based, in turn, on different sets of expectations and forms of knowledge that are valued in the particular context. As Hathaway (2015) points out, there is sometimes the assumption that students know or will find these things out naturally, a situation which, in the light of recent research, she argues, is "increasingly untenable" (p. 506).

Writing and Disciplinarity

Christie and Maton (2011) have argued that different subject areas and theoretical approaches build knowledge in different ways. People working in particular disciplines often share "ideals, beliefs, values, goals, practices, conventions, and ways of creating and distributing knowledge" (Flowerdew & Costley, 2016, p. 11). All of this is essential for students to understand if they are to succeed with the writing they are doing in their various areas of study. Hyland (2012), in his book on disciplinary identities, discusses how writers use language in a way that reflects the relationship between themselves and the disciplinary community in which they are writing. Writers' use of language reflects the values and conventions of the discipline as agreed on points of view are adopted and agreement is shown with those who hold these points of view (Hyland, 2012). In this way writers use language "to acknowledge, construct and negotiate social relations" (p. 63) between themselves and their disciplinary community. They take on roles and identities that align with institutional and disciplinary practices and "the attitudes one is expected to have toward these practices" (Martin, 2000, p. 161). Writers, thus, through their use of language, index ways of demonstrating membership of their particular disciplinary group (Hyland, 2012), something that student writers need to learn to do, no matter what their level of study and the discipline in which they are working.

To effectively use an academic genre, then, students need an understanding of the culture, circumstances, purposes, motives and epistemologies that prevail in particular academic disciplines (Johns, 1997; Wingate, 2015) and strategies they can employ to engage with them (Starfield, 2004). The teaching of academic writing, then, needs to take a sociocultural orientation, aimed at providing students with "an understanding of the values and social practices of the target communities, and to empower them with the knowledge of making informed choices" (Koutsantoni, 2007, p. 220) when writing their texts. The focus, then, in the teaching of academic genres, should be on "students gaining control over the range of genres specific to their disciplinary context," starting with the "authentic social practices of the disciplines" (Curry, 2016, p. 91). This view of literacy as social practice which sees academic literacy/ies "as emerging from disciplinary practices of knowledge making and communication" (Curry, 2016, p. 82) and learning to write as a matter of "disciplinary becoming" (Curry, 2016, p. 78), underlies a number of writing courses taught in the Faculty of Education and Social Work at the University of Sydney, each of which will be described below.

Bringing Together Theory and Practice

The courses described in this section of the chapter focus on undergraduate writing, postgraduate writing and thesis and dissertation writing. While all of the courses have very practical aims they also focus on theoretical matters related to writing in the academy in a way that aims to bring together both theory and practice in each of the courses.

Texts and Expectations

This first course, titled *Texts and Expectations*, is aimed at undergraduate students in the Faculty. This course draws on work in the areas of academic literacies (see below) and English for academic purposes as both share a lot of common ground and can both "contribute to a more mainstream and comprehensive approach to the teaching of academic writing" (Hathaway, 2015, p. 508). An academic literacies perspective (Blommaert, Street, Scott & Turner, 2008; Lea & Street, 1998; Lillis, 2006; Lillis & Tuck, 2016) sees learning to write as learning to acquire a repertoire of linguistic practices that is based on complex sets of values, viewpoints, beliefs, purposes, rules and ways of using language. Both academic literacies and English for academic purposes, Hathaway (2015, p. 508) argues:

> offer understandings of the epistemological, cultural and linguistic aspects of entering and participating in new knowledge communities and learning to generate legitimate meanings within them. Furthermore, both approaches position academic practices as relative constructs.

These practices, she argues, are not natural or given. Rather, they are the products of a specific time and place. From this, she suggests, it follows that these practices can be opened up to explicit examination. Students can be asked to both compare and question texts and contexts in order to enable them to better understand the academic forms and genres that are available to them (see also Wingate & Tribble, 2012; Wingate, 2015 for discussions of relations between academic literacies and English for academic purposes).

The first main topic covered in the course, then, is the notion of academic literacies and a discussion of what this means for writing in the academy. Next, following the work of Johns (1997, 2008, 2014, 2015), strategies for researching requirements and expectations for reading and writing in the disciplines are discussed. Other matters covered in the course include the role of reading in academic literacies development (Lillis & Tuck, 2016; Wingate, 2015), voice and identity in academic writing (Allison & Mei 2001; Hyland, 2012; Matsuda, 2015), intertextuality and academic writing (Creme & Lea, 2008; Pecorari & Shaw, 2012), genre (Paltridge, 2014; Swales, 2016a), and grammar, discourse and coherence in academic writing (Paltridge, 2012; Paltridge, 2017).

During the course, students write a series of online reflections in which they discuss their awareness of expectations for reading and writing in their academic classes, awareness of themselves as readers and writers, and awareness of the texts they are writing and appropriate language choices within these texts. At the end of the course they write a critical reflection on their literacy journey throughout the semester and then a critical reflection on a specific text they have written for one of their other courses during the semester. These tasks aim to develop students' capacity to reflect on literacy expectations in higher education, on texts and on themselves as readers and writers in order to provide them with a foundation they can use to develop their understanding of academic literacies during the course of their studies as well as to reflect on expectations surrounding reading and writing in their disciplines. The tasks, then, focus on the matters raised by Grabe and Kaplan (1996) referred to above which students consider in relation to their own developing literacy experiences.

English in Academic Settings

The Faculty also offers a course for master's students titled "English in Academic Settings," which, equally, explores in Hathaway's (2015, p. 509) words the "ways of being, valuing, knowing and expressing" that students need to understand in order to achieve their academic goals. As Hathaway points out, quoting Elbow (1998, p. 162), "learning new intellectual practices is not just a matter of practicing them; it is also a matter of thinking and talking about one's practice."

This course, as with the undergraduate course, was developed to enable students to reflect on the theory and practice of communicating in writing in an academic environment, so they can apply these reflections to their own writing. The course, thus, aims to enrich students' understanding of sociocultural influences on academic communication and, in particular, academic writing. Topics covered in the course include academic literacies (see above), genre, discourse communities (Canagarajah, 2002; Hyland, 2009; Swales 1990), disciplinary expectations (Hyland, 2012; Koutsantoni, 2007), characteristics of effective academic writing (Hinkel, 2004), ways of making claims (Hyland, 1996), writer voice and the ownership of ideas, critical thinking and argumentation (Durkin, 2008), and students as researchers.

In the course, students examine tasks they have been assigned in their disciplinary classes in terms of the values and expectations that underlie the tasks. To do this, students interview the teachers who have set the assignments and ask them questions, not just about what they want them to write, but also why they want them to write it. Students do this to try and gain an insider's perspective on institutional and audience expectations for their academic writing as well as unpack the values and requirements they need to negotiate in order to achieve their academic goals. Once they have completed their interviews, students write a report in which they discuss the findings of their analysis in both theoretical and practical terms. In their reports, the students are asked to consider matters such as:

- *Audience*: Who is the readership for the writing? What assumed knowledge do they have on this topic? How does this impact on what you need to explain?
- *Purpose*: What is the purpose of the writing? To what extent are you expected to contribute your own ideas?
- *Discourse community expectations*: What are some assumptions you are making about what represents a good piece of writing?
- *Structure*: How should you structure your writing? What decisions have you made, and why? In what ways have you considered the reader when structuring your writing?
- *Language*: What role does language play in your writing? How have you addressed issues of formality and hedging in your writing?

They also discuss what they have learned about the task in relation to theories of academic literacies, genre, audience and discourse communities and how these relate to the writing practices and expectations of the disciplines in which they are studying. As these students learn, texts and assignments tasks vary according to discipline, task type, topic, class, teacher and a number of other factors. It is essential, then, for students to explore these factors as they related to the assignments they are writing.

Thesis and Dissertation Writing

The course on thesis and dissertation[1] writing draws heavily on Grabe and Kaplan's (1996) framework for an ethnography of writing presented earlier in this chapter. In this course, students consider how features of the sociocultural context in which their text is written and associated roles, expectations and values impact on what they write, how their text will be read and, importantly, how it will be assessed. They complete the task shown in Figure 2.1 then discuss their answers with other students in the class before on open class discussion of what the analysis has revealed (see Paltridge, Starfield & Tardy, 2016 for a discussion of the context of thesis and dissertation writing).

The contextual features shown in Figure 2.1 are, of course, not as distinct or as neat and tidy as this task might suggest (Fitzpatrick & Costley, 2016). As Yates and Orlikowski (2007) point out, they are deeply intertwined and each, in its way, has an impact on what a writer writes and the way they write it, in the context of the genre and the discipline in which the student is working. These features, further, are not the same for all thesis and dissertation writers. Two students sitting beside each other in the same class and from the same academic department may have little in common with each other if their work

Setting of your thesis or dissertation

Focus and research perspective of your thesis or dissertation

Purpose of your thesis or dissertation

Your readers' role and purpose in reading your thesis or dissertation

The relationship between you and readers of your thesis or dissertation

Expectations, conventions and requirements for your thesis or dissertation

Background knowledge, values and understandings which underlie your thesis or dissertation

Relationship your thesis or dissertation has with other texts and genres

FIGURE 2.1 The social and cultural context of theses and dissertations

1 The terms "thesis" and "dissertation" are used in different ways in different parts of the world. In the US, master's students write "theses" whereas in Britain (and Hong Kong), they write "dissertations." At the PhD level, a US student writes a "dissertation" and a student at a British university writes a "thesis." In Australia, the term "thesis" is used for both the master's and doctoral degrees. The course described in this chapter is for both thesis and dissertation writers.

draws on different research methodologies, theoretical perspectives and orientations, even if they are working in the same academic discipline. The approach to research for example, may be quantitative, qualitative or naturalistic, or it may be mixed methods. This will influence the claims that can and cannot be made in the text, what will count as *evidence* and what will not. The research will also be influenced by departmental views on what *good* research is and the extent to which students are required to write a text (and carry out research) that fits with this perspective or paradigm.

Within all this, however, students are expected to meet "the scholarly expectations of the university as a whole" (Johns & Swales, 2002, p. 17) as well as meet expectations for research at this level of study such as originality and contribution to knowledge, criteria that are often interpreted differently in different disciplinary contexts (Clarke & Lunt, 2014). Students are also expected to demonstrate a command of appropriate research methods and techniques, an understanding of previous research (Bourke & Holbrook, 2013) and how their work fits with this previous research.

Conclusion

Students, then, need to learn what matters in their disciplinary area, what the expected ways are in which they should behave in their performance (Butler, 1990) as academic writers in the disciplinary culture and methodological orientation with which they are working, as well as what other ways might be available to them to do this (see French, 2016 for a discussion of this). That is, students need to learn how, through the use of language, to present themselves to their readers and, in doing this, how they can index (Ochs, 1992; Strauss & Feiz, 2014) their membership of their disciplinary community as they perform and position themselves (Devitt, 2015) through the genres they are writing.

We, thus, need to focus on both text and context (Johns, 2008, 2014, 2015, 2016) in the teaching of academic writing in ways that will enable students to both understand and meet the literacy requirements and expectations of the academy. The drawing together of work in the area of English for academic purposes and academic literacies, as shown in the courses outlined in this chapter, provides an example of how this can be done. This focus helps students understand what the texts that they are writing do and how they shape the production of knowledge (English, 2015). The view, thus, is of writing as knowledge making, rather than just transmission (Lillis, 2003) or technique, or a means of displaying knowledge (English, 2015). This approach, Lillis (2015) argues, is transformative in that it provides a way of exploring:

> what it is that prevailing academic conventions for meaning making have to offer—and to whom—and what it is they constrain or restrict. (p. 8)

This view acknowledges that student populations are not homogeneous, writing requirements and expectations are not one size fits all, and disciplines are not necessarily stable. University communities are changing, the student body in universities is changing, as are literacy expectations and requirements in the academy, especially with what has been called the *postmodern turn* (Best & Kellner, 1997) in the new humanities and social sciences. Even the boundaries between academic disciplines are changing (Whitchurch, 2010). Sometimes students can *border cross* (Giroux, 1992) between areas of study and sometimes they cannot. These borders, however, are becoming increasingly fluid and much less clear than they once were or seemed to be (Manathunga & Brew, 2012) (see Trowler, 2012, for further discussion of academic disciplines, domains and practices). All of this has implications for the teaching of academic writing and how we help students achieve their goals, taking account of the complex and changing demands of the disciplinary settings and discourse communities (Lockhart, 2016; Swales, 1990, 2016b) in which they are working.

Acknowledgments

My thanks to colleagues Marie Stevenson, Alyson Simpson, Bronwyn James and Arlene Harvey for sharing the course outline for *Texts and Expectations* with me, and to David Hirsh for the course outline for *English in Academic Settings*.

References

Allison, D., & Mei, W. S. (2001). Academic writing: Whose expectations? *RELC Journal, 32*, 52–71.

Best, S., & Kellner, D. (1997). *The postmodern turn*. New York: Guilford Press.

Blommaert, J., Street, B., Scott, M., & Turner, J. (2008). Academic literacies—What have we achieved and where to from here? *Journal of Applied Linguistics, 4*, 137–148.

Bourke, S., & Holbrook, A. P. (2013). Examining PhD and research masters theses. *Assessment and Evaluation in Higher Education, 38*, 407–416.

Bowles, H. (2012). Analyzing language for specific purposes. *Modern Language Journal, 96*, Focus Issue, 43–58.

Butler, J. (1990). *Gender trouble: Feminism and the subversion of identity*. New York: Routledge.

Canagarajah, S. (2002). Multilingual writers and the academic community: Towards a critical relationship. *Journal of English for Academic Purposes, 1*, 29–44.

Casanave, C. P. (2014). *Before the dissertation: A textual mentor for doctoral students at early stages of a research project*. Ann Arbor: University of Michigan Press.

Christie, F., & Maton, K. (2011). Why disciplinarity? In F. Christie & K. Maton (Eds.), *Disciplinarity: Functional linguistic and sociological perspectives* (pp. 1–9). London: Continuum.

Clarke, G., & Lunt, I. (2014). The concept of "originality" in the PhD: How is it interpreted by examiners? *Assessment and Evaluation in Higher Education, 39*, 803–820.

Creme, P., & Lea, M. R. (2008). *Writing at university* (3rd ed.). Maidenhead, UK: Open University Press.

Curry, M. J. (2016). More than language: Graduate student writing as "disciplinary becoming." In S. Simpson, N. A Caplan, M. Cox & T. Phillips (Eds.), *Supporting graduate student writers: Research, curriculum, and program design* (pp. 78–96). Ann Arbor: University of Michigan Press.

Devitt, A. (2015). Genre performances: *Genre Analysis* and rhetorical-linguistic genre studies. *Journal of English for Academic Purposes, 19*, 44–51.
Durkin, K. (2008). The adaptation of East Asian masters students to western norms of critical thinking and argumentation in the UK. *Intercultural Education, 19*, 15–27.
Elbow, P. (1998). Reflections on academic discourse: How it relates to freshmen and colleagues. In V. Zamel & R. Spack (Eds.), *Negotiating academic literacies* (pp. 145–170). Mahwah, NJ: Lawrence Erlbaum.
English, F. (2015). Genre as a pedagogical resource at university. In T. Lillis, K. Harrington, M. R. Lea & S. Mitchell (Eds.), *Working with academic literacies: Case studies towards transformative practice* (pp. 245–255). Fort Collins, CO: AC Clearinghouse.
Firth, J. R. (1964). Context of situation. In P. Strevens (Ed.), *The tongues of men and speech* (pp. 110–114). London: Oxford University Press.
Fitzpatrick, D., & Costley, T. (2016). Using annotated bibliographies to teach student writing in social sciences. In J. Flowerdew & T. Costley (Eds.), *Discipline-specific writing* (pp. 141–154). Abingdon, UK: Routledge.
Flowerdew, J. (1993). An educational, or process, approach to the teaching of professional genres. *ELT Journal, 47*, 305–316.
Flowerdew, J., & Costley, T. (2016). Introduction. In J. Flowerdew & T. Costley (Eds.), *Discipline-specific writing* (pp. 9–40). Abingdon, UK: Routledge.
Forest, R. W., & Davis, T. S. (2016). Investigating local sociocultural and institutional contexts for discipline-specific writing. In J. Flowerdew & T. Costley (Eds.), *Discipline-specific writing* (pp. 20–40). Abingdon, UK: Routledge.
Freedman, A. (1999). Beyond the text: Towards understanding the teaching and learning of genres. *TESOL Quarterly, 33*, 764–768.
French, A. (2016). Exploring post/graduate academic writing practices, research literacies and writing identities. In C. Badenhorst & C. Guerin (Eds.), *Research literacies and writing pedagogies for masters and doctoral writers* (pp. 113–131). Leiden: Brill.
Giroux, H. A. (1992). *Border crossings: Cultural workers and the politics of education*. London: Routledge.
Grabe, W., & Kaplan, R. (1996). *Theory and practice of writing. An applied linguistic perspective*. London: Longman.
Halliday, M. A. K. (2007). The notion of "context" in language education. In J. J. Webster (Ed.), *Language and education. M. A. K. Halliday* (pp. 269–290). London: Continuum.
Halliday, M. A. K. (2009). Context of culture and of situation. In J. J. Webster (Ed.), *The essential Halliday* (pp. 55–84). London: Continuum.
Hasan, R. (1995). The conception of context in text. In P. H. Fries & M. Gregory (Eds.), *Discourse in society: Systemic functional perspectives, meaning and choice in language* (pp. 183–283). Norwood, NJ: Ablex.
Hasan, R. (1999). Speaking with reference to context. In M. Ghadessy (Ed.), *Text and context in functional linguistics: Systemic perspectives* (pp. 219–328). Amsterdam: John Benjamins.
Hathaway, J. (2015). Developing that voice: Locating academic writing tuition in the mainstream of higher education. *Teaching in Higher Education, 20*, 506–517.
Hinkel, E. (2004). *Teaching academic ESL writing*. New York: Lawrence Erlbaum.
Hood, S. (2013). *Systemic functional linguistics. GXB Genre across borders*. Accessed 10 January 2017 from http://genreacrossborders.org/systemic-functional-linguistics.
Hyland, K. (1996). Writing without conviction? Hedging in science research articles. *Applied Linguistics, 17*, 433–454.
Hyland, K. (2009). *Academic discourse*. London: Continuum.

Hyland, K. (2012). *Disciplinary identities: Individuality and community in academic discourse.* Cambridge: Cambridge University Press.

Johns, A. M. (1990). L1 composition theories: Implications for developing theories of L2 composition. In B. Kroll (Ed.), *Second language writing: Research insights for the classroom* (pp. 24–36). Cambridge: Cambridge University Press.

Johns, A. M. (1997). *Text, role and context: Developing academic literacies.* Cambridge: Cambridge University Press.

Johns, A. M. (2008). Genre awareness for the novice academic student: An on-going quest. *Language Teaching, 41*, 237–252.

Johns, A. M. (2014). Contextualising texts in the EFL/ESP classroom. *Language Center Forum*, Sultan Qaboos University, *14*, 1, 2–15.

Johns, A. M. (2015). Students as genre scholars: ESL/EFL classroom approaches. In N. Artemeva & A. Freedman (Eds.), *Genre studies around the globe: Beyond the three traditions* (pp. 364–385). Edmonton, AB, Canada: Inkshed Publications.

Johns, A. M. (2016). Reader-culture-text mergence (RCTM): Seven pedagogical principles. In L. C. de Oliveira (Ed.), *The common core state standards in literacy in history/social studies, science and technical subjects for English language learners: Grades 6–12.* Alexandria, VA: Teachers of English to Speakers of Other Languages.

Johns, A. M., & Swales, J. M. (2002). Literacy and disciplinary practices: Opening and closing perspectives. *Journal of English for Academic Purposes, 1*, 13–28.

Koutsantoni, D. (2007). *Developing academic literacies: Understanding disciplinary communities' culture and rhetoric.* Oxford: Peter Lang.

Lea, M. R. (2008). Academic literacies in theory and practice. In N. Hornberger (Ed.), *Encyclopedia of language and education* (pp. 634–645). New York: Springer.

Lea, M. R., & Street, B.V. (1998). Student writing in higher education: An academic literacies approach. *Studies in Higher Education, 23*, 157–172.

Lea, M. R., & Street, B. V. (1999). Writing as academic literacies: Understanding textual practices in higher education. In C.N. Candlin & K. Hyland (Eds.), *Writing: Texts, processes and practices* (pp. 62–81). London: Longman.

Lea, M. R., & Street, B.V. (2006). The "academic literacies" model: Theory and applications. *Theory into Practice, 45*, 368–377.

Lillis, T. (2003). Student writing as "academic literacies": Drawing on Bakhtin to move from critique to design. *Language and Education, 17*, 192–207.

Lillis, T. (2006). Moving towards an "academic literacies" pedagogy: Dialogues of participation. In L. Ganobcsik-Williams (Ed.), *Teaching academic writing in UK higher education* (pp. 30–45). Basingstoke, UK: Palgrave Macmillan.

Lillis, T. (2013). *The sociolinguistics of writing.* Edinburgh: Edinburgh University Press.

Lillis, T. (2015). Towards transformative design. In T. Lillis, K. Harrington, M. R. Lea & S. Mitchell (Eds.), *Working with academic literacies: Case studies towards transformative practice,* (pp. 8–11). Fort Collins, CO: AC Clearinghouse.

Lillis, T., & Scott, M. (2007). Defining academic literacies research: Issues of epistemology, ideology and strategy. *Journal of Applied Linguistics, 4*, 5–32.

Lillis, T., & Tuck, J. (2016). Academic literacies: A critical lens on writing and reading in the academy. In K. Hyland & P. Shaw (Eds.), *The Routledge handbook of English for academic purposes* (pp. 30–43). Abingdon: Routledge.

Lockhart, T. (2016). Flexibility, hybridity and writing: Theory and practice for developing post/graduate literacies. In C. Badenhorst & C. Guerin (Eds.), *Research literacies and writing pedagogies for masters and doctoral writers* (pp. 371–388). Leiden: Brill.

Malinowski, B. (1923). The problem of meaning in primitive languages. In C. K. Ogden & I. A. Richards (Eds.), *The meaning of meaning: A study of the influence of language on thought and of the science of symbolism* (pp. 451–510). London: Routledge and Kegan Paul.

Malinowski, B. (1935). *Coral gardens and their magic*. Volume II. London: George Allen & Unwin.

Manathunga, C., & Brew, A. (2012). Beyond tribes and territories: New metaphors for new times. In P. Trowler, M. Saunders & V. Bamber (Eds.), *Tribes and territories in the 21st century: Rethinking the significance of disciplines in higher education* (pp. 44–56). Abingdon, UK: Routledge.

Martin, J. R. (1984). Language, register and genre. In F. Christie (Ed.), *Language studies: Children's writing* (pp. 21–30). Geelong, VIC: Deakin University Press. Reprinted with revisions in A. Burns & C. Coffin (Eds.) (2001), *Analyzing English in a global context* (pp. 149–166). London: Routledge.

Martin, J. R. (2000). Beyond exchange: APPRAISAL systems in English. In S. Hunston & G. Thomson (Eds.), *Evaluation in text* (pp. 142–175). Oxford: Oxford University Press.

Martin, J. R., & Rose, D. (2008). *Genre relations: Mapping culture*. London: Equinox.

Matsuda, P. K. (2015) Identity in written discourse. *Annual Review of Applied Linguistics, 35*, 140–159.

Ochs, E. (1992). Indexing gender. In A. Duranti & C. Goodwin (Eds.), *Rethinking context: Language as an interactive phenomenon* (pp. 335–358). Cambridge: Cambridge University Press.

Paltridge, B. (2012). *Discourse analysis* (2nd ed.). London: Bloomsbury.

Paltridge, B. (2013). Genre and English for specific purposes. GXB Genre across borders. Accessed 10 January 2017 from http://genreacrossborders.org/genre-and-english-specific-purposes.

Paltridge, B. (2014). Genre and second language academic writing. *Language Teaching, 47*, 303–318.

Paltridge, B. (2017). Discourse analysis for the second language writing classroom. In J. I. Liontas (Ed.), *The TESOL encyclopedia of English language teaching*. Malden, MA: Wiley.

Paltridge, B., Starfield, S., & Tardy, C. M. (2016). *Ethnographic perspectives on academic writing*. Oxford: Oxford University Press.

Pecorari, D., & Shaw, P. (2012). Types of student intertextuality and faculty attitudes. *Journal of Second Language Writing, 21*, 149–164.

Prior, P. (2004). Tracing process: How texts come into being. In C. Bazerman & P. Prior (Eds.), *What writing does and how it does it* (pp. 167–200). Mahwah, NJ: Lawrence Erlbaum.

Starfield, S. (2004). "Why does this feel empowering?" Thesis writing, concordancing, and the corporatizing university. In B. Norton Peirce & K. Toohey (Eds.), *Critical pedagogies and language learning* (pp. 138–157). Cambridge: Cambridge University Press.

Strauss, S., & Feiz, P. (2014). *Discourse analysis. Putting our worlds into words*. New York: Routledge.

Swales, J. M. (1985). ESP – the heart of the matter or the end of the affair? In R. Quirk & H. G. Widdowson (Eds.), *English in the world* (pp. 212–223). Cambridge: Cambridge University Press.

Swales, J. M. (1990). *Genre analysis: English in academic and research settings*. Cambridge: Cambridge University Press.

Swales, J. M. (1993). Genre and engagement. *Revue Belge de Philologie et d'Histoire, 71,* 687–698. Accessed 10 January 2017 from deepblue.lib.umich.edu/.../2027.../swales-genre_and_engagement.pdf.

Swales, J. M. (2014). Foreword. In C. P. Casanave, *Before the dissertation: A textual mentor for doctoral students at early stages of a research project* (pp. v–viii). Ann Arbor: University of Michigan Press.

Swales, J. M. (2016a). Prof. Swales on genre & English for academic purposes. Accessed 10 January 2017 from www.youtube.com/watch?v=W--C4AzvwiU.

Swales, J. M. (2016b). Reflections on the concept of discourse community. *ASp, 69,* 7–19. doi: 10.4000/asp.4774.

Swales, J. M., & Feak, C. B. (2012). *Academic writing for graduate students: Essential tasks and skills.* (3rd ed.). Ann Arbor: University of Michigan Press.

Trowler, P. (2012). Disciplines and interdisciplinarity: Conceptual groundwork. In P. Trowler, M. Saunders & V. Bamber (Eds.), *Tribes and territories in the 21st century: Rethinking the significance of disciplines in higher education* (pp. 5–29). Abingdon, UK: Routledge.

Whitchurch, C. (2010). Convergence and divergence in professional identities. In G. Gordon & C. Whitchurch (Eds.), *Academic and professional identities in higher education: The challenges of a diversifying workforce* (pp. 167–183). Abingdon, UK: Routledge.

Wingate, U. (2015). *Academic literacy and student diversity. The case for inclusive practice.* Clevedon, UK: Multilingual Matters.

Wingate, U., & Tribble, C. (2012). The best of both worlds? Towards an English for academic purposes/academic literacies writing pedagogy. *Studies in Higher Education, 37,* 481–495.

Yates, J., & Orlikowski, W. J. (2007). The PowerPoint presentation and its corollaries: How genres shape communicative action in organizations. In M. Zachry & C. Thrall (Eds.), *Communicative practices in workplaces and the professions: Cultural perspectives on the regulation of discourse and organizations* (pp. 67–92). Amityville, NY: Baywood Publishing Company.

3

LEARNING TO WRITE FOR ACADEMIC PURPOSES

Specificity and Second Language Writing

Ken Hyland

Introduction

The massive expansion of English as the academic lingua franca has meant that many students around the world are now studying their subjects in a second language. This means that the ability to write in ways valued by their tutors becomes a key part of their learning and how they demonstrate their competence in a discipline. Writing is the way students learn to display their critical and analytic skills, their use of English for reasoning and persuasion, their grasp of subject matter issues and their ability to shape an argument using the conventions of their field. This means being able to craft their writing in community-specific ways and it is at the heart of the conceptual understanding of a discipline. In this chapter I explore what it means to take this view seriously, addressing the theme of this volume by focusing on learning to write for academic purposes.

In advancing the idea of specificity in academic writing I will discuss our approach to reforming the undergraduate EAP curriculum at the University of Hong Kong and the notion of *English in the Discipline* that underpinned it. Rather than focus on the process, however, I will provide evidence in support of such an approach by drawing on my research into how features of academic writing vary across fields, how academics construct different disciplinary-based identities, how tutors have different perceptions and expectations about student writing and how the assessment tasks they assign differ considerably across fields. Overall, the chapter highlights the disciplinary-specific nature of writing and argues for targeting teaching to best support L2 students towards control of the discourses that disciplinary insiders are likely to find effective. In so doing, I hope to show how research into the practices of the disciplines can not only advance our understanding of disciplines and writing, but also inform curriculum and classroom practice.

Some Background: English Language and Hong Kong's Tertiary Reform

First, I should say something about the context. In September 2012, universities in Hong Kong launched a four-year undergraduate curriculum to replace the existing three-year system. This reduced the secondary school experience by one year and refocused on a more student-oriented approach to undergraduate education. The change is a major shift in educational philosophy and the most far-reaching change in Hong Kong's educational framework for two generations (Tsui, 2009). It is an attempt to move away from a specialized British undergraduate curriculum and adopt a more holistic approach to the educational experience. Instead of selecting their major on arrival, students enroll in a broad disciplinary area and take a variety of first-year courses before they choose a major. This first-year *Common Core Curriculum* is a range of optional courses designed to facilitate the transition from school to university and to provide students with a more liberal/humanistic education.

This was a huge leap in the dark—very few countries have totally restructured their entire secondary and tertiary education systems in such a radical way all at once. Almost 30,000 new students entered university in 2012 admitted under two different systems, following two different curricula and spanning two different time frames. This was a considerable challenge, and not least for English language centers. Because English is the official medium of instruction in Hong Kong higher education, a major element of the new curriculum is the provision of English, posing questions for language providers about the kind of English that we should be teaching.

These questions were particularly acute at the Centre for Applied English Studies (CAES) at Hong Kong University. As Hong Kong's leading research university, HKU attracts the best performing students from Hong Kong and around the world. However, despite being an English-medium campus, student survey and interview data indicate that a significant percentage of undergraduates experience difficulties in academic writing and speaking (e.g., Evans & Green, 2007; Li, 2009). The university reaffirmed the importance of English in implementing the university reform and mandated a doubling of required credits for all students from 6 to 12 credits, and we decided that half of these should be for more subject-focused *English in the Discipline* courses. This recognizes that, because academic communication conventions differ hugely across disciplinary communities, identifying the particular language features, discourse practices and communicative skills of target cultures becomes central to teaching English in universities. Writing, of course, is a core component of all these courses.

English in the New HKU Curriculum

Stimulated by the climate of innovation in the university at the time, CAES prepared for the changes with a committed, research-led engagement with the reform process. Our new curriculum refocused on academic literacy so that all undergraduates would take two English courses:

1. A General EAP course for all first-year students called *Core University English* (CUE)
2. A more disciplinary-specific *English in the Discipline* (ED) course in later years.

This progression attempts to first provide students with a general understanding of academic conventions and then assist them towards control of more specific practices. It therefore recognizes that because the conventions of academic communication differ considerably across disciplines, identifying the particular language features, discourse practices and communicative skills of target groups becomes central to teaching English in universities. Both types of course presented their own developmental challenges.

Under the new curriculum all 3,000 first-year students at HKU take the Core University English (CUE) course for 6 credits. This is a University-wide program designed to enhance students' proficiency in academic English and so bridge the gap between the kind of English they have learned at secondary school and what will be expected of them when they enter their disciplinary studies in their second year. Making a virtue of heterogeneity, classes are deliberately composed of students from a range of faculties and programs and the tasks ask students to draw on content material from their common core courses in developing their understanding of spoken and written texts.

There are obviously difficulties in identifying anything that might be considered a *core* in the language used across the university. It is, however, possible to help students to structure writing as a coherent argument, to show how they can present a stance through hedging and various kinds of evidence, and to develop critical reading skills by identifying how an author's opinions are expressed. Essentially, in CUE we want students to see that writing at university is very different from writing at school. We want them to take responsibility for clarity in their writing and give them the resources to do this, which means helping them to see that academic writing in English, compared with other contexts and languages, tends to:

- Be more explicit about its structure and purpose
- Use more citations to support arguments
- Focus on actions rather than actors
- Use fewer rhetorical questions than students tend to use in school essays
- Be generally intolerant of digressions
- Be cautious in making claims
- Package processes as things
- Spell out steps in an argument and connections between sentences very clearly

The course therefore focuses on writing and speaking to help students gain some control over these skills. The written genres are essays and reports that appear in most of the students' common core courses and the course introduces students to features like nominalization, impersonality, argument, metadiscourse, stance and citation.

CUE is therefore a *bridging course* in English that brings students up to speed with general academic English. After the first-year core curriculum, students select and study for their majors and take one of the 30 new *English in the Discipline* (ED) courses that are offered in the second, third or fourth year depending on the preference of the client faculty. These focus on the specificity of the language they need for their disciplines. These ED courses either (1) run parallel with a particular course or (2) collect courses together from a particular discipline.

The idea behind these courses is to offer students a more discipline-sensitive approach to English and has involved working in close collaboration with individual faculties and departments to ensure that the English courses align with the work students will do in their content courses.

The development of these ED courses presented opportunities to conduct research into disciplinary literacies and build closer relationships and understandings with departments. As far as possible we sought to engage in research-informed course design, but the process was not always smooth. Teachers encountered a range of attitudes from enthusiastic cooperation to cold indifference. In writing of an earlier attempt at collaboration at HKU, for example, Barron (1992) argued that the divergent philosophies of functionalism in EAP and realism in science can undermine cooperation and lead to the subordination of EAP to subject content. So while we sought to interview faculty, get samples of student writing judged to be *good* by their tutors and align assignments with specific courses, we avoided *partnership* arrangements with courses that might have left us vulnerable to a subordinate teaching role.

At its heart, the idea of *English in the Discipline* recognizes that writing is central to success at a university and that learning to write involves acquiring a new and challenging literacy rather than topping up generic writing skills learned at school. Moreover, because the conventions of academic communication differ considerably across disciplines, identifying the particular language features, discourse practices and communicative skills of target groups becomes central to teaching English in universities. Teachers at CAES therefore had to become researchers of the genres they were to teach and to devise courses around the principle of *specificity*.

Evidence for Academic Specificity

Having provided a sketch of the context, I will offer some evidence for the value of a specific approach to writing instruction drawing on four very different sources: the variations in the features used by academics from different disciplines creating the same genre, how academics seek to project a disciplinary identity in their bios, the differences in tutors' writing expectations and feedback practices in different disciplines and the disciplinary-specific writing assignments that confront undergraduate students. While only the last two of these feed directly into the design of our undergraduate program, all reinforce the importance of specificity as a core principle that informs our understanding of teaching EAP and that underpins our approach to teaching and learning.

Differences in Genre Features

First, rhetorical choices vary enormously across disciplines because they express very different epistemological and social practices. This means that students learn their disciplines as they learn its discourses. While the hard/soft distinction is a blunt instrument to elaborate these differences, it helps reveal some of the ways that authors seek to connect their rhetorical choices to wider social and academic understandings. Some examples of these differences are shown in Table 3.1. This combines a series of studies into features of a corpus of 120 research articles from the ten leading journals in eight disciplines, comprising 1.4 million words (Hyland, 2004, 2005).

Most predictably, we find that authors in the soft knowledge disciplines intrude into their texts through use of *I* or *we* almost three times more frequently than scientists. This allows them to claim authority through personal conviction and to emphasize their contribution. It sends a clear signal of the writer's perspective and distinguishes that perspective from others. But while self-mention can help construct an authoritative self in the humanities, authors in the hard sciences generally downplay their personal role to establish the objectivity of what they report uncontaminated by human activity. They're concerned with generalizations rather than individuals, and this is done by distancing the writer from interpretations using the passive, dummy *it* subjects, and by attributing agency to inanimate things like tables, graphs or results. By subordinating their voice to that of nature, scientists rely on the persuasive force of lab procedures rather than the force of their writing.

Similarly, citation practices also differ enormously, reflecting the extent writers can assume a shared context with readers. *Normal science* produces public knowledge through cumulative growth; problems emerge from earlier

TABLE 3.1 Selected Features across Fields (per 1,000 Words)

Fields	*Self-mention*	*Citation*	*Self-citation*	*Hedges*	*Boosters*	*Directives*
Arts/Humanities	34.2	11.1	0.4	17.5	6.9	1.2
Science/ Engineering	12.1	5.8	0.6	10.25	4.5	2.5

problems, which allows writers to rely on readers recovering the significance of the research without extensive referencing. They are often working on the same problems and are familiar with the earlier work. In the humanities and social sciences, on the other hand, research is less linear, the literature more dispersed and the readership more heterogeneous, so writers can't presuppose a shared context to the same extent, but have to build one far more through citation. This also helps account for the much higher proportion of self-citation in the sciences (12.5 percent of all citations in the sciences compared with 4.3 percent in the humanities). The linearity of research means that scientists are constantly building on their previous work far more than writers in the soft knowledge fields.

The table also shows that hedges and boosters index disciplinary practices, with both occurring more frequently in the arts and humanities papers. *Hedges* are devices that withhold complete commitment to a proposition; they imply that a claim is based on plausible reasoning rather than certain knowledge while *boosters* stress certainty and commitment to statements. Because they represent the writer's direct involvement in a text, they are twice as common in the social sciences as in hard sciences. So hedges indicate the degree of confidence the writer thinks it might be wise to give a claim while opening a discursive space for readers to dispute interpretations. One reason they are more common in the soft fields is that there is less control of variables, more diversity of research outcomes and fewer clear bases for accepting claims than in the sciences. Writers can't report research with the same confidence of shared assumptions so papers rely far more on recognizing alternative voices. Arguments have to be expressed more cautiously by using more hedges. But because methods and results are also more open to question, writers also use more boosters in some circumstances to establish the significance of their work against alternative interpretations, using forms like *definitely*, *prove* and *certain* to restrict alternative voices.

In the hard sciences positivist epistemologies mean that the authority of the individual is subordinated to the authority of the text and facts are meant to *speak for themselves*. This means that writers often disguise their interpretative activities behind linguistic objectivity. Scientists put greater weight on the methods, procedures and equipment used rather than the argument to suggest that results would be the same whoever conducted the research. Less frequent use of hedges and boosters is one way of minimizing the researcher's role, and so is the preference for modals over cognitive verbs as these can more easily combine with inanimate subjects to downplay the person making the evaluation. Modals, then, are one way of helping to reinforce a view of science as an impersonal, inductive enterprise while allowing scientists to see themselves as discovering truth rather than constructing it.

The final feature reflects the difference between hard and soft knowledge areas regarding the extent to which succinctness and precision are valued, or even possible: directives. These instruct the reader to perform an action or to see things in a way determined by the writer and are expressed through imperatives (like *consider, note* and *imagine*) and obligation modals (such as *must, should* and *ought*). They direct readers to three main kinds of activity:

- *Textual acts* direct readers to another part of the text or to another text.
- *Physical acts* direct readers how to carry out some action in the real world.
- *Cognitive acts* instruct readers how to interpret an argument, explicitly positioning readers by encouraging them to *note, concede* or *consider* some argument in the text.

They are not only more frequent in science texts, but also function differently. So while directives represent a writer's intrusion into a text and so might be expected to be more frequent in the soft fields, they are also a potentially risky tactic as they instruct readers to act or see things in a certain way.

If we exclude Philosophy, 60 percent of directives in the soft knowledge texts direct readers to a reference or table rather than telling them how they should interpret an argument. So examples like these are common:

1. *See* Steuer 1983 for a discussion of other contingencies' effects. (Marketing)
2. *Look at* Table 3.2 again for examples of behavioristic variables. (Marketing)
3. For transcription conventions *please refer to* the Appendix. (App Linguistics)

Those in the sciences, on the other hand, largely guide readers explicitly through an argument, emphasizing what they should attend to and the way they should understand it:

4. What has to be recognized is that these issues... (Mech Eng)
5. Consider the case where a very versatile milling machine of type M5... (Elec Eng)
6. A distinction must be made between cytogenetic and molecular resolution. (Biology)

Such differences, it might be supposed, are based in the fact that the linear, problem-oriented nature of the natural sciences enables research to occur within an established framework, allowing authors to presuppose considerable background knowledge among their readers. Arguments can therefore be formulated in a highly standardized code. Moreover, directives facilitate directness, contributing to the succinctness that is valued by both editors and information-saturated scientists.

These variations suggests that although teaching students general academic writing skills can certainly help sensitize them to key rhetorical features of research writing, it can never hope to accommodate the very distinctive ways that disciplines have of seeing, and talking about, the world. Such differences point to the advantages of aligning courses as closely as possible to these epistemological variations in academic writing practices.

Disciplinary Constructions of Identity

Another argument for the significance of disciplinary specificity is the different ways in which individuals talk about themselves, rather than the ways they talk about the world, that is, how they routinely represent a scholarly identity. Although this is not directly related to the development of our ED courses, how members of different disciplines understand themselves in relation to their communities offers strong support for treating the university as structured by specific fields of study. It not only points to the very clear distinctions in disciplinary value systems, and what individual members aspire to achieve, but also reflects what subject tutors might look for in the ways that students present themselves in their writing and behavior.

One of the clearest expressions of identity is in academic bios, a genre where, in 50 to 100 words, academics create a narrative of expertise for themselves. The bio is particularly interesting as it sits in stark contrast to the article itself, which has been stripped of identifying information for blind review. In this section I refer to a study conducted by Polly Tse and myself (Hyland & Tse, 2012) of 600 bios, with 200 from leading journals in each of Applied Linguistics, Electrical Engineering and Philosophy. The corpus was also stratified by status, using four categories from senior academics to technicians and students.

Because the content of bios indicates the kinds of identities likely to be approved by their peers, we first looked at what aspects of themselves writers included in these texts. We found that virtually everyone mentioned employment and together with research interests this comprised over half of the 1,853 moves in the corpus. As to be expected, there was increasing mention of research, employment, publication and achievements with increasing status, as experience brings more things that authors might feel worth mentioning. Discipline, however, was the most significant influence on what authors included in their bios and Table 3.2 shows the variation across the three fields.

The biggest disciplinary difference was the weight engineers gave to education. For them, this was typically linked with the area of study, thereby demonstrating a specific expertise and insider-competence:

7. She received the Ph.D. degree (on thin-oxide technology and novel quasi-nonvolatile memory) from the University of California, Berkeley in 1999.

TABLE 3.2 Acts by Disciplines (per 1,000 Words)

	App Ling	*Elec Eng*	*Philosophy*	*Total*
Employment	16.5	8.3	14.9	13.2
Research	13.1	9.2	8.7	10.3
Publications	6.7	2.1	11.9	6.9
Education	5.1	8.2	4.0	5.8
Achievement	1.5	2.7	0.6	1.6
Com Services	1.1	2.2	1.4	1.5
Personal Profile	0.6	1.4	0.8	0.9
TOTAL	44.6	34.1	42.3	40.2

8. Hyouk Ryeol Choi received the B.S. degree from Seoul National University, Seoul Korea, in 1984, the M.S. degree from Korea Advanced Institute of Science and Technology (KAIST), in 1986, and the Ph.D. degree from Pohang University of Science and Technology (POSTECH), Pohang, Korea, in 1994.

These results perhaps reflect the more apprenticeship-based system of research training common in the hard sciences, where inexperienced academics play a fuller role in the research and publishing process as part of a lab-based team while pursuing their studies. The focus of a PhD is often part of a wider collaborative study and so more likely to warrant early publishing and count as an original contribution. Research is typically less individually conceived and independently conducted than in the soft knowledge fields and so for many engineers educational training is a substantial aspect of their career profile. Education therefore tends to be given more attention in their bios.

In contrast, applied linguists crafted identities around their research interests:

9. Her research interests include human motivation and affect in a variety of applied contexts.
10. Jennifer Whistler's scholarship unpacks traditional and new media convergence within global markets. She is particularly interested in…

Here writers claim academic credibility through their scholarly endeavors, signaling both an insider expertise in areas of current interest to the field and seeking recognition of disciplinary membership. Philosophers, on the other hand, tended to emphasize their publications. Generally these are monographs and involve a greater time investment than the multiply authored and frenetically paced hard sciences articles, thus perhaps counting for more when constructing a self.

Identity is expressed not only in terms of *what* academics say about themselves but also about how they say it and here we borrowed from Systemic Functional Linguistics (SFL) to look at verbs, or process types. SFL sees rhetorical choices as signaling a bi-directional connection between language and context, so that the clause is the linguistic expression of experience. Most relevantly here, verbs express different processes by recognizing a distinction in the grammar between *mental* processes (relating to sensing, e.g., think, belief, feel) and *material* processes (concerned with doing, e.g., work, write, study). A third form is *relational* processes, which express *being*, or the relationship between these categories.

In our bio corpus, writers used relational and material processes in 95 percent of all clauses, stressing what they *are* and what they *do*. This is because bios have something to say about *who the author is*, or rather, how he or she wants to be seen. Other process types are far less significant in this corpus (Table 3.3). Discipline is once again the major influence. Most obviously, Philosophy, the most individualistic of the three disciplines studied, contained a higher proportion of relational processes, while engineering, the most collaborative, contained the least.

Applied linguists favored mental verbs, which project a distinctively intellectual identity to the writer. Linguists represent themselves as thinking academics rather than as intellectual workers grinding out a quota of papers and presentations:

11. Her recent work *considers* the intersections of civic rhetoric and digital spaces.
12. His fascination with computers leads him to *examine* why some technologies are taken up while others are abandoned.

TABLE 3.3 Process Types by Discipline (per 1,000 Words)

	AL	*EE*	*Phil*	*Total*
Relational	30.8	23.7	32.6	27.9
Material	23.6	23.6	22.0	23.2
Mental	2.1	0.7	1.4	1.2
Verbal	1.1	1.4	0.7	1.1
Behavioral	0.1	0.0	0.1	0.0
Existential	0.0	0.0	0.1	0.0
TOTAL	57.7	49.4	56.8	53.5

Engineers, on the other hand, used more verbal forms to present themselves as arguers and talkers, highlighting agency and constructing the author as an active scholar:

13. She *presents* at numerous meetings and *talks* in the area of organic and inorganic semiconductor devices.
14. He *proposes* the use of selectively grown epitaxial layers.

The biggest variations, however, were in relational processes. Philosophers used identifying relational clauses twice as frequently as linguists and four times more than engineers. Explicitly naming themselves as something is obviously key to identity and perhaps reflects the more individualistic ethos in philosophy. Here research represents the creative insights of the author and this is very different to the more humble scientific ideology, which sees results as the collective endeavors of a team using appropriate procedures.

So while the bio seems a standardized genre with limited options, these apparently bland descriptions are cross-cut by discipline, once again reinforcing a view of language use that is based on disciplinary specificity and an individual's membership of a rhetorical community.

Disciplinary Variations in Tutor Expectations

Another major disciplinary difference is tutors' attitudes to writing and feedback. Surprisingly, this is a relatively under-researched area of second language writing research as we have tended to focus our interest on the views of those that *teach* writing rather than those for whom most writing is *done*.

To discover something of faculty expectations about student writing I conducted an interview study of 20 academics, five from each of four faculties comprising eight disciplines at HKU (Hyland, 2013). The findings show broad differences in the attitudes and practices of these teachers. All teachers set written assignments—always as assessment and often as the only assessment. This is the principal means of establishing a visible and measurable form of quality control while developing skills of disciplinary appropriate description, argument and critique. Teachers in the soft knowledge fields, however, were agreed that this is not just a measure of quality control, but of developing skills of disciplinary argument. These quotes give some flavor of this:

> Writing is absolutely key, it embodies the discipline: the main discipline product. Teaching History is about teaching students to write. What I expect them to gain ultimately, as well as the ability to express themselves, is the ability to engage more effectively with discourses in the past. You can't do that unless you can articulate precisely what the discourse means.
>
> (History)

> I think writing is very important. It reflects the ways which students structure and express their thoughts. So, I am less concerned about correct spelling and grammar, what I am very concerned about is teaching them to write logical essays which take a research question and address it in a structured and thoughtful way with evidence and logical conclusions.
>
> (Business)

For teachers in the sciences writing was less important and the fact that students were writing in a second language was often treated as a minor issue:

> If they have problems with language errors, that means they are not working hard enough. They are 21 years old. I mean they should have a high level of ability already, not just what they have learnt since coming here. When I assess their writing I have to treat everybody equally so grade grammar less, a very small percentage, maybe 5%.
>
> (Engineering)

While science instructors recognized the difficulties students had in gaining control over disciplinary writing conventions, they were more likely to blame their lack of experience in using academic English than their L2 backgrounds. Simply, many recognized that students' prior learning experiences could not provide them with the skills required to successfully develop the kinds of elaborated arguments and expositions that are set as assignments. This was typically attributed to the school system:

> I found when students come in, organizing and making a clear argument was in fact pretty weak. Most of them haven't experienced writing or reading reports when they are in high school.
>
> (Biology)

> The biggest problem is they are not responsible for every sentence they write. Maybe this is the writing they do in school? But it is very important that every sentence is evidence for Engineering or professional writing, like in a court. But they write it not to the point. That is not good technical writing.
>
> (Engineering)

Looking at the feedback itself, teachers in the humanities and social sciences tended to offer more explicit commentary on language. These comments, moreover, were largely seen as aspects of disciplinary writing rather than just aiming for correct grammar. They seemed to be seeking an outcome of their feedback and teaching, which involved students gaining a conceptual understanding of the discipline, including both ideational and rhetorical aspects.

> I suppose my feedback focuses on trying to help them clearly state a claim or idea and then how they can develop it in an appropriate style. So, it's about encouraging clarity of thought and clearly defining a question to discuss.
>
> (English)

> Well, when I think about giving feedback, I reflect on what I received as a student as I would think that the comments didn't reflect the amount of work I put into the project. So when I give feedback, I break it down, I give them feedback on the overall impact of the piece, the argument in an essay. Then I would look at whether they got the basic structure, and then look at content. What about historical content? Is it accurate? Has it been persuasively argued? Are they thinking the right way?
>
> (History)

In the sciences, however, feedback was typically less frequent and more cursory, often just ticks or question marks and more commonly just a grade. The texts seem hurriedly checked, rather than carefully read. Tutors rarely required drafts and gave no feedback.

> Actually I don't ask for a draft. Their report is an assignment and they are graded on this. If we give them a chance to write a draft, if we correct a draft, we are just giving a grade to our own work. We don't write their exams for them so why write their reports?
>
> (Engineering)

In fact, tutors often delegated feedback to teaching assistants and several did not see improving students' disciplinary literacy as their job at all:

> They go to the postgraduates first and then to me if necessary. If the students send them their drafts then the demonstrator will give them feedback. But this isn't compulsory. It's up to them.
>
> (Chemistry)

> How helpful is the written feedback for improving students' work? I've no idea. I don't teach them how to write. They go to academic writing classes I think. I don't think my feedback would help them to write.
>
> (Engineering)

While reflecting the ideas of individual faculty members, the views reported here nevertheless display clear patterns of attitudes and practices towards writing by tutors acting as community members. Again, there are differences that underpin the need to adopt a specific approach to English language teaching as a way of best meeting the needs of students.

Variation in Assignment Types

Perhaps specificity is most obvious in the *kinds* of writing that students are asked to do. In most higher education contexts students are not attending academic writing courses in order to learn to *write*; they are learning to write for purposes that lay outside the English class. For them, writing is a tool they need in order to participate in their disciplines and to demonstrate their learning to readers in those disciplines.

Writing therefore contributes to learning in areas other than writing itself: instruction relates to the acquisition of an academic competence in both disciplinary knowledge and the ability to discuss it appropriately. This kind of writing often takes a very different form to that which goes on in writing classes, evoking a distinction made by Manchón (2011) between Learning-to-Write (LW), where students are learning to express themselves in writing, and Writing-to-Learn (WL), where they are using writing to develop their expertise in the practices of the discipline. A Writing-to-Learn perspective, then, sees writing as a mode of learning, of both content and the way to talk about that content, which means that teaching should account for the knowledge learners already possess and be situated in the context in which it is used.

The most obvious expression of this difference is the fact that different fields value different kinds of argument and set different writing tasks. Learners are required to think their way into their fields through writing, and professors across the curriculum seek to initiate students into these particular styles of thinking by setting specific writing assignments (e.g., Currie, 1993). Instruction in the concepts and content of a subject involves students gaining a familiarity with the norms, expectations and conventions of writing of that interpretive community and this social and epistemological diversity is the context in which second language students experience writing at university. Written genres themselves become the tools by which knowledge and learning are articulated for students. Because of this, writing has come to be seen as a social practice rather than a skill (Lillis, 2001) and specific genres are recognized as having a powerful influence on how students understand and engage with their disciplines.

Thus, the humanities and social sciences stress analyzing and synthesizing multiple sources while the sciences value activity-based skills like describing procedures, defining objects and planning solutions. We also know that different fields make use of different genres, so that in their large-scale corpus study of 30 disciplines in UK universities, Nesi and Gardner (2012) found 13 different *genre families*, ranging from case studies through empathy writing to reports. These differ considerably in their social purpose, genre structure and the networks they form with other genres.

Even in fairly cognate fields students write quite different texts. In looking at the assignments given to medical students, for instance, Gimenez (2009) found that nursing and midwifery students were given very different writing assignments. Our own research for our ED courses has discovered that students in the speech and hearing sciences write reflective journals, journalism students write narratives and pharmacy students produce drug profile presentations. Simply, different fields value different kinds of argument and set different writing tasks for their students. Again this underlines the different ways students are assessed and different expectations of how they should write.

Back to School: Specificity in the ED Classroom

Turning from the research back to HKU, I have space for just one example of an *English in the Discipline* course to show what a specific writing course looks like in practice.

English for Clinical Pharmacy is a third-year ED course focusing on common spoken and written genres in drug information and developed in collaboration with colleagues from the faculty of medicine. Collaboration with faculty can be a fraught process, dependent on good relations with imaginative individuals in the client faculty who are able to recognize the value of writing and communication skills to their students. *English for Clinical Pharmacy* represents a good example of what can be achieved through good relations and mutual respect.

The first part of the course involves introducing specific vocabulary and strategies for learning new medical terms as well as the citation conventions that students will need. This is to provide them with the ability to select vocabulary and rhetorical devices appropriate to drug information genres, and to synthesize and cite information and evidence from multiple sources to provide drug recommendations. In the first assignment, for example, students have to search for and select relevant drug information from reliable sources and respond to enquiries about drugs from different stakeholders, indicating their sources. Figure 3.1 shows how the exercise is formatted.

The second written assignment drives the course and involves students applying their genre knowledge in writing a comparative drug evaluation, synthesizing and properly citing information and evidence from multiple sources to provide recommendations. Drug evaluation is a basic part of a pharmacist's career, as many of the documents they write have to be based on some form of drug evaluation. Thus, together with the follow-up poster presentation of their recommendation, this mini project carries 45 percent of the marks for the course (half of these are given by colleagues in the Faculty of Medicine).

Here students, working in pairs, evaluate and recommend two drugs that can be used to treat the same medical condition. To make sure the exercise is meaningful,

City H☺spital
Drug Information Services

Online Forum
Post your question here and it will be answered by our registered pharmacists:

Question:
I bought some cimetidine from the pharmacy to try and help my reflux problems. I have also been taking antacids and the pharmacist said something about not taking antacids and other medications at the same time and also something about not taking cimetidine for too long. Can you please remind me of these details?

Response:

Email

From: Dr. Ho Man Wei
To: (Student's name)
Subject: Cimetidine
Dear (student's name),
My patient appears to have developed gynaecomastia and he believes that this is due to the cimetidine that I have prescribed him to treat his GORD symptoms. Could this be possible and if so, what alternatives would you suggest?
Best regards,
Dr. Ho
City Hospital, Hong Kong

Email: response

From: (Student's name)
To: Dr. Ho Man Wei
Subject:

FIGURE 3.1 Drug enquiry assignment

the drugs assigned to the students are selected by the Pharmacy department. The Pharmacy department also advised us on the writing task—this is a hospital bulletin article—as this is a common genre for clinical pharmacists who are working in a hospital. Students receive input on the hospital bulletin article by analyzing two exemplars of the genre, working in pairs to identify the moves/sections and key features, before planning the structure of their own drug evaluation article. Students need to conduct further research to make an informed comparison. The students have to decide which aspects of the drugs are worth evaluating and comparing and decide on an appropriate structure for the bulletin article. Each student pair writes a first draft and receives feedback before writing a final draft.

Thus the project provides an opportunity for learners to develop and practice useful and highly disciplinary-specific research and academic writing skills.

They have to search for and select relevant drug information from reliable sources, compare drugs and write a comparative drug evaluation article for publication in an online pharmacy bulletin. To ensure the authenticity of all this, the project has not only been jointly designed by Pharmacy and English tutors in partnership, but is also co-assessed with members of the Pharmacy department. The involvement of pharmacy tutors helps ensure motivation and authenticity and the students appreciate the efforts made to support their learning. While collaboration with faculty experts can be a difficult and bruising experience, often involving attempts to subordinate the writing course to faculty imperatives, this case shows how useful to students a successful partnership can be.

Conclusions

I have argued that the idea of specificity is central to teaching writing at university because students' success depends not on what they produce in their English class but on how far they can demonstrate a competence in disciplinary discourses. Disciplines are language-using communities where writers, texts and readers come together. They are the contexts within which students learn to communicate and to interpret each other's talk, gradually acquiring the specialized discourses of the group. Although the notion of discipline is not altogether straightforward, successful academic writing does not occur in a vacuum. Instead, it largely depends on the individual writer's projection of a shared context as they seek to embed their writing in a particular social world.

I have located my discussion in the context of one country and one language center within it, but my argument is, of course, much wider. The research I have drawn on shows that academic work is structured within frameworks of beliefs and practices and that to be taken seriously, students need to be able to engage in these practices and, in particular, in their discourses. This means that as writing teachers we need to understand the distinctive ways that disciplines have of asking questions, addressing a literature, criticizing ideas and presenting arguments, so we can help students participate effectively in their learning. Our role is not to top up students' language proficiency or polish composing skills but to help them develop new kinds of literacy. Writing teachers are literacy teachers and our task is to equip learners with the communicative skills they need to participate in particular academic cultures.

References

Barron, C. (1992). Cultural syntonicity: Cooperative relationships between the ESP Unit and other departments. *Hong Kong Papers in Linguistics and Language Teaching, 15*, 1–14.

Currie, P. (1993). Entering a disciplinary community: Conceptual activities required to write for one introductory university course. *Journal of Second Language Writing, 2*(2), 101–117.

Evans, S., & Green, C. (2007). Why EAP is necessary: A survey of Hong Kong tertiary students. *Journal of English for Academic Purposes, 6*(1), 3–17.

Gimenez, J. (2009). Beyond the academic essay: Discipline-specific writing in nursing and midwifery. *Journal of English for Academic Purposes,* 7(3), 151–164.

Hyland, K. (2004). *Disciplinary discourses: Social interactions in academic writing.* Ann Arbor, MI: University of Michigan Press.

Hyland, K. (2005). *Metadiscourse.* London: Continuum.

Hyland, K. (2013). Faculty feedback: Perceptions and practices in L2 disciplinary writing. *Journal of Second Language Writing, 22,* 240–253.

Hyland, K., & Tse, P. (2012). "She has received many honours": Identity construction in article bio statements. *Journal of English for Academic Purposes, 11,* 155–165.

Li, D. C. S. (2009). Learning English for academic purposes: Why Chinese EFL learners find EAP so difficult to master. *Revista Canaria de Estudios Ingleses, 59,* 33–46.

Lillis, T. (2001) *Student writing: Access, regulation, desire.* London: Routledge.

Manchón, R. M. (Ed.). (2011). *Learning-to-write and writing-to-learn in an additional language.* Amsterdam: John Benjamins.

Nesi, H., & Gardner, S. (2012). *Genres across the disciplines: Student writing in Higher Education.* Cambridge: Cambridge University Press.

Tsui, A. B. M. (2009). *HKU common core curriculum: What is "common" and what is "core"?* Presentation at the 3+3+4 Symposium on "Core Curriculum," May 12, 2009.

4

DEVELOPING A FLEXIBLE, IN-SESSIONAL EAP WRITING PROGRAM FOR UNDERGRADUATES AT A LARGE RESEARCH UNIVERSITY IN THE UNITED STATES

Tony Silva

Introduction

This chapter reports on an informal case study of the development of a university second language writing program over a period of roughly 25 years. My purpose is not to describe an exemplary program—that is, this will not be a *how to* piece; rather it is *a show and tell* account of how a program developed in a particular context. The chapter will include an account of the context, history and current status of the program (focusing on administration and staffing), the curricular approach adopted, a description of the focal course (ENGL 106i) and its contents (activities and assignments), my reflections and conclusions (thoughts about pedagogical implications) and appendixes (comprising relevant course documents).

Context

This context is Purdue University, a public state university located in West Lafayette, Indiana, in the United States. The university currently enrolls more than 37,000 students, around 28,000 undergraduates and 9,000 graduate students (Purdue University, 2016a). More than 9,000 of these students are international students (Purdue University, 2016b), which gives Purdue the third largest international student population of all public universities in the United States (Institute of International Education, 2016).

These international students currently represent 125 countries and constitute roughly 23 percent of the entire student body—about 18 percent of undergraduates and 40 percent of graduate students. Purdue's international students come primarily from East and South Asia—about 48 percent from China, 18 percent from India and 7 percent from South Korea, and are enrolled primarily in STEM areas—especially in engineering (41 percent), science (17 percent) and technology (6 percent) (Purdue University, 2015). This chapter will focus on Purdue's undergraduate international student population.

The ESL Writing Program is part of the Introductory Composition Program, which is housed in the English department. The focus of the Introductory Composition Program, which is administered primarily by the department's Graduate Program in Rhetoric and Composition, is *First-Year Composition* (ENGL 106), a required course for virtually all undergraduates at Purdue, serving roughly 6,000 students a year. The primary focus of the ESL Writing Program is *First-Year Composition for International Students* (ENGL 106i). This course is managed by the English department's Graduate Program in Second Language Studies/ESL and serves roughly 900 students a year.

A Brief History of the ESL Writing Program

In 1986, I came to Purdue as a faculty spouse/English department doctoral student in rhetoric and composition and linguistics. Soon thereafter, I was teaching in and informally coordinating Purdue's writing support courses for undergraduate international students—a two-course, first-year composition sequence (ENGL 101i and ENGL 102i). This sequence was parallel to the mainstream composition sequence required of all undergraduate students.

After graduating and teaching for a year at Auburn University, I returned to Purdue as an assistant professor, where part of my new job was to direct the incipient ESL Writing Program. As the program moved forward, curricula were reviewed and revised, a pool of teachers (primarily English department graduate students) was cultivated and enrollment in international sections of first-year composition was capped at 20 students. (The mainstream ENGL 106 course was capped at 27 at that time.)

In 2003, a major development in the English composition program caused some significant changes in the undergraduate ESL writing courses. The mainstream composition program went from a two-course sequence (ENGL 101 and ENGL 102) to a reconceived single composition course (ENGL 106) that would meet five days a week and include classroom instruction, digital technology and regular teacher–student conferences. The ESL Writing Program followed suit and, in addition, was allowed to cap enrollment at 15 students per section. This situation still holds today, except for the fact that the numbers of international students and, consequently, the number of international sections of first-year composition, has skyrocketed.

Current Status of the ESL Writing Program

Administration/Director

The Director of the ESL Writing Program has always been a member of the faculty of the Graduate Program in Second Language Studies/ESL. This was my job from 1991 to 2015. Currently, the ESL Writing Program Director's responsibilities include the ongoing development and modification of its courses and their instructional materials, the hiring of instructors, the mentoring and evaluation of new instructors (which involves a weekly meeting, two class observations of each new instructor, two post-observation conferences and a review of instructor evaluations) and staff supervision and development.

Teaching Staff

The ESL Writing Program's instructors are typically students in the Graduate Program in Second Language Studies/ESL (SLS); however, it does sometimes employ people from other programs in the English department (for example, Rhetoric and Composition, English Language and Linguistics, and Creative Writing) and from departments and programs outside the English department (for example, Education, Languages and Cultures, and Comparative Literature).

During their first year in the SLS program, these graduate students each teach one section of mainstream *First-Year Composition* per semester and receive a lot of support, including a week of intensive orientation before they begin their first semester and two semesters of mentoring. This mentoring comprises a three-hour-per-week course in each of their first two semesters. This course is a practicum in the teaching of writing that involves reading professional literature on the teaching of writing, the study of methodologies, assessment issues and the relationship between theory and pedagogy. Mentor groups (usually with 8–10 students) are typically led by faculty members or advanced graduate students from the Graduate Program in Rhetoric and Composition.

The Graduate Program in Second Language Studies/ESL typically requires its students to teach and get mentored in the mainstream composition program during their first year. The aim is to give them the opportunity to interact with students from other graduate programs in the English department and give them experience or additional experience in teaching a writing course—most of our SLS graduate students come in with quite a bit of ESL teaching experience, but sometimes have not taught writing per se. After students have taught mainstream composition for a year, and if they want to teach ESL writing, they must sign up for a practicum in teaching ESL Writing taught by the ESL Writing Program director. However, this mentoring is much less extensive. After a two-hour orientation meeting, the group meets for an hour once a week, basically to talk about what has been going on in their classes in the previous week, to share and discuss student papers (in the manner of a reading group), to address problems that come up and to preview the week to come.

At present, around 75 percent of the ESL writing instructors are international students themselves. Currently, we have instructors from Afghanistan, China, India, Iran, Japan, Libya, Poland, Russia, Saudi Arabia, Taiwan, Thailand and Turkey as well as instructors from the United States. Until very recently, these instructors have been almost exclusively teaching assistants. In recent years, due to increased demand, the program has brought on both short- and long-term lecturers.

Students

Our undergraduate international students these days come, for the most part, from East Asia, specifically China, India and South Korea, with small groups of students from numerous other countries. They are typically first-year students with a mean age of about nineteen. On average, they have studied English for more than eight years; they are more often men (58 percent) than women (42 percent), and most of them are majoring in science, engineering or business. They are typically well educated, affluent, cosmopolitan and technologically savvy. However, as most of them are in an English medium university for the first time, it takes a while for their latent English ability to manifest itself.

Curricular Approach

Before coming to Purdue, my primary experience in teaching second language writing had been with intermediate-level English learners in Intensive English Programs. Being young and foolish, I tried to use basically the same materials and approaches with my students at Purdue, even though they were matriculated students with more advanced levels of English proficiency. Unsurprisingly, this did not go very well. So I tried this and I tried that with various degrees of success until I ran across a journal article by Ilona Leki who was working in a similar context and with students similar to mine at the University of Tennessee.

The article, which appeared in *TESOL Journal* in 1991–1992, was entitled "Building expertise through sequenced writing assignments." In short, this article calls for helping students write with authority and knowledge on a topic of their choice. It combines elements of process, EAP and genre-based approaches and recognizes the rhetorical, linguistic and strategic dimensions of writing. Leki argues that many first-year undergraduate students may not have decided on a major and, therefore, may not have the requisite knowledge to write about disciplinary issues authoritatively.

Leki suggests that, if teachers are working for student empowerment, it is important for them to aid students in becoming acquainted and comfortable with a body of knowledge and to help them locate, analyze and synthesize information on a topic. To do this, it is advisable to not ask students to write on a variety of topics, but to link writing assignments and, thus, aid students in building a knowledge base and set of skills in a particular area.

In this approach, with input from their teacher, students are asked to pick a topic they find engaging enough to work with for an entire semester and on which they have substantial personal experience. Leki advises that student writing be done workshop style, wherein students work through multiple drafts and get input from their instructor and classmates on developing, revising and editing their texts. This approach is meant to help student writers develop their knowledge of, expertise with and commitment to their chosen topic in a specific rhetorical context, and thus give the course assignments continuity and purpose.

Obviously, I was intrigued by this approach. I gave it a try and found that it and my student population went together like peanut butter and jelly.

Back to the Course

At this time, our *First-Year Composition* course for international students enrolls those who feel they might be at a disadvantage in the mainstream *First-Year Composition* course, due to such factors as level of English proficiency, experience in writing in English or familiarity with American cultural or educational practices. Our course is not obligatory for undergraduate international students; enrolling in it is a choice made by students in consultation with their advisors. The primary goal of the course is to help students become more comfortable with and proficient in writing in English.

Both the mainstream and international sections of the course meet the same composition requirement; bear the same amount of credit; share a focus on strategic, rhetorical and linguistic issues; and integrate classroom instruction, individual and small group conferencing and the use of technology. Additionally, the mainstream and international sections are not distinguished on students' transcripts so that there will be no stigma attached to taking an international section.

All international sections meet one hour a day five days a week in a room set up as a wireless computer lab or in a regular computer lab, giving students and teachers constant and easy access to that technology. There is no required textbook, though instructors are free to use textbooks or reference books if they so desire. The program director provides instructors with materials to give to their students—a policy handout, a syllabus, assignment sheets, an analytic grading rubric and access to sample papers from a recently developed online corpus.

The course requires the completion of five major writing projects. Students write three drafts for each assignment and receive feedback from both their instructors and their peers. First drafts are typically responded to in small group conferences and focus on content and organization; second drafts are typically responded to in individual conferences and focus on language issues. Third drafts receive grades and written comments. Students spend roughly half of their time in class and the other half in conferences. They receive instruction on relevant rhetorical, textual and linguistic issues when each assignment is introduced in class as well as in their individual or small-group, draft-focused conferences with their teachers and peers. What information is provided and how it is presented is the prerogative of the teachers.

Preliminaries

The course begins with the provision of a policies and procedures document (see Appendix A), detailing course information and materials and addressing issues such as attendance, participation, assessment (formative and summative) and grading. There is also a detailed course schedule (see Appendix B) that indicates what will be covered and what will be due for each of the 74 class meetings. In addition, students do an in-class writing assignment, so that we can assess their English language writing ability, and complete a brief online survey to help us understand the demographics our student population.

Writer's Autobiography

The first major writing assignment is a writer's autobiography (see Appendix C). This assignment has three objectives (1) to help students develop their narrative skills, (2) to give us some insights into their experiences as writers and (3) to encourage students to think of themselves as writers. The focus of this assignment is one's development as a writer. Students are asked to consider their writing experiences, in all of the languages they write in, and to not limit their accounts to school experiences. They are asked to consider such things as people who have influenced their writing, their successes and failures in writing, whether writing is easy or difficult for them and why and their strengths and weaknesses in writing. They are told that they do not need to write about all of or only these areas nor follow this order in their papers—that the purpose of thinking about these topics is to help them recover and arrange relevant memories.

For this and the other major writing assignments, students are informed that their audience for their writing should be their fellow classmates.

Topic Negotiation

After the completion of the Writer's Autobiography unit, teachers meet one-on-one with their students to negotiate the topic a student will address in each of the subsequent writing assignments (see Appendix D). The sequenced writing project allows students, in consultation with their instructor, to choose their own topic, as long as this topic (1) interests and motivates them; (2) is one which they have personal experience with and an investment in; and (3) allows them to successfully complete the papers in the sequence, which include a proposal, a synthesis paper, an interview report and an argumentative essay.

Students are asked to bring along three topics to discuss with their teacher and to decide together on which topic will be the most viable. Some successful topics have included the causes of Alzheimer's disease—chosen by a student whose grandmother had recently died of this affliction; working with autistic children—chosen by a student who had an autistic younger brother; and my favorite, cures for baldness—chosen by a student terrified by the fact that male pattern baldness ran in his family. He chose to go with implants, by the way. This stage is also where a reading component for the course is introduced. Students are asked to locate and read at least one published source of information pertaining to their topic each week and to provide the instructor with publication information for the source.

Proposal

The first of the sequenced writing assignments is a proposal (see Appendix E). The purpose of this assignment is to build a foundation for the subsequent papers they will write for the class. They are asked to delineate the topic they will be writing about, explain why the topic is interesting and important, describe their personal experience related to their topic and develop and state questions addressing what they would like to learn about their topic. They are told that it is not necessary to address these issues in this order; for example, they might want to begin their proposal with a narrative about their experience with the topic.

Synthesis Paper

The second of the sequenced writing assignments is a synthesis paper (see Appendix F). This assignment's purpose is to have students engage with published work addressing their topic by asking them to find, read and summarize at least three relevant texts. The students are asked in their papers to include information about the publications, indicate the focus and aim of the paper, present and integrate their summaries and offer their thoughts on the information provided in the summaries.

Interview Report

The third of the sequenced assignments is an interview report (see Appendix G). The purpose of this assignment is for students to get additional information on their topic by interviewing someone who is very knowledgeable about the subject. This requires students to find and arrange a meeting with a willing expert, develop interview questions, meet and interview this individual and record (with permission) or take notes on the interview. They are asked, after deciding on three to five subtopics in the interview that they would like to address, to begin their report by identifying their topic, stating the purpose of conducting the interview, introducing and describing the qualifications of the interviewee, detailing the context in which the interview took place, presenting relevant material from the interviews and reflecting on what they learned from the interview.

Argumentative Essay

The final and culminating assignment is a formal argumentative essay (see Appendix H). The purpose of this assignment is to produce an argumentative essay on the chosen topic, using the knowledge gained in completing the previous assignments and any additional sources of information. Students are asked to begin by orienting readers to their topic, stating their position and previewing their arguments; they continue by developing support for their position while acknowledging potential opposition and rebutting it, and conclude by briefly summarizing their argument and suggesting what needs to be done. This paper requires the use of documentation and the inclusion of a reference list.

Reflection

Does the Course Work?

It seems to. Student writing seems to improve (as much as one can expect over a fifteen-week period). Students evaluate their instructors and the class favorably. Instructors tell me they enjoy teaching the course. I get very few complaints.

Why Does It Work?

Because our situation is optimal in many ways: we are fortunate to have a lot of support—from the English department, from the Introductory Composition Program, from the Graduate Programs in Rhetoric and Composition and Second Language Studies/ESL and from the world famous Purdue Writing Lab. We have outstanding instructors—dedicated, engaged, knowledgeable, experienced, humane people who are almost always multilingual and have international experience. It is clear that students appreciate being taught by professionals who have been in their situation. And we have, for the most part, world-class students—smart, hardworking and highly motivated—for whom our course is often a welcome port in a storm. They often comment on how comfortable they feel in the course because its relatively small size allows them to get to know their classmates better and because of the sense of camaraderie they feel with their international student peers. Given this context, it would be hard to fail.

Are There Challenges?

Yes. One challenge is meeting the demand for our course—given the rapid and continuing increase in the number of international undergraduate students at Purdue. Another, related, challenge is insufficient support both for the ESL Writing Program and for the Graduate Program in Second Language Studies/ESL on which it depends. To speak frankly, the university is run primarily as corporate entity, whose central focus is on meeting *revenue targets*. One way to meet these targets is to increase enrollment of international undergraduate students—who pay more than three times as much as students from the state of Indiana. Unfortunately, but predictably, the amount of money the university gets from these students is not matched by the funds allotted for the language support many of them desire and need. This situation makes the growth and maintenance of the quality of our program increasingly difficult.

Conclusion

I am well aware that writing courses reflect and are shaped by the context in which they were created. The course described in this chapter is no exception. It was designed for matriculated undergraduate international students with relatively advanced language proficiency in small classes at a large North American research university and is taught by highly motivated, well-prepared and well-supported instructors. These conditions allowed me, in my role as an ESL writing program administrator, to give my instructors the freedom and flexibility to adapt this course to fit their teaching styles, to encourage them to innovate and to give them as much or as little support and guidance as they felt was necessary. I believe that this arrangement worked well for me, and it is my hope that you will find something in this chapter that will be useful in your context.

References

Institute of International Education (2016). *Open doors data.* Retrieved July 28, 2016 from www.iie.org/en/Research-and-Publications/Open-Doors/Data/International-Students/Leading-Institutions/2014-15.

Jacobs, H. L., Zinkgraf, S. A., Wormuth, D. R., Hartfiel, V. F., & Hughey, J. B. (1981). *Testing ESL composition: A practical approach.* Rowley, MA: Newbury House.

Leki, I. (1991–1992). Building expertise through sequenced writing assignments. *TESOL Journal, 1*(2), 19–23.

Purdue University (2015). *International students and scholars enrollment and statistical reports: Fall 2015.* Retrieved July 28, 2016 from www.iss.purdue.edu/Resources/Docs/Reports/ISS_StatisticalReportFall15.pdf.

Purdue University (2016a). *University enrollment summary.* Retrieved July 28, 2016 from www.purdue.edu/enrollmentmanagement/researchanddata/enrollment-summary/2016/Spring/Spring%202016.pdf.

Purdue University (2016b). *International students and scholars enrollment and statistical reports.* Retrieved July 28, 2016 from www.iss.purdue.edu/ISSOffice/Reports.cfm.

Appendix A: Course Information and Policies

Course Information

Course/Section Number:
Course Meeting Time:
Classroom:
Instructor's Name:
Instructor's Office:
Instructor's Phone Number:
Instructor's Email:
Instructor's Office Hours:

Course Materials

Course materials will be provided by your instructor.

Grades

Course grades will be calculated on a 100-point scale
A = 90–100
B = 80–89
C = 70–79
D = 60–69
F = <60

Points will be awarded in the following amounts
Class Participation—10
Readings—10
Paper #1: Writer's Autobiography—10
Paper #1: Proposal—15
Paper #2: Synthesis Paper—15
Paper #3: Interview Report—15
Paper #4: Argumentative Essay—25

Course Policies

Attendance

You are expected to attend all class and conference sessions. You will be allowed three unexcused absences without penalty. Each additional unexcused absence may result in the deduction of 2 points from your course grade.

Lateness

You are expected to arrive on time for all class and conference sessions. You will be allowed three unexcused late arrivals. Every three additional unexcused late arrivals will be equivalent to one unexcused absence.

Late Work

You are expected to hand in all assignments on time. In the case of unexcused late submissions, for each day that a paper (a first, second or final draft) is late, two points may be deducted from your grade on that paper.

Class Participation

You are expected to participate cooperatively, constructively and to the best of your ability in all class activities.

Appendix B: Class Schedule

Class	*Day*	*Focus*	*Assignment Due*
1	M	Introductions	
2	T	Writing Sample	
3	W	Policies and Procedures	
4	R	Writing Lab Orientation	
5	F	Writers' Autobiography – Assignment/ Planning	
6	M	Writer's Autobiography – First Draft Review	First Draft (Autobiography)
7	T	Writer's Autobiography – First Draft Conferences	
8	W	Writer's Autobiography – First Draft Conferences	
9	R	Writer's Autobiography – First Draft Conferences	
10	F	Writer's Autobiography – Second Draft Review	Second Draft (Autobiography)
	M	Labor Day – No Class	
11	T	Writer's Autobiography – Second Draft Conferences	
12	W	Writer's Autobiography – Second Draft Conferences	
13	R	Writer's Autobiography – Second Draft Conferences	
14	F	Writer's Autobiography – Second Draft Conferences	
15	M	Writer's Autobiography – Second Draft Conferences	

(continued)

(continued)

Class	*Day*	*Focus*	*Assignment Due*
16	T	Topic Conferences	Final Draft (Autobiography)
17	W	Topic Conferences	
18	R	Topic Conferences	
19	F	Topic Conferences	
20	M	Topic Conferences	
21	T	Library Orientation	Reading 1
22	W	Proposal – Assignment/Planning	
23	R	Proposal – First Draft Review	First Draft (Proposal)
24	F	Proposal – First Draft Conferences	
25	M	Proposal – First Draft Conferences	Reading 2
26	T	Proposal – First Draft Conferences	
27	W	Proposal – Second Draft Review	Second Draft (Proposal)
28	R	Proposal – Second Draft Conferences	
29	F	Proposal – Second Draft Conferences	
30	M	Proposal – Second Draft Conferences	Reading 3
31	T	Proposal – Second Draft Conferences	
32	W	Proposal – Second Draft Conferences	
33	R	Synthesis Paper – Assignment/Planning	Final Draft (Proposal)
34	F	Synthesis Paper – Summarizing/Paraphrasing	
	M	October Break – No Class	
	T	October Break – No Class	

Class	*Day*	*Focus*	*Assignment Due*
35	W	Synthesis Paper – First Draft Review	First Draft (Synthesis)
36	R	Synthesis Paper – First Draft Conferences	
37	F	Synthesis Paper – First Draft Conferences	
38	M	Synthesis Paper – First Draft Conferences	Reading 4
39	T	Synthesis Paper – Second Draft Review	Second Draft (Synthesis)
40	W	Synthesis Paper – Second Draft Conferences	
41	R	Synthesis Paper – Second Draft Conferences	
42	F	Synthesis Paper – Second Draft Conferences	
43	M	Synthesis Paper – Second Draft Conferences	Reading 5
44	T	Synthesis Paper – Second Draft Conferences	
45	W	Interview Report – Assignment/Planning	Final Draft (Synthesis)
46	R	Interview Report – Interview Etiquette/ Questions	
47	F	Interview Report – Interview Question Review	Questions (Interview)
48	M	Interview Report – Interviews	Reading 6
49	T	Interview Report – Interviews	
50	W	Interview Report – First Draft Review	First Draft (Interview)
51	R	Interview Report – First Draft Conferences	
52	F	Interview Report – First Draft Conferences	
53	M	Interview Report – First Draft Conferences	Reading 7

(continued)

(continued)

Class	*Day*	*Focus*	*Assignment Due*
54	T	Interview Report – Second Draft Review	Second Draft (Interview)
55	W	Interview Report – Second Draft Conferences	
56	R	Interview Report – Second Draft Conferences	
57	F	Interview Report – Second Draft Conferences	
58	M	Interview Report – Second Draft Conferences	Reading 8
59	T	Interview Report – Second Draft Conferences	
60	W	Argumentative Essay – Assignment/Planning	Final Draft (Interview)
61	R	Argumentative Essay – Paraphrasing	
62	F	Argumentative Essay – Quotation	
63	M	Argumentative Essay – Documentation	
64	T	Argumentative Essay – First Draft Review	First Draft (Argument)
	W	Thanksgiving Break – No Class	
	R	Thanksgiving Break – No Class	
	F	Thanksgiving Break – No Class	
65	M	Argumentative Essay – First Draft Conferences	
66	T	Argumentative Essay – First Draft Conferences	
67	W	Argumentative Essay – First Draft Conferences	

Class	*Day*	*Focus*	*Assignment Due*
68	R	Argumentative Essay – Second Draft Review	Second Draft (Argument)
69	F	Argumentative Essay – Second Draft Conferences	
70	M	Argumentative Essay – Second Draft Conferences	
71	T	Argumentative Essay – Second Draft Conferences	
72	W	Argumentative Essay – Second Draft Conferences	
73	R	Argumentative Essay – Second Draft Conferences	
74	F	Course Wrap-up	Final Draft (Argument)

Appendix C: Writer's Autobiography Assignment

Audience

Your audience for this paper will be the members of this class.

Focus

The focus of this assignment is your development as a writer—in both your native and second or foreign language(s). Consider your entire life, including pre-school years, and do not limit yourself to school experiences. Some areas of your experience you might want to consider include: people who have influenced your writing, your memories of successes and failures in writing, your feelings about writing (whether it is easy or difficult for you and why) and your strengths and weaknesses in writing. You do not need to write about all of or only these areas nor follow this order in your paper. The purpose of thinking about these topics is to help you recover and arrange relevant memories. Please note that although the assignment asks you to focus on your *writing* history, you might have to include certain experiences that do not explicitly relate to writing but provide a context for those experiences.

Format

Your Writer's Autobiography should be in the form of a Word document. Your document should be double-spaced, have one-inch margins on all sides and be done in a 12-point font.

Contents

In your Writer's Autobiography, which should run about 750–1,000 words, you will need

- A title
- An introduction that contextualizes your narrative
- A body that details your experience as a writer—you may want to do this in chronological order
- A conclusion that brings a sense of closure to your account

Suggestion for Drafting Your Proposal

- Give yourself at least two to three uninterrupted hours to develop your draft
- Start by making some notes regarding what you would like to include in your narrative
- Consider writing the body of your paper first and then developing your introduction and conclusion
- Give your draft a title *after* you have completed it

Appendix D: Sequenced Writing Project Overview

For this course you will need to complete a sequenced writing project, in which you will produce four papers on the same subject. The assumption behind this is that you will write best when each assignment builds directly on the previous assignment. You are free to choose, in consultation with your teacher, your own topic. This topic must be one that you:

- Find interesting and want to learn more about, because you will be working with it all semester
- Have had some personal experience with
- Can address in all four papers (the Proposal, Interview Report, Synthesis Paper and Argumentative Essay) required by this project—which are described below

Proposal: involves introducing the topic you will be writing about, explaining why you believe this topic is interesting and important, describing your personal experience related to this topic and developing and stating a research question or questions.

Interview Report: involves writing up a report of an interview with someone who is an expert on your topic.

Synthesis Paper: involves finding credible published material on your topic and summarizing and integrating the information in this material.

Argumentative Essay: involves using all the previously gained information on your topic (and more) to create an essay that essentially answers your research question or questions.

Appendix E: Proposal Assignment

Audience

Your audience for this paper, as well as for all the papers to follow, will be the members of this class.

Purpose

The purpose of this assignment is to build a foundation for the other papers you will write for this class—the Synthesis Paper, the Interview Report and the Argumentative Essay. You can build this foundation by recounting everything your currently know about the topic you have chosen, including the significance of the topic and your personal involvement with it.

Format

Your Proposal should be in the form of a Word document. Your document should be double-spaced, have a one-inch margin on all sides and be done in a 12-point font.

Contents

In your Proposal, which should run about 750 words, you will need to:

- Develop a title
- Introduce and delineate the topic you will be writing about
- Explain why you believe your topic is interesting and important
- Describe your personal experience related to your topic
- Develop and state questions addressing what you would like to find out about your topic

Note: It is not necessary to address these issues in this order; for example, you might want to begin your proposal with a narrative about your experience with the topic.

Suggestions for Drafting Your Proposal

- Give yourself at least two to three uninterrupted hours to develop your draft
- Start by making some notes regarding what you would like to include in each section
- Draft each section separately before trying to tie them together
- Give your draft a title *after* you have completed it

Appendix F: Synthesis Paper Assignment

Audience

Your audience for this paper, and all of the other written assignments, will be the members of this class.

Purpose

The purpose of this assignment is to continue building a foundation for the other papers you will write for this class—the Interview Report and the Argumentative Essay. You can continue to build this foundation by finding, reading and summarizing three pieces of publicly available published material on your topic and by integrating the relevant information from your summaries.

Format

Your Synthesis Paper should be in the form of a Word document. Your document should be double-spaced, have a one-inch margin on all sides and be done in a 12-point font.

Contents

Your Synthesis Paper, which should run about 1,000 words, should have two main parts:

- Summaries of each of your three pieces of published material
- A framework for your summaries

The framework for your synthesis paper should include an introduction, conclusion and transitional material. Your introduction should identify your topic, include information about the publications you will summarize and indicate what you will do in this paper. Your conclusion should include your thoughts on the information provided in the summaries (this constitutes your synthesis, that is, your combining of separate elements into a coherent whole) and provide a sense of closure. Your transitional material should link the sections of your paper (introduction, summaries and conclusion).

Suggestions for Drafting Your Synthesis Paper

- Give yourself at least two to three uninterrupted hours to develop your draft
- Start by closely reading and summarizing your three publications one at a time
- Decide on the order of presentation of your summaries
- Draft your introduction
- Draft your conclusion
- Link the parts of your paper
- Give your draft a title

Appendix G: Interview Report Assignment

Audience

Your audience for this paper, as with all of the other written assignments, will be the members of this class.

Purpose

The purpose of this assignment is to continue building a foundation of knowledge for your Argumentative Essay.

Format

Your Interview Report should be in the form of a Word document. Your document should be double-spaced, have a one-inch margin on all sides and be done in a 12-point font.

Contents

Your Interview Report, which should run about 1,000–1,500 words, involves:

- Choosing an interviewee
  - Finding someone who is very knowledgeable about your topic and available
- Preparing for the interview
  - Contacting your potential interviewee and requesting an interview
  - Working out a time and place to conduct the interview
  - Developing questions for the interview
- Conducting the interview
  - Informing your interviewee of the purpose of the interview
  - Getting permission to record the interview
  - Asking and following up on your questions and taking notes
  - Concluding by thanking your interviewee for participating
- Writing the interview report
  - Reviewing your recording and notes
  - Deciding on three to five topics you would like to address in the body of your report
  - Developing an introduction that identifies your topic, states the purpose of conducting the interview, introduces and describes the qualifications of the interviewee, describes the context in which the interview took place and indicates what you will be doing in this report
  - Developing the body of your report around the topics you chose to focus on, addressing each topic in a separate section

- Developing a conclusion in which you reflect on the interview and provide a sense of closure
- Providing transitional material to link the sections of your paper.

Suggestions for Drafting Your Interview Report

- Give yourself at least two to three uninterrupted hours to develop your draft
- Start by reviewing the information from the interview
- Draft the body of your report, considering the order of presentation of material
- Draft your introduction
- Draft your conclusion
- Link the parts of your paper
- Give your draft a title

Appendix H: Argumentative Essay

Audience

Your audience for this paper, as with all of the other written assignments, will be the members of this class.

Purpose

The purpose of this assignment is to produce an Argumentative Essay on your chosen topic, using the knowledge you have gained in completing the previous assignments and any additional sources of information.

Format

Your Argumentative Essay should be in the form of a Word document. Your document should be double-spaced, have a one-inch margin on all sides and be done in a 12-point font.

Contents

Your Argumentative Essay, which should run about 1,250–1,500 words, should include:

- An appropriate title
- An introduction in which you:
  - Orient your readers to your topic
  - State your position
  - Preview the rest of your paper
- A body in which you:
  - Provide support for your position in three to five paragraphs
  - Acknowledge potential opposition to your argument
  - Rebut this opposition
- A conclusion in which you:
  - Briefly summarize your argument
  - Suggest what you think needs to be done to improve the current situation
- A list of sources of information you have used in your paper

Suggestions for Drafting Your Argumentative Essay

- Reread the papers you have written for the Sequenced Writing Project, review any additional information you have collected and seek out new information on your topic as needed
- Decide on a position statement that you would like to argue for

- Decide on what information you will use to support your argument
- Consider potential opposition to your argument
- Give yourself at least two to three uninterrupted hours to develop your draft
- Draft the body of your report, considering the order of presentation of material and citing your sources of information in APA style
- Draft your introduction
- Draft your conclusion
- Link the parts of your paper
- Give your draft a title
- Assemble a list of references in accordance with APA guidelines

Appendix I: Final Draft Evaluation Form (Adapted from Jacobs et al., 1981)

Student: *Paper:*

Content (30 points: very good = 27–30; good = 24–26; adequate = 21–23; fair = 18–20; poor = <18)

Comments: Score:

Organization (20 points: very good = 18–20; good = 16–17; adequate = 14–15; fair = 12–13; poor = <12)

Comments: Score:

Vocabulary (20 points: very good = 18–20; good = 16–17; adequate = 14–15; fair = 12–13; poor = <12)

Comments: Score:

Grammar (20 points: very good = 18–20; good = 16–17; adequate = 14–15; fair = 12–13; poor = <12)

Comments: Score:

Conventions (10 points: very good = 9–10; good = 8; adequate = 7; fair = 6; poor = <6)

Comments: Score:

Total (100 points: very good = 90–100; good = 80–89; adequate = 70–79; fair = 60–69; poor = <60)

Comments: Score:

PART II

Instruction in Specific EAP Knowledge and Skills

Academic Genre-Based Instruction

5

THE CHALLENGE OF GENRE IN THE ACADEMIC WRITING CLASSROOM

Implications for L2 Writing Teacher Education

Christine M. Tardy

Introduction

Within second language writing, pedagogical and theoretical discussions of teaching academic writing have recognized the important role of genre for at least two decades. Writing in educational and academic contexts occurs primarily through established genres, and students' chances for successful participation in academic communities depends in part on writing in ways that approximate expected patterns within those genres. Genre pedagogies have garnered attention as valuable in raising learners' awareness of generic patterns of writing and facilitating their own use of such patterns. A hallmark of genre pedagogies is their focus on the relationships between purpose, audience and form through "inductive, discovery-based" (Hyland, 2007, p. 150) approaches to learning. Though approaches vary, they typically engage students in scaffolded and guided analysis of genre samples. In English for Specific Purposes (ESP) and English for Academic Purposes (EAP), it is common to focus this analysis on very specific genres that students need to learn and use, but in contexts where students encounter a wide range of genres, the focus may instead be on raising students' awareness of the complexities of genre more generally.

Interest in genre pedagogies within second language writing is evidenced by a high presence of genre-related topics in the *Journal of Second Language Writing*'s most downloaded and most cited articles, a fairly heavy emphasis on genre and socioliterate approaches in the well-known teacher education textbook *Teaching L2 Composition* (Ferris & Hedgcock, 2013), and the prominence of genre scholarship at conferences like TESOL and the Symposium on Second Language Writing. It is somewhat surprising, then, that there has been very little research into the kinds of knowledge that teachers should hold in order to successfully address genre in the L2 academic writing classroom. Teacher knowledge of genre and genre pedagogies is important because of the often-described danger that genres may inadvertently be taught as prescriptive formulas or templates rather than as dynamic, socially preferred conventions.

Despite a lack of systematic research into teachers' knowledge of and experiences with genre in the classroom, there is some evidence that teachers find it challenging to implement a genre approach that is not overly prescriptive or rigid. Two decades ago, Kay and Dudley-Evans (1997) investigated this issue, pointedly asking, "To what extent, and how successful, are genre-based approaches used in classrooms?" (p. 308). They summarized the voices of 48 teachers describing their experiences trying to put genre into practice in a variety of L2 teaching contexts. The participants in Kay and Dudley-Evans' study pointed to many practical benefits of genre approaches (finding them to be empowering, liberating and confidence-raising), but they also expressed several concerns, including:

- The danger of the approach becoming prescriptive rather than descriptive
- The danger of the approach becoming restrictive, leading to lack of creativity and demotivation
- The danger of it becoming *boring and stereotyped*
- Concerns of it becoming too text-centered and focused on reproduction

These reservations have also been voiced by some scholars who have argued that genres cannot be meaningfully taught in classroom settings and that attempts to do so may fall into the trap of prescriptivism (e.g., Dixon, 1987; Freedman, 1993). In responding to such critiques, Hyland (2007) acknowledges that "the dangers of a static, decontextualized pedagogy are very real if teachers fail to acknowledge variation and apply what Freedman (as cited in Hyland, 2007) calls 'a recipe theory of genre.' But there is nothing inherently prescriptive in a genre approach" (p. 152).

I agree whole-heartedly with Hyland's (2007) characterization; after all, the success of *any* teaching approach is contingent on an array of factors, including the teacher's experience and practices, institutional constraints and policies, and its appropriateness for the backgrounds, interests and motivations of the learners. Yet, unfortunately, these factors have not been studied in any depth in relation to genre pedagogies. Instead, most published studies or descriptions of genre teaching are carried out by experienced teacher–researchers in contexts in which the teacher has some degree of curricular autonomy (e.g., Cheng, 2008, 2011; Swales & Lindemann, 2002; Yasuda, 2011). We know far less about attempts of novice teachers to employ such approaches in the classroom, and we have few examples of experienced teachers who struggle with genre pedagogy (cf. Tardy, 2009). In an attempt to address this gap in part, this chapter explores EAP teachers' perspectives on implementing genre approaches in their academic writing classrooms, identifying key challenges and considering how teacher education might minimize—or at least support teachers in addressing—these challenges.

I am particularly interested in this issue within the context of early under graduate writing instruction in the United States, a context of learning that differs in many ways from the environments in which postsecondary genre pedagogy has typically been described and studied: English for *specific* academic purposes, such as discipline-specific undergraduate writing or the genre-specific graduate-level writing (e.g., thesis writing). In the next section of this chapter, I will describe some of the factors that make genre pedagogies challenging in early undergraduate writing, and I will then draw on an in-progress study of writing teachers to identify some of the key obstacles that these teachers faced in teaching with genre. Finally, I will consider some implications for supporting L2 writing teachers in genre approaches with the contexts of early undergraduate writing but not limited to that context.

Early Undergraduate Writing in the United States

As a teacher, I have had good success adopting genre approaches in ESP workplace contexts and in EAP courses for graduate student writers, but I admit that I have struggled a bit more in trying to integrate genre when teaching writing to first-year undergraduates in the United States. It seems that I am not alone. In a 2008 article, Ann Johns wrote of her own challenges implementing genre approaches in this setting:

> A few years ago, when I felt I was sufficiently theoretically mature, I devoted five years to the development of a genre-based textbook for first year university students—and I failed miserably in the effort. (pp. 237–8)

Johns goes on to state that we still lack "a genre-based pedagogy that is … satisfactory for the novice tertiary student, relatively new to college or university, and naïve about academic languages, texts, and cultures" (p. 238).

The context of teaching that Johns is referring to is somewhat unique to the United States. First-Year Writing (FYW), also known as Freshmen Composition, is a required course at most US universities and includes one or two semesters of writing instruction typically taken in the first year. At many large research universities, FYW is taught primarily by graduate students in English departments, who may be studying literature, creative writing, rhetoric and composition or TESOL/applied linguistics. At institutions without a pool of graduate student teachers, these courses are usually taught primarily by non-tenure-track instructors, often part-time and earning low wages for their teaching. Today, many writing programs offer streams or sections of FYW courses that are designated for second language writers as an effort to meet the distinct needs of these students, many of whom are international students. These L2 writing sections are sometimes (though not always) taught by instructors with a background in TESOL or applied linguistics, but teachers may or may not have familiarity with scholarship in second language writing.

Perhaps surprising to readers outside of the US, there is no clear consensus on the goal of FYW instruction. While university administrators and faculty across the disciplines often understand the course to be a place in which students can learn to write error-free and well-developed prose, FYW administrators and instructors may see the course as being primarily about critical thinking, creative expression, social justice or development of academic literacies. As Leki (2006) noted, many L1 writing professionals have worked hard to counter the perception that first-year writing programs are "mere service courses" (p. 68), but at the same time, most L2 writing professionals and students do tend to see these courses as EAP courses, preparing students for future academic writing. Therefore, there are often competing, or at least unclear, views about the aims of instruction for first-year L2 writing.

An additional issue at play is that FYW courses are typically taken before students have completed much, if any, work in their major programs of study. Therefore, they are still not engaging extensively, or even minimally, with a disciplinary community (and its genres) while enrolled in FYW. Instead, as part of a liberal arts education, US students spend the first year or two of their university studies taking general introductory courses across the curriculum in areas as diverse as history, psychology, biology, philosophy and astronomy. They are, in a sense, caught between the more general writing that they experienced in secondary school and the disciplinary writing that they will later be asked to do in their majors.

In composition studies, Devitt (2009) has advocated for teaching *genre awareness* in this context, which she describes as "a conscious attention to genres and their potential influences on people and the ability to consider acting differently within genres" (p. 347). As Bawarshi and Reiff (2010) explain, this approach is often implemented through students' systematic analysis of a genre's rhetorical context and textual patterns. The analysis may be followed by a formal *genre analysis essay* or by production of the target genre. Johns (2008) has similarly advocated for an approach that emphasizes meta-awareness, arguing that what might be most beneficial to first-year L2 writers is "developing the *rhetorical flexibility* necessary for adapting their socio-cognitive genre knowledge to ever-evolving contexts" (2008, p. 238). Johns argues that such an approach might include elements from ESP, rhetorical genre studies and systemic-functional linguistics, such as:

- Exploration, analysis and reproduction of texts that are characteristic of a variety of disciplines
- Ethnographic-type analysis of texts and contexts
- Interviews with instructors across disciplines about the writing they do and value
- Teaching of *the language of texts* with an emphasis on disciplinary-specific elements

Devitt and Johns both make a compelling argument that genre awareness and rhetorical flexibility are valuable goals for early undergraduate writing. However, these skills are not easy to teach and therefore pose a significant challenge or obstacle to the use of genre approaches in the first-year L2 writing classrooms.

Challenges to Teaching with Genre in First-Year Writing: Teachers' Perspectives

In August 2015, I began following the experiences of six teachers (see Table 5.1) who chose to integrate genre in some way into their first-year writing courses—some were teaching courses made up solely of L2 writers, some were teaching both L1 and L2 courses and some were teaching courses primarily made up of L1 writers. All could be characterized as EAP courses, as these instructors' main aim was to prepare students for concurrent and future university-level academic writing. Each of the six instructors had previous experience teaching FYW, ranging from one to four years, all were graduate students in applied linguistics or rhetoric and composition, and all were enrolled in my graduate seminar on genre theory and pedagogy in early 2015. Therefore, these were not novice teachers at the start of the study, and all had some background and interest in genre scholarship. Individual teachers in this study adopted slightly different approaches to genre pedagogy, but all aligned generally with the *genre awareness* orientation described by Devitt (2009) and Johns (2008, 2011). Jim, Rebecca, Ruby and Wanda all taught genre analysis as a major course assignment, in which students selected a genre of their choice to systematically examine and then wrote an analytic essay sharing their findings. Gustav designed a one-day activity in which students analyzed a common genre that they would later write in, and Sydney designed a content-based course that engaged students with concepts of genre, discourse community and literacy and integrated genre analysis throughout the semester.

TABLE 5.1 Research Study Participant Teachers

Participant	*# of years teaching FYW (at start of study)*	*PhD program enrolled in*
Gustav	1 years	Applied linguistics
Jim	3 years	Rhetoric and composition
Rebecca	1 year	Applied linguistics
Ruby	3 years	Applied linguistics
Sydney	2 years	Rhetoric and composition
Wanda	3 years	Rhetoric and composition

Although the study is longitudinal and took place over two semesters, I focus in this chapter on data collected over the first four months, during which I conducted three interviews with each teacher and observed each of their classes at least one time. The goal of my research has been to understand how teachers implement genre into their early undergraduate EAP writing courses and what kinds of challenges and opportunities they encounter in doing so. In the remainder of this section, I identify the most common challenges faced by these teachers.

Unclear Rationale for Students

All of the teachers in this study incorporated some kind of activity in which students explicitly analyzed a genre or a set of genres using guiding questions, aiming to build at the kind of genre awareness described by Devitt (2009) and Johns (2008). For some instructors (Jim, Rebecca, Ruby and Wanda), this analysis took the form of a major paper assignment in which students analyzed a genre of their choice; for others (Gustav and Sydney), genre analysis was carried out through in-class activities. In both cases, the teachers expressed concern about whether the students understood the purposes of the activities. They often noted that the students were able to work through a set of analysis questions in class but didn't seem to understand *why* they were doing so. Rebecca explained that "it was difficult for them to understand *what* the genre is, and I still think that they don't have a firm grasp on what is genre" (Interview #2), suggesting that without this basic understanding the task of analyzing a genre lacked a sense of purpose for many students. Others commented that a genre approach to writing instruction was very different to what students were accustomed to, and they may not have understood the aims; however, some teachers felt that the uniqueness of the approach could be a strength because students were able to feel that they were learning something new.

Potential for Transfer

Nearly all of these teachers expressed uncertainty about whether students would be able to transfer tools for analyzing genres to their own academic writing later on, which was the underlying goal of the analysis tasks. Even if students were able to do so, would it ultimately make a difference in their writing development and academic participation, they wondered. One teacher, Jim, described his concerns this way:

> I'll be curious to know, like, next semester, even two months from now, three months from now, if there's *anything*- what, if anything, students are finding that they're using from this semester. I don't know. And they may not know. That's the thing, right? They might not ever know.

> They might forever talk about their first-year writing class that made no sense to them. (laughs) [...] When is it just frustrating, and when is it helpful? (Interview #2)

Other teachers similarly expressed a lack of confidence in the likelihood for transfer, despite it being a major theoretical rationale for teaching meta-awareness of genre. The teachers noted as well, though, that this issue was not unique to genre pedagogy but was instead a persistent concern in teaching FYW, regardless of the teacher's approach.

Time and Scaffolding

In many cases, the teachers in my research altered their original course plans to spend more time on genre analysis activities, because the tasks went much more slowly than they had anticipated. In their interviews, all six identified time as a major challenge in implementing genre analysis activities. They universally felt that they had underestimated the time required for students to complete the analysis tasks in a meaningful way, and they often felt constrained by their syllabi and institutional expectations for including a certain number and type of assignments in the course.

For the four teachers who incorporated a major genre analysis writing assignment, scaffolding was mentioned as critical for success, and all four teachers described needing to do more scaffolding if they were to teach a similar assignment in the future. They noted the need to break down analysis tasks into smaller parts and to introduce activities that explore genres much earlier on in the course so that students could gradually become familiar with the idea of looking at writing in this way. One instructor, who taught a short genre analysis activity but did not require a major genre analysis paper, was disappointed in the lack of depth that his students were able to go into during a single in-class activity in which they analyzed literacy narratives as a genre. During this activity, which I observed, students were asked to identify conventional features of the genre, but they struggled to identify any meaningful patterns or to connect those to the larger rhetorical context of the genre. In reflecting on the activity, the teacher, Gustav, explained that "they probably didn't have enough either experience or guidelines to identify key elements (like register, style) because it was something I assumed they know, but they didn't necessarily" (Interview #2). In the future, Gustav realized, he would need to spend much more time familiarizing students with these concepts. The challenge of time also appeared to be related to the novelty of the genre approach for students, who needed to learn both the metalanguage and practice of analyzing genres, and for teachers, who often needed to restructure their syllabi in order to provide sufficient time for introducing students to genre analysis.

Integrating a Focus on Language

One somewhat surprising trend in the teachers' interview was the difficulty they faced in incorporating discussions of language into their classrooms. This challenge may have been in part related to instructors' feeling that there was not sufficient time in their class schedules to focus on linguistic patterns in genres. However, all six teachers also expressed some lack of confidence in their own abilities to integrate discussions of language into writing instruction, and this was true for both those studying applied linguistics and those studying rhetoric and composition. The applied linguistics PhD students, in fact, noted that while they were comfortable teaching language in a language classroom, they felt they had fewer strategies for doing so within a writing classroom, where the focus tended to be on macro-level issues such as content development, organization, rhetoric and revision. The teachers were unsure of how to integrate discussions of language with these concerns.

Wanda and Jim, both rhetoric and composition students, reflected on their class activities that had focused on move analysis and linguistic patterns as being some of the most effective parts of their courses, but despite this, they both felt less equipped for this kind of teaching. Jim, for example, described feeling that a focus on language was exactly what his students needed but that he lacked a wide pool of strategies for teaching this.

> I guess the thing that seems to make sense to me the most is really focusing on specific linguistic strategies. And I haven't done it. I guess because I'm a little afraid of it myself, because it's not really my speciality, you know. [...] I've done a little bit here and there, but like not- You know, like the stuff that Ken Hyland has done with engagement and stance and that kind of stuff. Where actually picking out- you know focusing on specific words and even sentence length and that kind of stuff, I think that *can* be really valuable. (Interview #2)

One possible reason for some of these difficulties might be the lack of a textbook for teachers to draw on, specifically one that incorporated a focus on language through genre exploration. Instead, the textbooks available to these teachers gave little attention to linguistic features. One teacher, Ruby, explicitly identified this as a concern during her course:

> I'm not using any flat-out text that tells me how to do it or what to do. So, it feels a little ad hoc. I don't think it necessarily has to be as ad hoc as I'm doing it, but I don't know. (Interview #2)

While observing the teachers' classes and talking with them in interviews, I often wondered if a genre-based textbook (something that is currently missing from the FYW textbook market) would have been helpful for them. Somewhat surprisingly, though, none of the teachers expressed a desire for such a textbook when I asked them about this at the end of their course. Instead, they appreciated the opportunity to develop their own activities and materials. Instead, they pointed to a lack of pre-service teacher support in how to integrate language into writing courses in general, not specifically in relation to genre pedagogies.

Summary

Following these six teachers has been revealing and also somewhat eye-opening for me as a genre scholar, L2 writing administrator and teacher educator. These are not brand new teachers; they have completed an entire graduate course on genre, and some are themselves emerging scholars of genre and academic writing. If these interested and knowledgeable teachers are struggling, the challenges facing novice teachers, especially those with limited L2 writing education, must be much more significant. In the US at least, a large number of postsecondary EAP writing teachers will learn about genre solely through a single reading, workshop or textbook. Given the challenges that even more experienced teachers face in teaching genre, such limited support is insufficient for novice teachers. Though research is clearly needed, it seems very plausible that the dangers of prescriptivism or teaching genre as formulas are very real in many teaching contexts.

Implications for Teacher Education

Having outlined some of the challenges of genre pedagogy in one EAP context, I turn now to the question of how L2 writing teacher educators can support pre-service and in-service teachers in addressing genre in the L2 writing classroom, particularly in early undergraduate EAP. I begin, though, with a few assumptions:

1. Genre and rhetorical flexibility are important in the teaching of early undergraduate L2 writing.
2. In most cases, teachers in this setting have relatively little background in genre pedagogies.
3. Without such background, the task of developing students' genre awareness is difficult at best. At worst, attempts to do so may end up inadvertently adopting prescriptive or just plain confusing approaches to writing.

Looking now at the knowledge that the six teachers in my study *successfully* drew on, and at principles of genre scholarship that are now fairly well established, I'd like to outline four practices that I believe can play a valuable role in L2 writing teacher education.

Destabilize and Expand Teachers' Genre Theories

Johns (2002) has described the importance of *destabilizing* students' theories of genre, and I think this principle is very valuable for teachers as well. New teachers may hold relatively static views of writing, often established through the writing courses they took as students and then reinforced through the writing textbooks that they use as teachers. Therefore, teacher education offers an important opportunity for challenging those existing assumptions and expanding their resources for understanding and describing academic writing. Genre theories offer a valuable lens through which to do so because they help demonstrate the social nature of common patterns, disrupting any assumptions of universal rules that apply across contexts. Genre theories helps us see rules as conventional (and variable) patterns that are created through social preferences and that, therefore, vary across social spaces.

For new EAP writing teachers, it would seem that there is great value in having at least an introduction to genre theories. First, knowledge of genre theories provides teachers with language to use when talking about genre with students. In the classes that I observed, for example, the teachers repeatedly talked with students about how writers make choices from available options, clearly influenced by Ken Hyland's work. They referred to genres as common responses to situations that repeat, drawing on Carolyn Miller's (1984) seminal paper. And they described genres as used and shaped by discourse communities, in ways similar to John Swales' (1990) early work. As teachers, they were able to highlight the importance of purpose and audience in shaping text form, helping them to avoid portraying genres as formulas or recipes. It seems to me that they would have had great difficulty reframing this theoretical knowledge for students without holding a fairly strong understanding of the theoretical issues themselves. By engaging pre- and in-service teachers with current scholarship on genre theory, then, we help equip them with broad knowledge that they can employ strategically when working with their students.

Explore Pedagogical Models, Their Techniques and Their Potential Adaptations

In this chapter, I have referred to genre pedagog*ies*, rather than pedagog*y*, recognizing the variation in approaches that aim to increase students' awareness of and tools for writing in genres. While genre scholars may debate the merits of different pedagogical approaches across contexts, there is value for teachers to be familiar with a range of approaches. The teachers in the study described here, for example, had read about genre pedagogies from ESP/EAP (Johns, 2002; Swales, 1990; Swales & Feak, 2004), systemic-functional linguistics

(SFL) (e.g., de Oliveira & Lan, 2014; Martin, 1993; Rose & Martin, 2012) and rhetorical genre studies (Bawarshi, 2003; Devitt, 2009); they drew on this broad knowledge strategically in their classroom, employing a range of approaches and techniques in their teaching. For example, all of the teachers offered students sets of questions to guide analysis of sample texts, similar to approaches described in rhetorical genre studies. Five of the teachers required that students locate multiple examples of a genre they wanted to analyze, knowing the importance of dealing with variation across genre samples as emphasized in ESP/EAP genre approaches. Four of the six teachers taught students to analyze texts' rhetorical moves, another common technique in ESP/EAP genre teaching. Two teachers (of L1 writing, in fact) expressed concern that their current approaches were insufficiently focused on language, and they discussed possibly using the teaching/learning cycle from SFL-oriented genre approaches in the future. They felt that this scaffolded approach to genre teaching—which involves a cycle of modeling, deconstructing, jointly constructing and independently constructing the genre-text (Martin & Rose, 2005)—could bring some helpful explicitness and guidance to the process for students.

What is important to emphasize here is that these six teachers *had* pedagogical options from which to choose. When something did not seem to go as hoped in the classroom, they had a few other tools in their toolbox to work with and try. They were also all able to focus on key principles of genre pedagogy, such as consciousness-raising, student exploration of texts as social practices and the value of making visible the normalized conventions of genres—but these principles were only of use to these teachers *because* they had become familiar with them through their reading and discussion of genre scholarship in a graduate-level course. Without such knowledge, they would not have had access to these tools, and it is unclear how they might have approached the teaching of genres.

To support novice L2 writing teachers in developing similar repertoires of knowledge and teaching strategies, exploration of multiple pedagogical approaches would seem to be of great value. Familiarity with the scaffolded approach of the teaching–learning cycle, tools like move analysis, or frameworks for analyzing rhetorical contexts gives teachers a range of techniques to turn to as they troubleshoot what might be most effective in their own context. Fortunately, there are numerous chapters, articles and books that can provide examples to teachers (e.g., Hyland, 2004; Johns, 2002; Paltridge, 2001), though very few are written for the context of early undergraduate EAP writing. Unfortunately, we still have few examples of undergraduate writing textbooks successfully adapting genre approaches, and I think that this poses significant challenges to new teachers, for whom concrete examples of instructional strategies may be even more important than theoretical explorations.

Create and Adapt Frameworks and Metalanguage for the Exploration of Language and Discourse

Perhaps the biggest challenge faced by the teachers in this study was the use of frameworks and metalanguage for helping students to explore writing—" a systematic means of describing texts [for] making our students' control over them more achievable" (Hyland, 2007, p. 163). A strength of SFL-oriented approaches is that they familiarize teachers with such a metalanguage, which can then be adapted for students. But in my context, many new teachers find the language of SFL to be confusing and even overwhelming, and the coursework that they take as graduate students offers little if any support in this area.

In the United States, most writing teachers, including many L2 writing teachers, have very little background in language analysis, which is almost certainly a reason that they struggle with this aspect of genre pedagogy. But, as Hyland (2007) has aptly stated, "Teachers of *writing* clearly need to be teachers of *language*.... A knowledge of grammar, focusing on how students can codify meanings in distinct and recognisable ways, becomes central to teacher education programs" (p. 151). Numerous scholars, including the New London Group (1996), have echoed this need for teachers to develop a functional metalanguage.

The teachers in my research were able to discuss some linguistic features of text with their students—most commonly, the use of first-person pronouns—but all of them still felt that language integration was a challenge or even a gap in their teaching, as described earlier. Without having tools for language analysis themselves (including the relevant metalanguage), they may be less successful helping students to analyze texts in meaningful and illuminating ways. I was struck by this need most recently during a class session of my graduate course in teaching second-language writing. As we read about genre and socioliterate approaches in Ferris and Hedgcock's (2013) book, one teacher asked, "How do we know what aspects of language to explore with students? Where do I start? Are there existing frameworks out there that I can use?" While some examples do exist, they are most often for teachers in primary school, secondary school or discipline-specific academic writing contexts, so they are less relevant to the needs of teachers in early undergraduate writing courses. Perhaps even more significantly, most teachers of first-year L2 writing are unlikely to encounter resources prepared for school settings or discipline-specific university contexts.

L2 writing teacher education, therefore, offers an opportunity to engage teachers with existing frameworks through courses and workshops, and—crucially—provide them the space to practice *adapting* those frameworks for different purposes and teaching settings. Modeling such adaptations throughout teacher education, by exploring the genres that TESOL professionals themselves engage in, is also extremely valuable. Though this may require the integration of additional content in our curricula, it appears to be *critical* content. One study by Gebhard, Chen, Graham and Gunawan (2013), for example, found that the teaching of and practice with using metalanguage from SFL in teacher education courses *did* make a difference in teachers' abilities to adapt such metalanguage for students and even to design context-appropriate genre-based courses.

Reflection

If there is anything we know for certain about teacher learning, it is that it is complex. Research into L2 writing teacher education is still relatively limited, but a few studies offer important insight. For example, based on case studies of four L2 writing teachers, Icy Lee (2010) has emphasized the value of *conscious deliberation* and *reflection* on teachers' goals and practices. Teacher learning, she notes, involves "teachers battling with the realities of teaching within their own classrooms" (p. 154). Providing opportunities for them to encounter and reflect on "the realism and idealism" (Ortega as cited in Lee, 2010, p. 154) of teaching seems to be essential.

We might also look to principles of transfer that have become increasingly visible in writing studies. DePalma and Ringer's (2011) notion of *adaptive transfer* is particularly useful here. As the authors note, the *reuse* or direct application of knowledge is likely quite rare in learning. In contrast, *adaptive transfer* is described as the dynamic *reshaping* and adaptation of existing knowledge to new problems and contexts. In teacher education, adaptive transfer seems to be a far more important goal than the simple reuse of content learned in a graduate course. As teacher educators, we want to support L2 writing teachers' processes of drawing on a broad pool of knowledge and to employ that knowledge strategically in addressing the concerns encountered in their own classrooms. Reflection has been suggested as an important metacognitive facilitator in this process. Engaging novice teachers in explicit reflection and *mindfulness* regarding their practice may encourage the adaptation of their knowledge about genre and teaching in order to *reshape* it to address challenges in different instructional contexts.

Conclusion

While I am afraid that I have provided few solutions to the challenges of implementing genre pedagogy in early undergraduate EAP writing, I hope that these four strategies for teacher education can at least offer a starting point for supporting teachers in this endeavor. I also acknowledge that the issue that I'm tackling is to some extent about the complicated and fraught context of First-Year Writing in the United States. At the same time, I suspect that other undergraduate contexts in which writing is taught might share some of these complicating factors: vague or uncertain genre expectations for students, lack of genre-based teaching materials and limited teacher support in genre theory and pedagogy. Therefore, the teacher education practices outlined here should hold value across contexts as well.

I continue to feel that genre approaches have a great deal to offer in the teaching of academic writing, even at the early undergraduate level—yet, we need to be cautious. Without fairly robust teacher preparation, genre approaches may be confusing to EAP teachers and students or even fall into the trap of rigid prescriptivism. There is, therefore, a great deal that can be learned from teachers' own experiences in the classroom, including their challenges and successes. It is my hope that we see, in the future, more research into those experiences and the unique ways in which teachers contend with and adapt genre into early undergraduate L2 writing.

References

Bawarshi, A. (2003). *Genre and the invention of the writer: Reconsidering the place of invention in composition*. Logan, UT: Utah State University Press.

Bawarshi, A. S., & Reiff, M. J. (2010). *Genre: An introduction to history, theory, research, and pedagogy*. West Lafayette, IN: Parlor Press and the WAC Clearinghouse.

Cheng, A. (2008). Individualized engagement with genre in academic literacy tasks. *English for Specific Purposes, 27*, 387–411.

Cheng, A. (2011). Language features as the pathways to genre: Students' attention to non-prototypical features and its implications. *Journal of Second Language Writing, 20*, 69–82.

de Oliveira, L. C., & Lan, S. W. (2014). Writing science in an upper elementary classroom: A genre-based approach to teaching English language learners. *Journal of Second Language Writing, 25*, 23–39.

DePalma, M.-J., & Ringer, J. M. (2011). Toward a theory of adaptive transfer: Expanding disciplinary discussions of 'transfer' in second-language writing and composition studies. *Journal of Second Language Writing, 20*(2), 134–147.

Devitt, A. (2009). Teaching critical genre awareness. In C. Bazerman, A. Bonini, & D Figueiredo (Eds.), *Genre in a changing world: Perspectives on writing* (pp. 337–351). Fort Collins, CO: The WAC Clearinghouse and Parlor Press.

Dixon, J. (1987). The question of genres. In I. Reid (Ed.), *The place of genre in learning: Current debates* (pp. 9–21). Deakin, Australia: Deakin University Pres.

Ferris, D. R., & Hedgcock, J. (2013). *Teaching L2 composition: Purpose, process, and practice* (3rd ed.). New York: Routledge.

Freedman, A. (1993). Show and tell? The role of explicit teaching in the learning of new genres. *Research in the Teaching of English, 27*, 222–251.

Gebhard, M., Chen, I.-A., Graham, H., & Gunawan, W. (2013). Teaching to mean, writing to mean: SFL, L2 literacy, and teacher education. *Journal of Second Language Writing, 22*, 107–124.

Hyland, K. (2004). *Genre and second language writing*. Ann Arbor: University of Michigan Press.

Hyland, K. (2007). Genre pedagogy: Language, literacy, and L2 writing instruction. *Journal of Second Language Writing, 16*, 148–164.

Johns, A. M. (2002). Destabilizing and enriching students' genre theories. In A. M. Johns (Ed.), *Genre in the classroom: Multiple perspectives* (pp. 237–246). Mahwah, NJ: Lawrence Erlbaum.

Johns, A. M. (2008). Genre awareness for the novice academic student: An ongoing quest. *Language Teaching, 41*(2), 237–252.

Johns, A. M. (2011). The future of genre in L2 writing: Fundamental, but contested, instructional decisions. *Journal of Second Language Writing, 20*, 56–68.

Kay, H., & Dudley-Evans, T. (1997). Genre: What teachers think. *ELT Journal, 52*(4), 308–314.

Lee, I. (2010). Writing teacher education and teacher learning: Testimonies of four EFL teachers. *Journal of Second Language Writing, 19*, 143–157.

Leki, I. (2006). The legacy of first-year composition. In P. K. Matsuda, C. Ortmeier-Hooper, & X. You (Eds.), *The politics of second language writing: In search of the promised land* (pp. 59–74). West Lafayette, IN: Parlor Press.

Martin, J. R. (1993). Genre and literacy – Modeling context in educational linguistics. *Annual Review of Applied Linguistics, 13*, 141–172.

Martin, J. R., & Rose, D. (2005). Designing literacy pedagogy: Scaffolding democracy in the classroom. In R. Hasan, C. Matthieson, & J. Webster (Eds.), *Continuing discourse on language: A functional perspective, Vol 1* (pp. 251–280). London: Equinox.

Miller, C. R. (1984). Genre as social action. *Quarterly Journal of Speech, 70*, 151–167.

New London Group. (1996). A pedagogy of multiliteracies: Designing social futures. *Harvard Educational Review, 66*, 60–92.

Paltridge, B. (2001). *Genre and the language learning classroom*. Ann Arbor: University of Michigan Press.

Rose, D., & Martin, J. R. (2012). *Learning to write, reading to learn: Genre, knowledge and pedagogy in the Sydney School*. Bristol, CT: Equinox.

Swales, J. M. (1990). *Genre analysis: English in academic and research settings*. Cambridge, UK: Cambridge University Press.

Swales, J. M., & Feak, C. B. (2004). *Academic writing for graduate students* (2nd ed.). Ann Arbor: University of Michigan Press.

Swales, J. M., & Lindemann, S. (2002). Teaching the literature review to international graduate students. In A. M. Johns (Ed.), *Genre in the classroom: Multiple perspectives* (pp. 105–119). Mahwah, NJ: Lawrence Erlbaum Associates.

Tardy, C. M. (2009). *Building genre knowledge*. West Lafayette, IN: Parlor Press.

Yasuda, S. (2011). Genre-based tasks in foreign language writing: Developing writers' genre awareness, linguistic knowledge, and writing competence. *Journal of Second Language Writing, 20*, 111–133.

6

CREATING AN EFFECTIVE ARGUMENT IN DIFFERENT ACADEMIC GENRES

A Scaffolded Approach

John Bitchener

Introduction

Creating an effective argument in different academic genres can sometimes be a challenge for second language (L2) writers. This may be the result of a limited understanding of what constitutes an academic argument as well as factors relating to an accurate and appropriate use of the L2. The aim of this chapter is to identify the knowledge and skills that writers need in order to create an argument, to explain why they may encounter issues with argument creation, to describe some of the pedagogical approaches that have been recommended and to present a seven-stage scaffolded approach that supervisors, EAP teachers and instructors can follow to help their students create effective arguments. The seven-stage approach is described as it applies to the creation of an argument in (1) the literature review of a thesis or dissertation (hereafter *dissertation* will be used to also refer to *thesis*), (2) other part-genres of a dissertation and (3) other academic texts that are commonly associated with proposing a research project and disseminating its findings (e.g., grant application, research proposal, journal article, book chapter). The chapter concludes with a discussion of the advantages of using this approach and some suggestions on how supervisors, EAP teachers and instructors can use the approach at undergraduate level as well as at postgraduate level.

Knowledge and Understanding of the Concepts of Argument and Argumentation

An understanding of the difficulties that L2 writers might encounter in the creation of an academic argument presupposes an understanding of what constitutes an academic argument and an awareness of how it may vary from genre to genre. In academic writing, the term *argument* can refer to individual claims or to the argument of a whole text (or units within a wider text). With individual claims, *argument* refers to a proposition that is supported with evidence and reasoning, but with the whole text, it refers to "a connected series of statements intended to establish a position and implies a response to another (or more than one) position" (Andrews, 1995, p. 3) or to "a sequence of interlinked claims and reasons that, between them, establish content and force of the position for which a particular speaker (writer) is arguing" (Toulmin, Reike, & Janik, 1984, p. 14). Thus, the first defining characteristic of an argument is the development of a position (i.e., the development of an argument). The second feature is a presentation of the position through the logical sequence of propositions that establish the position. The third characteristic of an argument is the selection of relevant information for inclusion in the development of the position. As Wu (2006) explains, this requires an ability to analyze and evaluate content knowledge to determine its relevance and appropriateness for inclusion in the argument. If writers understand, first of all, that these are three defining characteristics of an effective argument, it would seem that they will be more likely to be successful in writing an effective argument.

Knowledge and Understanding of Genre-Related Factors That Determine the Nature of Argument

Writers also need to understand that the specific nature of an academic argument is determined by different genres or discourse/text types (e.g., a dissertation, a research proposal, a journal article, an essay) because, as genre theory explains, the defining features of each genre are determined by factors such as its communicative purposes or functions, the expectations of the intended audience or readership of the genre and the expectations/requirements of different disciplines in which it is used (each with their particular value systems, epistemologies and histories).

The type of argument presented in dissertations (as one type of academic genre) may vary according to the type of research being reported. For the traditional dissertation that reports on an empirically based piece of research, the communicative purposes include a presentation of the problem/issue that was investigated, reasons it was considered an issue and needing investigation, its importance to the context in which it is situated, how it was investigated, what the investigation found and the contribution of the research to new knowledge (e.g., theory-building, new empirical knowledge, research methodology and practice). Thus, the dissertation genre develops its argument from an identification of a problem to a series of claims and conclusions about what the research has found. It does this by means of a logical presentation of propositions about each of these areas of focus. In the traditional dissertation, these areas are typically presented in separate chapters and, given the different purposes and functions of each chapter, they are frequently referred to as part-genres. As such, each part-genre seeks to develop a separate argument or position. For example, the literature review develops an argument to explain and justify the focus of the research (justifying the research questions that were investigated or the hypotheses that were tested) by means of a series of thematic/topic units that background and justify the overall aims of the research. Each of these units develops its own argument and, together, they produce a series of unit arguments that lead to the overall argument justifying the focus of the research.

Why Student Writers May Have Difficulty with the Creation of an Argument

Broadly speaking, student writers may have difficulty with the creation of an effective argument because they do not have sufficient knowledge of what is expected or because they do not have all the skills necessary to make use of their knowledge. Although L1 student writers may experience similar difficulties to L2 student writers, the latter may encounter additional challenges because they may not have the same level of linguistic competence as L1 student writers. The first part of this section considers the types of issues that both L1 and L2 student writers may encounter while the second part discusses some of the issues that L2 student writers may be more likely to encounter.

Issues Common to Both L1 and L2 Student Writers

L1 and L2 writers may have a limited knowledge or understanding of what is required for the effective creation of an academic argument. This may be the result of (1) the text being situated within a genre that is new to them, (2) insufficient instruction, (3) insufficient advice and feedback and (4) a limited range of resources (e.g., guidebooks) that focus on argumentation.

First, if the genre for which writers are creating an argument is new to them, it is understandable that they will not know what is expected of them. Thus, for students who have not written a literature review for a research thesis at master's level or for a research paper at undergraduate level, it is likely that they will be unclear about (1) the particular purposes/functions of a dissertation literature review, (2) how to manage the range and type of literature typically included in a dissertation and (3) how to organize the content of the argument in the most rhetorically effective manner.

The second reason that student writers may not have the necessary knowledge to create an effective argument is the limited amount of explicit teaching in universities about what is expected. While it is acknowledged that most institutions provide some form of guidance about doctoral processes and procedures, it is also frequently noted by supervisors and students that there is a lack of teaching on the type of text expected and on how to go about creating the text (Bitchener, Basturkmen, & East, 2010). As a result, text-level guidance is most often provided by supervisors and learning/writing support center advisors in the form of feedback on what a student has written. Some supervisors provide advice and discuss the intended focus of a text before their students start writing but many seem to prioritize feedback over pre-writing advice and direction. While providing some form of feedback on their students' texts, not all supervisors provide explicit, focused feedback on the argument of their students' texts (Hyland & Hyland, 2006). Students sometimes say that while their supervisors have tacit knowledge of what is expected, they are not always able to articulate in explicit terms what is needed or how to meet their expectations (Lea & Street, 1998; Walker, 2009). Specifically, with regard to providing feedback on the argument of a text, it has been noted that supervisors may not be clear about the concept of argument and/or may not be able to provide students with adequate guidance (Lea & Street, 1998; Mitchell & Riddle, 2000).

Student writers often seek information from university websites/handbooks and guidebooks about the type of content (including the argument informed by the content) to include in their texts and about how to organize it in a way that meets the expectations of the discipline. Apart from guides such as those by Bitchener (2010) and Paltridge and Starfield (2007) where a discourse analytical approach to understanding the type of content expected in different genres or part-genres like the dissertation literature review is described, these resources are typically silent on text-level expectations (Andrews, 2010; Groom, 2000).

Once writers have an understanding of these broad characteristics of an argument and of how they can vary from genre to genre, they also need to have a certain set of skills to be able to apply such knowledge. For example, in creating a literature review argument, they need, first of all, to be able to select literature (e.g., theoretical, empirical, philosophical, methodological and practical) that is relevant to the argument and this presupposes they can read with understanding and identify the purpose and focus of each piece of literature. Second, a literature review argument requires an ability to critically analyze and evaluate the extent to which each piece of literature is relevant to the focus of the unit for which it is being considered. Third, writers need to have an understanding of how each piece of literature can play a part in the development of the argument. Once the relevant literature has been selected, analyzed and evaluated, the writer then needs to be able to know how to present each piece of literature so that, as a series of propositions, they build rhetorically to an argument or case that can be defended. Because dissertation writers need to be able to manage a wide range of literature, the amount of difficulty encountered by some student writers may be considerable.

Issues More Specific to L2 Student Writers

There are several issues in relation to creating an argument that may present L2 writers with additional challenges to those of L1 writers: (1) adapting to a different epistemological background, (2) reading and understanding academic texts written in English, (3) understanding what constitutes a critical assessment of a text and (4) coping with a linguistic repertoire that may not be sufficiently development to produce complex arguments in the L2.

The epistemological background of L2 writers may be such that they are unaccustomed to the type of logical reasoning or argument that L1 writers are more familiar with. If instruction and/or discussion about any possible differences is provided in the early stages of writing, L2 writers are less likely to be disadvantaged through any lack of awareness of what is expected. Nevertheless, even though some attention may be given to what is expected, some L2 writers may struggle to apply their new knowledge in early iterations of their argument.

Reading in a second language can present challenges for L2 readers/writers who may have had little experience in navigating their way through academic texts that can often be quite dense for even L1 readers/writers. Thinking about the meaning of propositions at the sentence level can sometimes mean that conceptualizing the overall meaning of the discourse is neglected until further readings of the text take place. Thus, the amount of time that needs to be given to reading may reduce the amount of time that is given to an overall understanding of the key ideas of the literature.

Some L2 writers may be unaccustomed to what is involved in a critical evaluation of the ideas of others if it has not been required of them in their earlier education. Being able to select literature that is relevant to an argument requires a level of criticality that supervisors and teachers/instructors may need to address. Critical judgment is necessary if writers are going to create an effective argument from a series of relevant and connected ideas. L2 writers who may be more familiar with cultures of learning that regard highly an uncritical acceptance of what is published and an ability to summarize and synthesize ideas without critical assessment may, for example, struggle to argue a case for accepting, questioning or rejecting certain lines of argument.

L2 writers of a dissertation may not always have the same level of linguistic knowledge that their L1 peers possess. The task of creating a coherent and cohesive series of propositions can often be aided by a judicious use of discourse markers. It may sometimes be that L2 writers overuse discourse markers rather than rely on content connections between propositions to reveal a relationship between one statement and the next. Similarly, as a result of not fully understanding the precise meaning of some discourse markers (especially if they have similar but not identical meanings), they may use an incorrect marker and, as a result, fail to produce a clear connection between ideas. Additionally, L2 writers may have a more limited linguistic repertoire than L1 writers and therefore struggle to explain ideas as clearly and accurately as L1 writers. The use of an imprecise word or a vague expression by an L2 writer may cloud the intended meaning of the claim made. Also, writers who are able to accurately use a range of syntactic structures are more likely to write with precision and make connections between ideas than writers who do not have that level of knowledge. In this regard, L2 writers may struggle more than L1 writers.

Having identified a number of issues that L2 writers may encounter as they create academic arguments, it is necessary to consider briefly the extent to which the writing of an argument has been addressed pedagogically.

Pedagogical Approaches to the Creation of an Effective Argument

The need for pedagogical approaches that specifically focus on what constitutes an effective academic argument and on how to create such texts has been called for by a number of supervisors and EAP teachers/instructors over the years (Andrews, 2005, 2007, 2010; Davies, 2008; Mitchell & Andrews, 2000; Mitchell & Riddle, 2000). However, little attention has specifically been given to pedagogical approaches at both undergraduate and postgraduate levels.

A few models (Andrews, 1995; Toulmin, 1958; Toulmin et al., 1984) have sought to define what constitutes an academic argument and explain the process of argumentation but most have tended to focus more on the traditional essay required of undergraduate writers (Davies, 2008; Mitchell & Riddle, 2000). In this regard, teaching argumentation through the use of the Toulmin approach using syllogisms (conclusions drawn from two given or assumed propositions) has been supported as long as its use is considered in conjunction with disciplinary priorities. On the other hand, its use at the macro level of argument has only been accepted if it includes additional approaches like those suggested by Bacha (2010), Davies (2008) and Mitchell and Riddle (2000). Bacha (2010) proposed a five-step cycle (building the context, modeling and deconstructing texts, constructing texts jointly, constructing texts independently and linking related texts), while Davies (2008) argued for a six-step procedure for planning and developing whole essays (where the syllogism argument approach is used to connect premises and conclusions) and Mitchell and Riddle (2000) suggested a four-stage procedure for the organization of macro arguments.

At the postgraduate level, it is more often assumed that student writers know what an academic argument is and know how to create it. While postgraduate writers may have discovered, by this stage, how to write the traditional essay, they are unlikely to have fully understood (1) the nature of argument expected in dissertation part-genres and (2) how to create an effective argument at both the macro level and the micro level (thematic/topic units within the part-genre's macro structure). Swales (1990, p. 84) explains that students need (1) appropriate content and formal schemata in order to make "allowable contributions" to a genre and (2) some form of instruction on both content and schemata. However, despite a widespread understanding of the need for pedagogical options that focus on argumentation, universities often tend to take a hands-off approach and leave this task to supervisors or EAP instructors/advisors in learning/writing support centers and, as the previous section explained, neither may be able to explicitly articulate their tacit knowledge.

Guidebooks rarely address the argument-writing needs of students. However, two guides by Bitchener (2010) and Paltridge and Starfield (2007) explain, by means of a discourse analytical approach, how the macro argument of texts may be created. They describe the type of content expected in different part-genres like the dissertation literature review and how the rhetorical structure of the argument, drawing upon the type of content identified, can be effectively created. This approach introduces readers to the typical discourse moves (units of content) that have been identified in discipline-specific research. From the specific advice that this research has made possible, a more generic set of typical discourse move options have been formulated. This advice not only refers to what the typical discourse moves are, it also identifies how they can be rhetorically organized to create an effective argument. To a large extent, this advice can help student writers with the macro argument of a text. However, many students continue to have difficulty when it comes to creating an effective argument for a particular discourse move, especially if the move includes a wide range of theoretical and research literature across a number of thematic or topic units.

To illustrate, one of the discourse moves identified in these guides for the dissertation literature review is "a presentation of knowledge claims and statements about theories, beliefs, constructs and definitions." This is a broad, multi-faceted discourse move and, as such, needs to include a wide range of moves and units. The question arises, then, about how to create an effective argument for this move. Clearly, the argument will comprise a series of thematic/topic units and, within each of these, further arguments that explain and justify the literature that is selected. It can be seen, then, that this is an issue that both L1 and L2 student writers are likely to encounter. In the next section, an approach that scaffolds student writers through seven stages in the creation of an argument for one thematic/topic unit of a dissertation literature review is discussed.

A Seven-Stage Scaffolded Approach to the Creation of a Dissertation Literature Review Argument

Stages 1–3 of the approach refer to the selection of a wide range of literature relevant to the thematic/topic unit. Stages 4–5 focus on a scoping of the relationship between aspects of the selected literature so that a series of logically connected propositions can be formed and therefore lead to the central argument of the unit. Stages 6–7 refer to the writing of an overview of the argument. To illustrate each stage, reference will be made to the theoretical justification of one of five research questions from a doctoral dissertation: Can written corrective feedback (CF) be expected to facilitate L2 development? In order to answer this question, the writer needs to consider, from a theoretical position, whether or not it is reasonable or not to expect that written CF might be useful for the development of the target language. One would expect there to be not only a wide range of theoretical literature to support the claim but equally a range of literature that does not support the position.

Stage 1: Reading and Understanding the Literature

The first challenge for student writers is to identify the literature that is relevant to the unit. Given the focus of the research question, two broad areas of literature would seem to be relevant: (1) literature on how an L2 is learned/acquired and (2) literature on the contribution that written CF may be able to make to L2 development—a focus that would lead readers to consider the interface between the SLA (second language acquisition) and L2 writing literatures. Reading and understanding a wide range of theoretical literature can be a challenge for L2 readers as well as L1 readers but it is possible that the former may encounter more difficulties than the latter given their more limited experience in reading literature in English and their more limited lexical repertoire. Reading with an understanding of the focus of each piece of literature is critical to the creation of a strong argument.

Stage 2: Identify the Focus of Each Piece of Literature

This stage helps the reader/writer to identify whether or not a certain piece of literature may be relevant to the unit. There may be more than one foci for each piece of literature so each of these foci needs to be identified. Stage 2 suggests that readers record these and, as Figure 6.1 illustrates, key words can be chosen to represent each focus. Arrows can be added to show any important relationship between the various foci of the piece of literature. Gass (1997) refers to seven key topics on how written CF input can be used to modify input. If readers discover this piece of literature early in their reading program, they may not necessarily know how important and relevant each of these foci is to an explanation about how and why written CF may facilitate L2 development. However, they are likely to realize from the signposting (use of key headings) and the discussion about each foci that they are potentially important areas for inclusion. Readers/writers will have their own method for recording this information.

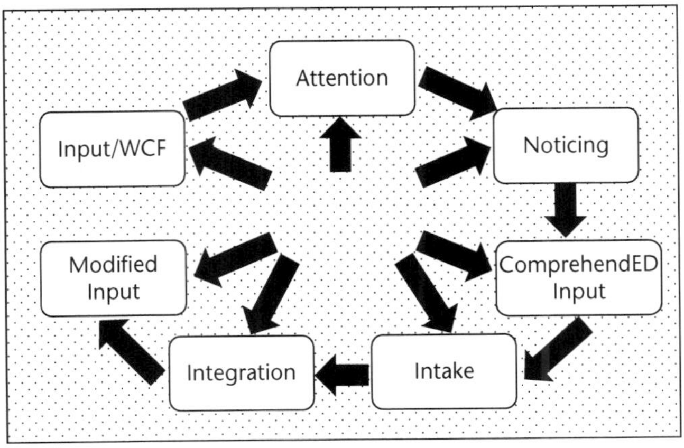

FIGURE 6.1 Focus of literature

Stage 3: Allocating Each Piece of Literature to a Key Heading

It is likely that readers will come across a number of pieces of literature on the headings they create so one way of bringing all these pieces together is to record each one (by name of author and year of publication) under each key heading. In Figure 6.2, it can be seen that "Noticing" is one of the areas of focus identified by Gass (1997) in Figure 6.1 and that the student has identified five additional pieces of literature on this topic. It should be noted that some authors will appear under a number of different headings if, like the Gass (1997) piece, they cover a number of key areas of relevance to the research question. As more reading is completed, readers are likely to start seeing connections between key headings and subheadings. As soon as they start to see relationships between key ideas, they should start to record these as they will be used to build the argument of the unit.

Stage 4: Identifying and Recording Relationships between Key Ideas

The creation of a mind-map on which key ideas/headings are recorded (with key authors and dates of publication) is a very effective means of developing an understanding of the relationship between key ideas. As the reading progresses, so too will the size of the mind-map. Separate mind-maps can then be created for certain headings. During the reading process, some initial headings may be subdivided into two or more additional headings while others may be collapsed into fewer headings. In order to show whether the key idea of one heading needs to be understood before that of another heading, horizontal arrows can be used to signal which aspect should be referred to first. It may sometimes be necessary to show that, of two headings, either one could precede the other. In Figure 6.3 below, it can be seen that *Acquired vs. Learned Competence* is a topic that may be explained before *Implicit vs. Explicit Knowledge* or, vice versa, that the latter may be explained

Noticing + Attention to CF Input

- Gass (1997)
- Tomlin and Villa (1994)
- Schmidt (1990, 2001)
- DeKeyser (1998, 2007)
- Ellis, N. (2005)

FIGURE 6.2 Literature on an area of focus (noticing and attention to CF input)

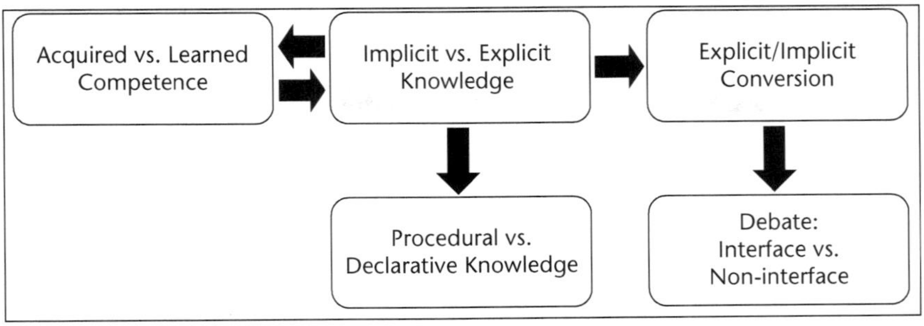

FIGURE 6.3 Mind-map (acquired vs. learned competence)

before the former. In this situation, arrows indicating both directions can be used. As more and more reading is completed, readers may want to divide certain headings into subheadings if, for example, a new heading indicates an expansion of an idea related to the original heading. We see in Figure 6.3 that *Implicit vs. Explicit Knowledge* can be subdivided into *Procedural vs. Declarative Knowledge*. Thus, the use of a vertical arrow pointing downwards reveals this relationship. The expansion could relate to either a similar or an alternative topic.

Stage 5: Scoping the Literature Relationship

Some reader/writers find no difficulty moving from stage 4 to the writing of the argument underpinning their unit. Others find it helpful to scope more fully the ideas informing each key heading. Creating a detailed Table of Contents for the unit or creating PowerPoint slides to reveal a more detailed outline of ideas are two approaches that have been reported anecdotally to benefit many students. Both of these approaches give writers the opportunity to show themselves and their supervisors that they have a clear understanding of the relationship between each heading and whether the argument is likely to be logical and cohesive. It can also reveal whether or not there are any gaps in the series of propositions informing the argument. The Table of Contents in Figure 6.4 identifies the key ideas/propositions to be included in a discussion of two of the headings shown in Figure 6.3. Subheadings within major headings can be shown by means of indentation and/or a numbering system. Each one of these headings or subheadings could be further expanded by means of PowerPoint slides. Writers who follow this additional stage tend to produce more coherent and cohesive arguments.

Stage 6: Articulating an Overview of the Argument

So that both the student writer and the supervisor can feel sure that the argument is going to be clear and logically developed, writers can be asked to write a single page overview (e.g., approximately 300–350 words) of the argument from the

Table of Contents and/or the PowerPoint slides. This task helps them to articulate in writing the connection of ideas from one proposition to another. Any gaps in the relationship between propositions can then be addressed before the whole unit is written. The overview can also serve as an introduction to the unit. The argument overview in the box below indicates that the argument that the writer will later construct about the contribution of written CF to L2 development is likely to be clear, logical and cohesive.

It can be seen that care has been taken by the writer to reveal clear connections between propositions. This has been achieved in several ways. First, there is either a reference back to the key idea of the preceding proposition or a reference forward to the key idea of the next proposition. Second, the use of meta-text to inform the reader about what s/he has done or will do can make the connection explicit. Third, the use of accurate and appropriate discourse markers and pronouns can be used to establish a connection of ideas. It may be useful for supervisors and EAP teachers/instructors to model this type of overview and have a discussion with their students about the effectiveness of different samples.

1.0 Goal of L2 learning: native/near-native competence
1.1 Two types of competence: learned and acquired
2.0 Two types of knowledge: explicit and implicit
2.1 Relationship between knowledge and competence types
2.2 Explicit – implicit conversion debate
  2.2.1 Interface position vs non-interface position
3.0 Explicit information processing
3.1 Skill acquisition theories
  3.1.1 Anderson
  3.1.2 McLaughlin
  3.1.3 DeKeyser
3.2 Information processing stages

FIGURE 6.4 Table of Contents for a key heading (explicit and implicit knowledge)

Overview of the argument:

1. The aim of this section is to present a case that supports a role for written corrective feedback (CF) in L2 development, drawing upon theoretical perspectives that have something to say about the cognitive processing of L2 information and the potential of written CF as explicit L2 input to facilitate such processing.

(continued)

(continued)

2. I begin by explaining that the central goal of L2 learning is the acquisition of native or near-native speaker competence.
3. In doing so, I argue that acquired competence that draws upon implicit knowledge can be developed from learned competence that draws upon explicit knowledge such as that provided by written CF.
4. Explaining this process, I refer to the skill acquisition models of Anderson and McLaughlin to show how explicit, declarative L2 knowledge can be proceduralized through meaningful, contextualized practice over time to a point where it may be converted to implicit, acquired knowledge.
5. Then, I describe the specific information processing stages that have been identified by cognitive theorists like Tomlin and Villa, and Schmidt and Swain, for example, and that have been represented in frameworks such as the one designed by Gass (1997).
6. In processing written CF as input, Gass' framework explains that learners need to attend to written CF as input if they are to progress through the other stages that will enable them to produce modified accurate output and ongoing accurate output in new written texts over time.
7. The other stages include an understanding (i.e., comprehendED input), an internalization and an integration of written CF as input.
8. Producing accurate output as a result of this conscious processing is the beginning of a longer consolidation process during which practice is believed to facilitate acquired competence.
9. I acknowledge the possibility that this linear route towards acquisition may be both facilitated and interrupted as a result of the type of written CF a learner is provided with and as a result of intervening individual internal (cognitive and motivational/affective) factors and individual external factors.
10. The extent to which these theoretical proposals are valid explanations of the acquisition route is something that only empirical research can investigate. This will be the focus of the next section.

Stage 7: Writing Up the Unit in Sections or as a Whole Text

Depending on the size of the unit, some writers may want to write a few subsections and have their supervisors comment on their effectiveness before they write the whole unit. Once the unit has been successfully completed, other units of the literature review can then be created using some or all of these stages. From the final statement of the sample overview in the box above, we see that the next unit would be one that considers the extent to which research evidence supports the theoretical argument that has been presented.

Advantages of the Approach

Because the writing of a literature-based unit involves a consideration of a wide range of literature, this approach has the advantage of helping readers/writers consider the direction of their argument as soon as they have read their first piece of literature. It provides an approach that helps them to (1) think about the relationship between various topics and ideas across many pieces of literature and (2) shape the direction of the argument as they read. What could be a daunting task is made easier as the thinking is done "en route" rather than at the end of a period of reading. The second advantage is the clarity that can arise from a diagrammatic representation of the writer's thinking. It is easier to see gaps in an argument from a diagrammatic outline than it is from a reading of twenty or more pages of text. Third, the sense of progress that can be made through this approach may help some readers/writers stay focused and help them see the relevance of certain pieces of literature more easily. Another advantage of the approach is the likelihood that fewer iterations will be required to make the argument effective. Saving time and energy (including emotional energy) for both writers and supervisors can lead to a more positive experience for both parties. Student writers sometimes say that they experience a writing block or that they tend to procrastinate when the hard work of writing is required. Because the thinking is done during the reading process, there is less likelihood that student writers will experience these issues if they have thought about what they want to say before they commit to paper. It could be argued by some that delaying the writing of the argument means that writers miss out on the experience of developing their thinking as they write. However, the approach described here does not suggest, for example, that writers should not write up paragraphs on aspects of a unit when they feel that they have a clear understanding of what the literature says.

Application of the Approach to Other Genres and Part-Genres

The type of argument required for three other part-genres of a traditional, empirically based dissertation (e.g., an introduction, a discussion of findings and a conclusion) is, to some extent, similar to that of the literature review, so the approach described in this chapter may also be applied to these part-genres. Each of these chapters requires that a range of information be organized as a series of logically connected propositions to create an argument that aligns with the expected purpose and focus of the part-genre. In each case, the range of information presented may not be quite as extensive as that which is included in a literature review. Adopting some or all of the seven stages discussed above may enable student writers to produce a text that meets the expectations of readers familiar with the part-genres.

Other part-genres like the methodology and results/findings chapters also require a clear and logical presentation of information but the argument is likely to involve a more linear presentation of procedures or results. It might be argued, though, that a discussion of the methodological approach and the philosophical approach underpinning the methodology calls for a similar type of argument to that of a literature review unit. Any unit that requires a careful consideration of the relevance of information to be included and a focus on the most effective way to rhetorically organize it may find this approach useful.

Writers of other genres that relate to, but sit outside, the dissertation may also find the seven-stage approach helpful. Students, academics and EAP teachers may find the type of processing described above is helpful for the writing of journal articles, book chapters, research proposals, grant applications and report writing because each of these genres requires that a range of literature (e.g., theoretical, empirical, practice-based, background) be selected and logically organized. At the undergraduate level, the same approach may be considered by students writing essays that require the selection and processing of information (e.g., both regular length essays and extended essays).

Who Can Make Use of This Approach?

Supervisors who have the responsibility for guiding their students through a dissertation are likely to find this scaffolded approach useful if any of their students experience difficulty in writing an effective argument. The approach can be employed by supervisors in any discipline as well as by EAP advisors or instructors. EAP teachers in pre-degree and undergraduate programmes may also consider including it in their syllabi. In doing so, they could (1) instruct their students about how the approach works, (2) discuss activities that involve a deconstruction of sample arguments and (3) provide students with opportunities to practice using it. Students starting their doctoral journey are likely to benefit from all stages of the approach but those who are introduced to it after a program of reading, thinking and scoping the direction of their argument for a whole chapter or for major units/sections may find stages 5–7 particularly relevant to their needs.

References

Andrews, R. (1995). *Teaching and learning argument.* London: Cassell.

Andrews, R. (2005). Models of argumentation in educational discourse: Text interdisciplinary. *Journal for the Study of Discourse, 25*(1), 107–127.

Andrews, R. (2007). Argumentation, critical thinking and the postgraduate dissertation. *Education Review, 59*, 1–18.

Andrews, R. (2010). *Argumentation in higher education: Improving practice through theory and research.* New York: Routledge.

Bacha, N. (2010). Teaching the academic argument in a university EFL environment. *Journal of English for Academic Purposes, 9*, 229–241.

Bitchener, J. (2010). *Writing an Applied Linguistics thesis or dissertation: A guide to presenting empirical research.* Houndmills, UK: Palgrave Macmillan.

Bitchener, J., Basturkmen, H., & East, M. (2010). The focus of supervisor feedback to thesis/dissertation students. *International Journal of English Studies, 11*, 79–97.

Davies, W. (2008). 'Not quite right': Helping students to make better arguments. *Teaching in Higher Education, 13*, 327–340.

Gass, S. (1997). *Input, interaction, and the second language learner.* Mahwah, NJ: Lawrence Erlbaum.

Groom, N. (2000). A workable balance: Self and source in argumentative writing. In S. Mitchell & R. Andrews (Eds.), *Learning to argue in higher education* (pp. 65–145). Portsmouth: Boynton/Cook Heinemann.

Hyland, K., & Hyland, F. (2006). Interpersonal aspects of response: Constructing and interpreting teacher written feedback. In K. Hyland & F. Hyland (Eds.), *Feedback in second language writing* (pp. 206–224). Cambridge: Cambridge University Press.

Lea, M., & Street, B. (1998). Student writing in higher education: An academic literacies approach. *Studies in Higher Education, 23*, 157–172.

Mitchell, R., & Andrews, R. (Eds.). (2000). *Learning to argue in higher education.* Portsmouth: Boynton/Cook Heinemann.

Mitchell, S., & Riddle, M. (2000). *Improving the quality of argument in higher education.* Final report. School of Lifelong Learning and Education: Middlesex University.

Paltridge, B., & Starfield, S. (2007). *Thesis and dissertation writing in a second language: A handbook for supervisors.* New York: Routledge.

Swales, J. (1990). *Genre analysis.* Cambridge: Cambridge University Press.

Toulmin, S. (1958). *The uses of argument.* Cambridge: Cambridge University Press.

Toulmin, S., Reike, R., & Janik, A. (1984). *An introduction to reasoning.* New York: Macmillan.

Walker, M. (2009). An investigation into written comments on assignments: Do students find them usable? *Assessment and Evaluation in Higher Education, 34*, 67–78.

Wu, S. (2006). Creating a contrastive rhetorical stance: Investigating the strategy of problematization in students' argumentation. *RELC Journal, 37*, 329–353.

7

L2 UNDERGRADUATE STUDENTS LEARNING TO WRITE USING SOURCES

A Trajectory of Skill Development

Rosemary Wette

Introduction

Since it is now generally acknowledged that proficiency in writing using sources is an important goal for all undergraduate students who want success in their university essays and assignments, my aims in the chapter are to explore what we now know about this challenging skill, and to make some practical suggestions for EAP writing instruction. I outline shifts in focus in research and scholarly interest in source text use by L2 students over the past thirty years, and describe the multiple components of this skill. I review current research and scholarship on the particular challenges it poses for inexperienced L2 writers, on the benefits of explicit instruction and on the developing skills of post-novices. In the final part of the chapter, I propose a trajectory of skill development in source text use for undergraduate L2 writers, and make a number of suggestions for course content and instructional tasks that would be appropriate at each stage of skill learning.

There are a number of possible explanations for the difficulties that academic writing using sources poses for all novices, and particularly for L2 writers. One is that the definitions of key constructs such as *common knowledge* and *plagiarism* are contested and imprecise. While common knowledge is often described as information that is *generally accepted* or *easily located in reference texts* (England, 2008), the definition glosses over the fluid, discipline-specific nature of this type of information. Any simple definition of plagiarism becomes problematic if one acknowledges that all academic texts are collaborative, intertextual productions and that, in reviewing and extending disciplinary knowledge, all academic writers to some extent "stand on the shoulders of giants" (Partington, 1996, p. 493, attributed to Isaac Newton). This lack of clarity is one reason for the difficulties that many L2 novice writers experience when trying to decide if their citations are appropriate, with L2 novice writers more likely to consider near-copied or minimally revised texts acceptable, and to miss clear examples of plagiarism (Shi, 2006). However, even university staff (both within and across disciplines) have been found to disagree about the legitimacy of sample citations (Bloch, 2012), including about the acceptability of reusing generic, formulaic phrases such as: *Research to date has tended to focus on ...*; *The study acknowledges a number of limitations* (Davis & Morley, 2015, p. 24).

Scholarly Understanding: From *Plagiarism* to *Language Reuse*

In the 1980s and 90s, it was believed that cultural differences in attitudes towards individual ownership and the importance of originality in academic content were the most influential sources of difficulty for L2 novice writers, especially students from Confucian heritage cultures of learning coming to study in Anglo-Western academic cultures (Pennycook, 1996). However, scholars with extensive experience of both types of cultures have pointed out that there are no "hard-wired cultural distinctions" (Bloch, 2012, p. 76) between the stance of Asian and Western societies towards copying and intellectual property, that attitudes and practices in all cultures are complex and dynamic, that students from similar cultural backgrounds often express quite different attitudes and that writers from English-speaking backgrounds also have difficulties mastering this skill (Howard, Serviss, & Rodrigue, 2010; Pecorari, 2003; Shi, 2006). It is now generally recognized that the linguistic or cultural background of an L2 writer is unlikely to be the only or principal source of difficulty when learning to write using sources.

Discussion of issues associated with plagiarism has been ongoing in the literature for more than thirty years, and a long-term goal of L2 writing scholars has been to convince university authorities that plagiarism by novice L2 writers is unlikely to be the result of deliberate deception. They have also argued that although limited academic English proficiency is one source of difficulty, the challenges posed by sophisticated academic literacies go well beyond their lexico-grammatical features. In recent years, these efforts have had some success, and there now seems to be a more general acceptance within tertiary institutions that plagiarism by L2 writers is primarily an academic literacy issue rather than a moral one, or one that can be resolved simply by requiring students to improve their proficiency in academic English. In the research literature, investigations of causes of and ways to combat *plagiarism* are therefore now much less common than exploratory studies of L2 writers' *textual borrowing* (Keck, 2014; Shi, 2004, 2010), *language reuse* (Flowerdew & Li, 2007) and *writing using/from sources* (Howard et al., 2010; Thompson, Morton, & Storch, 2013; Wette, 2010). Rebecca Howard's coinage *patchwriting*, or "copying from a source text and then deleting some words, altering grammatical structures, or plugging in one-for-one synonym substitutes" (Howard, 1993, p. 233), is now commonly used to describe a strategy that is frequently employed by L2 novice writers who are trying to learn from the language of published authors, and at the same time to bring the quality of English in their own texts to an acceptable level of accuracy and comprehensibility (Pecorari, 2003; Shi, 2004).

The Multiple Skill Components of Writing Using Sources

Writing using sources is a complex, multi-faceted, academic literacy skill set with a number of technical, linguistic, rhetorical, disciplinary and cultural elements. Expertise requires proficiency in comprehending and transforming source text material, as well as the ability to create an original text that builds on previous published knowledge. As a first step, writers need to know how to access and evaluate the quality (i.e., trustworthiness, newsworthiness and relevance) of sources, particularly in disciplines that draw on unpublished *grey* literature produced by business, government and industry sources. They must endeavor to fully comprehend the source and select relevant information (Hirvela & Du, 2013), as well as to use it to stimulate, confirm or challenge their own ideas and arguments. Repeated *top-down* and *bottom-up* readings are likely to be necessary in order for writers to compare and synthesize information from different sources, and decide what and how much to extract and whether the most appropriate type of borrowing is to select a quotation, summarize or paraphrase.

Moving from reading/thinking processes to writing, a combination of cognitive (critical reflection) and metacognitive thinking skills (planning, reflection, assessment and repair) are needed in order to compose a successful summary or paraphrase citation. These require the writer to draw on their prior knowledge, existing English language resources and personal composing strategies in order to successfully synthesize source content using superordinate terms such as *these circumstances*, *these practices*, *this situation* or *this belief*. In so doing, the writer reconceptualizes source contact by bringing it into contact with other sources, and with the writer's own ideas; however, in the process of integrating citations with their own positions, writers need to also clearly indicate the boundaries between the two in order to establish an authorial voice, and a dialogic relationship between themselves and their sources (Hyland, 2012; Shi, 2010).

Current Research and Scholarship

The Specific Challenges of Writing Using Sources for L2 Writers

The majority of empirical studies to date have been concerned with identifying specific difficulties and shortcomings in the attitudes and practices of inexperienced L2 writers, following Pecorari's observation that "recognizing the existence of the problem is the beginning of the solution" (2003, p. 343). Text-based studies have analyzed the extent of undergraduate students' paraphrasing abilities through texts produced under test conditions (e.g., Plakans & Gebril, 2012; Shi, 2004; Storch, 2012; Wette, 2010), as well as in their assignments, theses and dissertations (Howard et al., 2010; Pecorari, 2003; Shi, 2004). Studies have drawn on data gathered from interviews, think-aloud protocols and questionnaires to reveal the considerable uncertainty that exists among students about what constitutes acceptable writing using sources. From this research we have learned that novice writers appear to have difficulties selecting appropriate, citation-worthy content, and are likely to produce closely paraphrased portions of the source, rather than summaries of key points from one or more sources (Howard et al., 2010; Keck, 2014). Attribution is often partial or missing (either accidentally or deliberately so that cited content will appear to be original), and L2 novice writers frequently present secondary sources as primary (Pecorari, 2003). They are likely to overuse quotations (Plakans & Gebril, 2012), especially block quotations (Shi, 2004). They also have difficulties establishing an appropriate authorial voice, and tend to use source content to supply ideas, rather than to support their own propositions (Shi, 2004). One study (Plakans & Gebril, 2012) reported that L2 student writers used source texts as a learning tool by noting appropriate vocabulary and technical terminology for possible use elsewhere in their assignments.

To summarize, in the absence of clear, universally accepted guidelines and as a consequence of the many challenges involved in becoming proficient in this particular skill set, it is predictable that novice L2 writers will face difficulties in writing using sources, starting with the basic decision about whether an item of information is "supportive or irrelevant, new or learnt, owned by a particular author or shared by others" (Shi, 2010, p. 21). Explanations of the unskilled practices of these writers encompass a range of language-related, disciplinary and personal factors. They include shortcomings in students' reading and writing strategies, and their limited knowledge of text content, text language, disciplinary citation practices and the rhetorical purposes of citations (Keck 2014; Shi, 2004). Research evidence also suggests that inexperienced L2 writers often lack the linguistic resources to use appropriate superordinate terms and synonyms or to make appropriate syntax changes, and the self-confidence to position themselves as contributors to disciplinary discussions (Hyland, 2002; Petrić, 2007).

Proficiency in Writing Using Sources before and after Instruction

A small number of studies have been conducted to measure changes in students' ability after completing targeted L2 writing courses. Through pre- and post-instruction comparisons, this research has revealed clear progress in students' ability to select appropriate source texts (Thompson et al., 2013), their knowledge of rule-governed aspects of writing using sources such as choice of reporting verbs and correct formatting of end-of-text and in-text citations, and their ability to integrate information from multiple sources (Wette, 2010). Studies have also revealed a marked reduction in the incidence of extended copying without attribution after instruction, although this is usually associated with a concurrent increase in patchwriting (Storch, 2012; Wette, 2010). Other post-instruction gains (as well as ongoing difficulties) that have been noted include progress in students' ability to evaluate sources, produce accurate and well-written paraphrases, consider the reader and project an appropriate authorial voice (e.g., Morton, Storch, & Thompson, 2015; Thompson et al., 2013).

One study investigating post-instruction gains involved 78 L2 writers in their second year of undergraduate university study (Wette, 2010). Findings identified clear progress in students' general knowledge of basic rules and conventions of writing using sources, measured by two versions of an eight-item quiz completed before and after a unit of instruction. Nearly 90 percent of participants scored at least six correct answers in the post-quiz, compared with 63 percent before instruction. Modest but clearly discernible gains were evident in the quality of students' citations in comparable pre- and post-instruction tests, and in students' end-of-course assignments. In the tests, copying from source texts was much less frequent in the post-test (a decrease from 35.11 percent to 4.85 percent), while the percentage of citations evaluated as acceptable increased from 16 percent to 39 percent. In a referenced essay produced by students independently for their final course assignment, nearly half (45.5 percent) of the 466 citations produced by the cohort of 78 participants were acceptable from an originality perspective; however, many students referenced items of information that were trivial or common knowledge, and instances of patchwriting were much more frequent than in the post-test task in which sources had been provided.

While source text use in students' independently produced post-course assignments revealed progress in their skill development, limitations in their ability to cite noteworthy information, capture the nuances of source texts and integrate source material with their own arguments and ideas were evident. These findings were supported by those of a related investigation of texts on discipline-specific topics produced by L2 undergraduate writers under test conditions (Storch, 2012). Post-instruction texts produced by students in both studies featured less copying and a higher percentage of accurate citations, but also their limited abilities in the more sophisticated aspects of this skill such as its role in supporting the writer's propositions and progressing disciplinary knowledge, and the importance of establishing a relationship with the reader.

Ongoing Challenges for Post-Novice L2 Writers

Research into the achievements and difficulties of inexperienced writers is more limited. It comprises a small number of longitudinal studies tracing the ongoing skill development of one or two individual students (e.g., Spack, 2004), and studies that have gathered data from larger cohorts of student writers at one particular point in time during their second, third or final years (e.g., Hyland, 2012; Shi, 2010). Both types of studies report that, regardless of the progress made during the initial phase of undergraduate studies, source text use by post-novices tends to be adequate but not yet effective or accomplished. Students still have difficulties accessing appropriate high-quality sources (Morton et al., 2015; Thompson et al., 2013), understanding source content and using texts for purposes other than attribution, for example, to support their own claims or to provide alternative views (Plakans & Gebril, 2012; Thompson et al., 2013). Many post-novice L2 writers continue to rely on quotations, to patchwrite or copy without acknowledgement (Hirvela & Du, 2013), and to cite individual sentences or a small portion of information from a single source rather than providing syntheses of relevant information from multiple sources (Howard et al., 2010).

As inexperienced writers, undergraduate L2 students' knowledge of appropriate vocabulary, correct spelling and coherent text organization is not yet completely assured, and this may explain why they sometimes resort to direct (unacknowledged) copying from texts. There also appears to be a continuing reliance on description of portions of source content, rather than the reconceptualization and synthesis that is needed to produce summary citations (Hirvela & Du, 2013; Howard et al., 2010; Spack, 2004). On a more positive note, an emerging sense of personal identity and voice as an academic writer was evident in texts analyzed for some studies (Morton et al., 2015; Thompson et al., 2013). However, post-novice L2 writers appear to still be reluctant to express a clear point of view, to defer to the authority of the reader and source text and to have only limited understanding of metadiscourse strategies related to voice and stance (Hyland, 2012).

In the follow-up to the 2010 study (Wette, forthcoming) a small cohort of six students was tracked throughout the year following the L2 writing course where they received basic instruction in source text use. Participants were all international students from Malaysia and China in the final semester of their second year and first semester of the third year of their four-year undergraduate degrees, and majoring in Arts and Social Science subjects. At the end of the L2 writing course, which they had all passed with average or above-average grades, these six students had produced referenced essays on one of two topics: *Challenges of Adapting to an English-Medium University Context*, or *Key Academic Literacy Skills Needed for Success at an English-Medium University*. An average of approximately 60 percent of citations produced by this group in their L2 writing course assignments had been evaluated as satisfactory; 16 percent were reasonably accurate but included patchwriting or more extensive copying, and a further 24 percent were inaccurate representations of the source (with or without unattributed copying).

During the two semesters after the end of this course, task requirements, assessment criteria and all citations (n = 228) from 27 essays and reports submitted by these six students for 14 different assignment tasks in 10 undergraduate courses that included *Media Analysis, Instructed Second Language Acquisition, Comparative Literature* and *Educational Psychology* were collected and analyzed. I also interviewed each student twice in order to elicit their personal perspectives on source text use. The main findings of citation analysis were that, partly on account of task instructions, more than 80 percent of citations were paraphrases or summaries of information taken from recommended book, chapter or article sources. In students' assignments, the balance of one-third (35 percent) integral and two-thirds (65 percent) non-integral citations was very similar to the percentage listed for citations in published texts (Hyland, 2000), and technical aspects of in-text and end-of-text citations were generally error-free (85 percent accuracy). The quality of students' citations was also evaluated. This revealed that while just over half of the 210 summary or paraphrase citations were satisfactory and legitimate, in 18 percent of citations attempted reformulations had resulted in some misrepresentation or distortion of source content, while 15 percent included items of content copied from the source without attribution. In about 10 percent of citations, copying was more extensive. Unacknowledged secondary citations (18 percent) were evident in these post-novice L2 writers' texts, but were less frequent than in other studies reported in the literature (e.g., Shi, 2004).

On a positive note, the results of this analysis of the citations of six post-novice L2 writers in disciplinary assignments suggests that they were able to maintain a similar level of achievement in the less demanding assignment on a general academic topic that they had produced at the end of the L2 writing course. However, students' citations did not match the skill level demonstrated by expert writers in published literature in many important respects. First, less than 10 percent of students' citations drew on a single source, whereas around 30 percent of those produced by expert writers are from multiple sources (Hyland, 2000). Second, the citations of these post-novice L2 students were, like the students in the Shi study (2010), used for a relatively narrow range of rhetorical purposes. The aim of more than three-quarters of citations was to attribute an idea, theory, point of view, research finding or item of information to a source. In the absence of any indication of the writer's stance through a comment or use of a particular reporting verb, this conveys a clear impression that the writer implicitly endorses the views of the source. A further 10 percent of citations acknowledged the source of a particular definition or concept. On the whole, it appears that these inexperienced writers were still heavily reliant on sources for ideas and information, and that they did not feel sufficiently knowledgeable or confident to challenge source content. Only 5 percent of citations placed source content in a supporting role with regard to the writer's own propositions and arguments.

The influence of assignment task instructions on students' source text use was also examined. For many assignments, students were instructed to use a specific number of sources (usually between five and ten) and specific types of sources (usually prescribed and recommended texts) in assignments with a required length of 1,000 to 2,000 words. These directives had clearly guided the citation content and density of students' work. Another influence was the task specifications for many assignments, which called for analysis of a particular data set, text or texts, for example a DVD excerpt of classroom instruction, an incomplete research report or one or more literary texts. Task instructions emphasized that assignments should clearly show students' responses and analysis, and should not be mere compilations of the views of source text authors. Students were informed that sources should be used primarily for supplying evidence and examples. Assessment criteria provided students with guidance in the form of explicit criteria that included the ability to smoothly integrate their own views with evidence and examples from source texts. Feedback from assignment markers included comments about students' use of evidence from appropriate literature, but also warnings about making strong claims from a limited knowledge base, and advice that they should make more frequent use of core and recommended readings to support their claims.

This study also interviewed each of the six students twice over the course of the year that followed their attendance at the L2 writing course. Their interview statements revealed a deferential attitude to sources, which as post-novices they still tended to regard as remote and infallible authorities, usually referred to as *professionals*, *people in authority* or *experts*. Although students acknowledged the need to avoid creating the impression that their work was merely *a compilation of other people's views* and aimed to *make claims and get support from the sources*, the vast majority of their citations were in fact non-integral (information-prominent), with no reporting verb to indicate stance, or with only the neutral phrase *according to*. Interview statements also revealed their awareness of the limitations on their current knowledge base, and their dependence on source texts to provide authoritative support: *My opinion is not so valid—I need to cite someone to make it stronger*; and *I don't have the authority to say this on my own*.

From this study and others that examined source text use by post-novice L2 writers (e.g., Pecorari, 2003; Shi, 2010; Storch, 2012), it is clear that while their citations showed some degree of proficiency, most students at this stage of skill development are not yet consistently effective or accomplished in the skill of writing using sources. They still need to develop their ability to:

- Reliably compose citations that are accurate without relying on patchwriting or copying
- Smoothly integrate sources with own ideas and propositions
- Provide sufficient acknowledgement of sources without appearing to be overly reliant
- Synthesize key ideas expressed over several paragraphs, pages or longer texts
- Construct accurate citations that draw on multiple sources
- Utilize source content for a broad range of rhetorical purposes
- Evaluate or question the authoritativeness of sources where appropriate
- Recognize the fundamentally persuasive nature of academic discourse by interacting with the reader and handling information flow using metadiscourse strategies
- See themselves as authors and managers of the texts they compose

A Trajectory of Skill Development in Writing Using Sources

Based on my own research (Wette, 2010; forthcoming), and from examination of the scholarly and research literature, I would now like to propose a trajectory of development by L2 writers that identifies four stages of development in writing using sources, consisting of novice, post-novice and intermediate stages of development, with proficiency as the final phase (Figure 7.1). It summarizes the key phases of development that L2 writers are likely to pass through, and I hope that teachers will find it useful for locating the current proficiency in source text use of the students in their classes. It may assist with the selection of appropriate instructional materials and tasks, and reduce the likelihood that teachers will underestimate the complexity of this skill set, or have unrealistic expectations about what can be expected of a class at a particular stage of development. Students may also appreciate information that will help them to locate their current level of ability, and to inform themselves about future stages and goals.

Novice/entry-level writer
Basic knowledge of procedures for quality source selection and evaluation
Uncertainty about whether a citation is needed or not (i.e., what is common knowledge)
Unattributed copying from sources
Heavy use of patchwriting and copying (sometimes unattributed)
Heavy use of paraphrasing of phrases or individual sentences
Heavy use of integral/author prominent citations
Heavy/excessive use of quotations
Heavy use of sources to provide ideas (attribution)
Single-author citations only
Little evidence of personal authorship or text management
Little evidence of any interaction with the reader through metadiscourse strategies
Post-novice writer
Improved ability to select quality sources
Still some uncertainty about what is/is not common knowledge
Marked decrease in unattributed copying from sources
Patchwriting and copying (sometimes unattributed)
Some development in ability to summarize and paraphrase
Increase in use of non-integral/information prominent citations
Use of sources to provide ideas
Limited range of rhetorical purposes for source use (e.g., explanation, definition, example)
Some knowledge of disciplinary citation practices (e.g. source selection, citation type)
Intermediate-level writer
Well-established ability to select relevant, quality sources
Patchwriting is less frequent but still evident
Generally appropriate use of integral and non-integral citations
Increasing use of multiple-source citations
Citations are used for a broad range of rhetorical purposes
Continuing progress in knowledge of disciplinary practices
Growing confidence in self as author and manager of information
Proficient writer
Ability to compose accurate, original, integrated paraphrases and summaries
Quotes are used sparingly, and are integrated with the writer's arguments and propositions
Frequent, appropriate use of multiple-source citations
Knowledge of disciplinary citation practices
Awareness of self as participant in a disciplinary dialogue on assignment issues
Awareness of the need to balance acknowledgement of sources with own arguments and ideas
Awareness of the importance of a personal stance and the persuasive objectives of texts
Confidence in self as author and manager of information

FIGURE 7.1 Source text use by L2 writers at four stages of skill development

Suggestions for Units of Instruction in Writing Using Sources

The final section of this chapter discusses a number of ways in which an enhanced awareness of the complex skill of writing using sources can lead to innovations in practice. I list possible course content for a progressive, guided development of students' abilities at (a) novice/post-novice and (b) intermediate/proficient stages of ability. At all stages, of course, tasks will be most effective if they are challenging but achievable, and if assessment criteria reflect realistic teacher expectations, based on students' current stage of development.

Course Content: Novice and Post-Novice L2 Writers

The initial focus of instruction needs to cover the basics of writing using sources including all technical and rule-governed components of this skill, reading, thinking and writing processes, as well as the main purposes for which source text citations are used. The aim of instruction for L2 novice writers is for students to develop an acceptable level of ability, and for expectations to be realistic.

Course content for learners at this stage will include the *mechanics* of writing using sources, legitimate and illegitimate source text use, and the range of rhetorical purposes of citations:

1. Technical and rule-governed skill components.
   - Accurate formatting and punctuation for in-text and end-of-text formatting (e.g., APA, MLA)
   - Evaluation of source quality, e.g., currency, relevance, trustworthiness, authorship and purpose, especially internet sources and *grey literature*
   - Decisions about whether to paraphrase, summarize or use a quotation
   - Decisions about when and how frequently to include a citation in extended paraphrases; marking the borders of citations
   - Knowledge of when it is permissible to use a secondary citation
   - Selection of appropriate reporting verbs
   - Appropriate use of integral and non-integral citations
2. Plagiarism, patchwriting and legitimate source text use.
   - Awareness of the difference between common knowledge and information requiring a citation
   - Skill in *top-down* synthetic reading processes to extract main ideas
   - Practice in paraphrasing tasks involving the transformation of source content through changes that transcend lexical and syntactic substitutions
   - Use and adaptation of commonly used content-free language patterns and sentence stems, such as: *A number of studies have investigated …*; *This section examines research into …*
   - Awareness of the need for transparency with regard to the relationship between the writer's text and the source text
   - The ability to compare and synthesize information from two or more sources to construct multiple-source citations

3. Analysis of citations to introduce students to the range of rhetorical purposes, and tasks to provide guided practice that familiarize students with a broader range of functions.
   - Demonstrating familiarity with research and scholarship
   - Acknowledging the origin of particular theories, concepts and terms
   - Supporting the writer's claims, choices and findings
   - Identifying sources with a similar focus

Course Content: Intermediate-Level L2 Writers

Instruction for students with reasonable proficiency in linguistic aspects of this skill set needs to emphasize its conceptual and disciplinary aspects. Course content may include:

- Selection of reporting verbs that evaluate the positions of sources towards the content to be cited (e.g., X *claims, maintains, neglects to consider* …)
- Integration of citations with the writer's own ideas and arguments, and how originality can be expressed in academic writing
- Development of confidence and skill in the use of non-integral and multiple-source citations
- Development of awareness of the different rhetorical purposes of citations, and the ways in which they can support a writer's views and propositions
- Use of interactive metadiscourse strategies to reveal the writer's stance, e.g., transition markers such as *however* and *in addition*, and frame markers such as *first* and *to summarize*
- Use of textual metadiscourse strategies to engage with readers and anticipate their responses to the text, e.g., hedges such as *tends to, can* and *may*, and boosters such as *clearly* and *demonstrate*
- Familiarity with the way people write in particular disciplines, including who and what is cited, and how citations are constructed, e.g., integral vs. non-integral citations, multiple citations
- An introduction to the broad range of rhetorical purposes (in addition to attribution) for which citations can be used to support the writer: acknowledgement of the originator of a concept, term or theory; identification of sources with a similar focus or argument; identification of sources with similar research findings; identification of sources with examples to support the writer's claim
- Compilation of an item bank of formulaic content-free language patterns and sentence stems commonly used in the students' disciplinary area, such as: *Recent years have seen increased research attention directed towards* …; *This essay has addressed the issue of* …
- Development of students' confidence in their ability to contribute to disciplinary discussion on topics where they have some knowledge and familiarity (Hyland, 2002, 2012)

Suggested Instructional Tasks and Activities

Extensive practice using achievable tasks requiring a limited number of citations from traceable sources such as a book review, or the application of a theory to a specific disciplinary example or situation will be helpful, as will constructive feedback on drafts. Plagiarism detection software such as *Turnitin* can be useful as a deterrent, but also as a guide for evaluating the quality of aspects of students' source text use. Students can be required to include page numbers so that the teacher can locate and check the cited portion of the source, and to submit copies of their sources (with cited content highlighted) for all or some of the citations in their assignments. Instructional tasks may include:

- Tasks to locate and comment on the quality of citations in well-written published or student-authored texts as models by comparing citations with the sources that are cited
- Critical analysis and evaluation of examples of expert (published outputs), accomplished and flawed (high- and low-scoring student assignments) citations
- Teacher-led class modeling (using graphic organizers where appropriate) of the process of constructing a paraphrase or summary citation, including selecting content, reconceptualizing content to form a paraphrase or summary, synthesizing multiple sources into a single citation and integrating the citation into a text
- Preparation and delivery (working in pairs or groups) of oral summaries of source extracts, and group tasks to construct and review draft citations
- Exploration (in groups or individually) of disciplinary citation practices and differences, and assembling of a text portfolio of quality exemplars from specific disciplinary areas
- Teacher-led class discussions of key topics and challenges, e.g., patchwriting, rhetorical purposes of citations, marking borders between citations and one's own ideas
- Writing conferences in which students show assignment drafts and discuss their use of sources with the teacher
- Peer draft reviews to provide students with practice in analyzing source text quality, and evaluating it against specific criteria

Conclusion

Just as the focus of attention has shifted over the years from a narrow focus on plagiarism to a more comprehensive understanding of various forms of ineffective or inappropriate writing using sources, a more recent shift in attention has resulted in increased emphasis on instructional approaches to assist learners in overcoming the challenges that they face in becoming proficient in this sophisticated academic literacy. It is my view that sustained, explicit instruction and discussion, supported by a variety of task types contextualized into specific disciplines and outputs, and constructive, targeted feedback are needed in order to build confidence and skill in novice and post-novice L2 writers. Writing using sources is clearly an incremental skill that develops gradually throughout the undergraduate years: while rule-governed and technical components of writing using sources are readily learned, proficiency in transforming and integrating sources takes longer, and inaccurate citations and patchwriting are likely to feature to some extent throughout students' undergraduate years. Students' development can be assisted through instruction, practice and feedback, but also through the growing sophistication of their understanding of disciplinary concepts and citation practices, and increased confidence in the ability to contribute to disciplinary discussions.

Looking to the future, there is still much to be learned about how L2 writing instruction can help students to develop the most important and potentially problematic aspects of this skill. More longitudinal studies of the writing development of cohorts of L2 writers would provide corroborating evidence of the trajectory that has been suggested in this chapter. In view of the speed and direction in which research and scholarship has progressed over the past thirty years, there is every reason to be confident that it will continue to provide valuable information and empirical evidence to enhance our knowledge of how to assist L2 writers towards proficiency in this challenging but essential academic skill.

References

Bloch, J. (2012). *Plagiarism, intellectual property and the teaching of L2 writing*. Bristol: Multilingual Matters.

Davis, M., & Morley, J. (2015). Phrasal intertextuality: The responses of academics from different disciplines to students' re-use of phrases. *Journal of Second Language Writing, 28*, 20–35.

England, A. (2008). The dynamic nature of common knowledge. In C. Eisner & M. Vicinus (Eds.), *Originality, imitation, and plagiarism: Teaching writing in the digital age* (pp. 104–113). Ann Arbor: University of Michigan Press.

Flowerdew, J., & Li, Y. (2007). Language re-use among Chinese apprentice scientists writing for publication. *Applied Linguistics, 28*, 440–463.

Hirvela, A., & Du, Q. (2013). "Why am I paraphrasing?": Undergraduate ESL writers' engagement with source-based academic writing and reading. *Journal of English for Academic Purposes, 12*, 87–98.

Howard, R. M. (1993). A plagiarism pentimento. *Journal of Teaching Writing, 11*, 233–246.

Howard, R. M., Serviss, T., & Rodrigue, T. K. (2010). Writing from sources, writing from sentences. *Writing and Pedagogy, 2*, 177–192.

Hyland, K. (2000). Academic attribution: interaction through citation. In K. Hyland, *Disciplinary discourses: Social interactions in academic writing* (pp. 20–40). Harlow: Pearson.

Hyland, K. (2002). Options of identity in academic writing. *ELT Journal, 56*, 351–358.

Hyland, K. (2012). Undergraduate understandings: Stance and voice in final year reports. In K. Hyland & C. Sancho Guinda (Eds.), *Stance and voice in written academic genres* (pp. 134–150). Houndmills, Basingstoke: Palgrave Macmillan.

Keck, C. (2014). Copying, paraphrasing, and academic writing development: A re-examination of L1 and L2 summarization practices. *Journal of Second Language Writing, 25*, 4–22.

Morton, J., Storch, N., & Thompson, C. (2015). What our students tell us: Perceptions of three multilingual students on their academic writing in first year. *Journal of Second Language Writing, 30*, 1–13.

Partington, A. (Ed.). (1996). *The Oxford dictionary of quotations*. Oxford: Oxford University Press.

Pecorari, D. (2003). Good and original: Plagiarism and patchwriting in academic second language writing. *Journal of Second Language Writing, 12*, 317–345.

Pennycook, A. (1996). Borrowing others' words: Text, ownership, memory, and plagiarism. *TESOL Quarterly, 30*, 201–229.

Petri , B. (2007). Rhetorical functions of citations in high-and low-rated master's theses. *Journal of English for Academic Purposes, 6*(3), 238–253.

Plakans, L., & Gebril, A. (2012). A close investigation into source use in integrated second language writing tasks. *Assessing Writing, 17*, 18–34.

Shi, L. (2004). Textual borrowing in second-language writing. *Written Communication, 21*, 171–200.

Shi, L. (2006). Cultural backgrounds and textual appropriation. *Language Awareness, 15*, 264–282.

Shi, L. (2010). Textual appropriation and citing behaviours of university undergraduates. *Applied Linguistics, 31*, 1–24.

Spack, R. (2004). The acquisition of academic literacy in a second language: A longitudinal case study, updated. In V. Zamel & R. Spack (Eds.), *Crossing the curriculum: Multilingual learners in college classrooms* (pp. 19–46). Mahwah NJ: Erlbaum.

Storch, N. (2012). Incorporation of source material: the effect of instruction. *TESOL in Context, 22*, 38–55.

Thompson, C., Morton, J., & Storch, N. (2013). Where from, who, why and how? A study of the use of sources by first year L2 university students. *Journal of English for Academic Purposes, 12*, 99–109.

Wette, R. (2010). Evaluating student learning in a university level EAP unit on writing using sources. *Journal of Second Language Writing, 19*, 158–177.

Wette, R. (forthcoming). Source text by undergraduate post-novice L2 writers in disciplinary assignments.

Instructional Tasks and Activities

8

LITERATE TALK

Supporting EAL Students' Academic Writing

Jennifer Hammond

Introduction

This chapter addresses academic writing instruction within the context of school education. Specifically, it addresses the notion of "literate talk" and the insights offered by this concept for teachers of academic writing across different curriculum disciplines. Although the notion of literate talk is perhaps better known within the context of school education, I would argue it is a concept that is equally relevant for those working with adult students who are seeking to develop their abilities with academic writing—whether those students are second language learners or native English speakers. As with a number of other educational metaphors (such as scaffolding), the value of literate talk lies both in its ability to capture something that is recognizable to teachers, and in the theoretical insights it offers. A key argument in the chapter is that theoretical understandings of the notion of literate talk can assist teachers in planning and implementing programs in ways that provide a bridge between students' everyday oral language and their academic writing.

The chapter begins by addressing questions regarding the nature of literate talk and its implications for the broader issue of teachers' knowledge about language. Here, it draws on the work of a number of researchers who have highlighted the role of talk in learning, as well as aspects of systemic functional theory. The chapter then turns to research that my colleagues and I have undertaken over a period of time into the education of students for whom English is an additional language (EAL students) within the context of mainstream schooling in Australia. Here it highlights insights and pedagogical implications that can be drawn from the notion of literate talk for teachers working with second language learners of academic writing.

Literate Talk and Teachers' Knowledge about Language

Literate talk is a term used by a number of researchers, particularly in the school context, to refer to the nature of talk that introduces educational concepts to students, and provides discipline-specific ways of talking about those concepts (Gibbons, 2009, 2014; Luk & Lin, 2015; Wallace, 2002; Wells, 1999; Wells & Chang-Wells, 1992). As students engage with educational knowledge, they are required to engage with language that constructs and disseminates knowledge, and, whether spoken or written, where texts are more written-like in character. It involves not just "talk as social action," but "the acquisition and development of more complex conceptual structures and cognitive processes" (Wallace, 2002, p. 113). Although spoken, literate talk thus differs from everyday spoken language in that it introduces discipline-specific vocabulary, as well as patterns of grammar and texts that enable students to discuss, classify, explain and argue and persuade. As Gibbons argues, such talk includes characteristics of explicitness, connectivity and coherence that differ from characteristics of everyday conversational English (Gibbons, 2009).

As with other educational metaphors (again scaffolding comes to mind here), general descriptions of "literate talk" require some unpacking. My own understanding of the term draws on researchers whose work has been described as constituting a *dialogic turn* in analysis of classroom interaction and learning (for example, Alexander, 2001, 2008a; Mercer, Dawes, & Kleine Staarman, 2009; Myhill, 2006; Skidmore, 2006; Wells, 1999). My understanding also draws on aspects of systemic linguistics (Halliday, 1978, 1993, 2008; Halliday & Hasan, 1989; Halliday & Matthiessen, 2014), particularly the notion of mode within that theory (Halliday, 1989; Gibbons, 2009, 2014). While the work of Alexander and others highlights the role of talk in learning, systemic theory provides resources that enable more detailed articulation of the textual and lexico-grammatical features that characterize differences, as well as areas of overlap, between spoken and written language. Together, I suggest, these perspectives provide valuable insights into the relation between different types of classroom tasks and the language and literacy demands and learning opportunities they pose for students. The two perspectives also provide insights into the demands faced by students in learning academic writing.

For those working in the TESOL field, the difference in demands placed on students in learning everyday spoken language in comparison with academic language and literacy are familiar. Following the work of Cummins (2000, 2008), there is wide acknowledgement that while EAL students are likely to require only a year or so to become fluent in everyday conversational spoken English, they will require around five to seven years to achieve peer-like abilities with academic language and literacy (Cummins, 2008; Gibbons, 2014). As Thomas and Collier (1997) point out, this time frame for academic language proficiency is substantially longer for *at-risk* students who have experienced disrupted or minimal access to formal schooling prior to arrival in their host country.

Most schoolteachers recognize differences between the demands of everyday spoken language and academic language and literacy, and are well aware of the importance, especially with EAL students, of supporting students' academic writing development. However, there is consistent and ongoing evidence that many teachers lack confidence in the extent and depth of their professional knowledge about language and literacy, and their ability to teach it effectively. For example, a recent large-scale survey of 5,128 Australian teachers in the state of New South Wales showed that 90 percent of teachers identified English language and literacy as a major need for EAL students (Watkins, Lean, Noble, & Dunn, 2013). However, the majority of those teachers also indicated that they lacked the skills to provide such support, and considered that they required access to professional support to develop the required expertise. Outcomes from a recently completed project that addressed the needs of refugee students in Australian schools confirm such findings (Hammond, 2014b). Interviews with teachers and students indicated that both groups recognized the challenges posed by academic language, and the importance of teacher support for students' academic language and literacy development. However, classroom observations showed that the kind of systematic and explicit teaching of language and literacy necessary to provide high levels of support for refugee and other EAL students within mainstream classes was a *hit and miss affair*. Such findings are consistent with outcomes from other research conducted with EAL and mainstream teachers in school contexts within Australia and other English-speaking countries (Hammond & Macken-Horarik, 2001; Hammond; 2008; Jones & Chen, 2012; Macken-Horarik, Love, & Unsworth, 2011).

Concerns about teachers' knowledge about language do not appear to be restricted to the school context. For example, amongst contributors to this book, the majority of whom work within various adult education contexts, the issue of teachers' knowledge about language arises again and again: Manchón (this volume) addresses the relationship between (knowledge of) language and writing, and points to the predominance of testing rather than teaching of academic writing in educational contexts; Hyland (this volume) highlights the discipline-specific nature of academic language (and writing) and argues the need for targeted teaching to support students' developing control of disciplinary discourses; Tardy (this volume) poses the question of what teachers need to know in order to effectively address genres in undergraduate writing classes; and Paltridge (this volume) argues the value of teachers encouraging students to *act as researchers* to explore implications of the relationship between theories of genre, audience and discourse communities for writing practices and expectations of specific academic disciplines.

My own view is that teachers' theoretical and practical knowledge about language is central to any program designed to support students' academic writing. And it is within this context that I suggest the notion of literate talk can be useful. Needless to say, the notion of literate talk by itself will not address the kind of knowledge about language and literacy required of teachers. However, I suggest it can offer theoretical and practical insights that may impact positively on the teaching of academic writing. It may also contribute to a theoretical framework that teachers can build on to further enhance their knowledge and confidence in teaching language and literacy across diverse curriculum disciplines.

In what follows, I first elaborate my own understanding of literate talk, and then turn to our research to tease out what I see as implications of the notion of literate talk for program planning and implementation, and more generally for teachers' knowledge about language and the teaching of academic writing.

Elaborating Literate Talk: Talking to Learn and Learning to Talk

In recent years, a substantial body of educational research has highlighted the role of talk in learning (Alexander, 2001, 2008a, 2008b; Mercer & Litttleton, 2007; Mercer, Dawes, & Kleine Staarman, 2009; Myhill, 2006; Skidmore, 2006; Wells, 1999). A consistent argument within this work is that extended, dialogic and in-depth talk about substantial curriculum concepts opens up genuine opportunities for learning. Further, interactions that enable such talk support students' thinking and mediate their developing understanding of curriculum knowledge. The argument put forward by Alexander is representative of this work. He writes (2008b):

> Of all the tools for cultural and pedagogical intervention in human development and learning, talk is the most pervasive in its use and powerful in its possibilities. Talk vitally mediates the cognitive and cultural spaces between adult and child, among children themselves, between teacher and learner, between society and the individual, between what a child knows and understands and what he or she has yet to know and understand. Language not only manifests thinking but also structures it, and speech shapes the higher mental processes necessary for so much of the learning that takes place, or ought to take place at school.... It follows that one of the principal tasks of the teacher is to create interactive opportunities and encounters that directly and appropriately engineer such mediation. (p. 92)

Such work not only highlights the pivotal role of talking to learn, it highlights the need for students to be supported to learn how to engage in the kind of dialogic talk that supports learning. While researchers such as Alexander generally do not use the term *literate talk*, their descriptions of dialogic talk resonate closely with this term. Amongst others, Mercer and his colleagues (Mercer, 2002;

Mercer & Littleton, 2007; Mercer et al., 2009) argue that students need to be supported to use language in joint activity for reasoning and for problem-solving. They also argue that if students are to engage in talk as a tool for thinking, where that talk is genuinely exploratory, and where it shapes higher mental processes, they need to be shown how to engage critically and constructively in that talk (Mercer, 2002). In a similar vein, Alexander (2008b, p. 118) argues that if programs are to "provide the best chance for children to develop the diverse learning talk repertoire on which different kinds of thinking and understanding are predicated" then teachers need to address the conduct and ethos of classroom talk, as well as the content.

While I totally accept arguments regarding the importance of *talking to learn*, my own view is that students, especially EAL students, need explicit support to ensure they also *learn to talk*. (Manchón [2011] addresses a parallel distinction between learning to write and writing to learn in her work on academic writing development for second and foreign language learners.) The emphasis on talking to learn within dialogic approaches tends to focus on the dynamics of classroom interaction, rather than explicit teaching about language and literacy. That is, the emphasis is on ensuring classrooms are structured in ways that offer affordances for extended dialogic interaction, and where students are taught to engage with others respectfully and thoughtfully. Yet, as Baynham (1993, p. 5) has argued, learning academic language and literacy involves not just a process of learning more language, but of functional diversification, where students are required to move between their everyday (and primarily spoken) world, and the more specialized and formal domains of schooling. It also requires students to take up different roles and relationships, deal with different kinds of knowledge, move between different registers and also move between spoken and written modes of language. While it is vitally important for teachers to provide students with opportunities to engage in extended dialogic talk that involves exploratory reasoning and problem solving, for second language learners, such opportunities, in themselves, are not enough. Students also need explicit support to develop control of the literate talk that will enable them to take up such opportunities. And this raises once again the issue of teachers' knowledge about language, and the nature of literate talk.

Systemic linguistics provides a powerful complement to dialogic approaches to teaching and learning (Hammond, 2016). The resources available within systemic theory, I suggest, provide a framework for developing more explicit knowledge about language and literacy—including knowledge of the similarities and differences between conversational talk and the literate talk of academic disciplines—and their similarities and differences to academic writing. So what are these resources and how can they contribute to teachers' developing knowledge about language? And where does the notion of literate talk fit within systemic theory?

Systemic theory is a functional, rather than formal theory of language, and its chief concern is with ways in which language is used in real situations. As Halliday (1978, 1993) has argued, language has evolved to satisfy human needs, and the way it is organized is functional with respect to these needs. He further argues, that as speakers or writers, we make selections from the lexical and grammatical systems of language, but those selections are constrained at a general level by the context of culture in which the language user is located, and at a more specific level by three major variables within any context of situation—namely, field (topic or activity of discussion), tenor (roles and relationships between participants) and mode (channel of communication—spoken, written, multimodal). Proponents of the theory argue that the relationship between the form of language (choice of vocabulary, patterns of grammar) and context in which this language is used is systematic and mutually predictable—enabling language users to predict from text to context and from context to text. While of course it is not possible to predict precise choices of vocabulary and grammar on the basis of context, it is possible (and indeed essential to meaningful functioning within any society) to be able to predict consistent patterns of language use. Within systemic theory the resulting patterns, or varieties of language, are known as registers (Christie & Martin, 2007; Eggins, 1994; Halliday & Matthiessen, 2014).

As indicated, mode is one of the variables within a context of situation, that, together with field and tenor, shape the choices that are made by speakers or writers in the construction of any text. While it is just one aspect of register theory, the notion of mode is especially relevant here because of the insights it provides into the nature and value of classroom talk, and into the nature of academic English, including the relationship between academic talk and academic writing.

Within systemic theory, mode is usually conceptualized as a continuum or cline, involving two kinds of distance: interpersonal and experiential distance (Eggins, 1994). Interpersonal distance refers to the distance in space and time between interactants. For example, face-to-face interactions involve less physical distance between interactants than telephone conversations or email exchanges; radio or television programs involve greater distance between speaker and audience; written academic texts involve still greater distance between writer and reader. Experiential distance refers to the distance between language and the social processes that are taking place. For example, for players in a football match, language accompanies the action of the game, and if separated from the action of the game, the language would be largely incomprehensible. In a later news report of outcomes from the game, language reconstructs the action of the game, and hence the language is somewhat distanced from the action; and for a social commentator writing about the impact of contact sports such as football, language is further distanced from the action and enables reflection on action. As we move from one end of the continuum (close physical proximity between interactants, language accompanying action) to the other end (physical distance, language as reflection) we also tend to move from spoken to written language. This notion of the mode continuum is summarized in Figure 8.1.

While the characterization of mode as spoken or written language is overly simplistic, conceiving of the relationship as a continuum from *very spoken* (language in action) to *very written* (language as reflection) remains useful. Some years

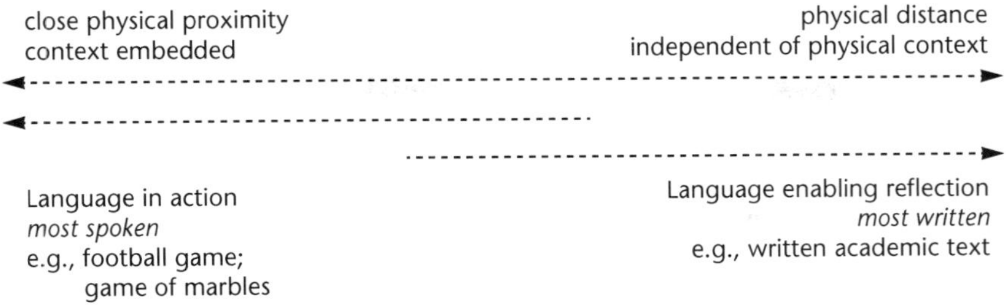

FIGURE 8.1 The mode continuum

ago, in his work on spoken and written language, Halliday (1989) demonstrated that written language is typically lexically dense, and often contains complex nominal groups characterized by nominalization and by grammatical metaphor. Conversely, spoken language is typically lexically sparse, but grammatically intricate in the sense that *sentences* are frequently long and contain numerous clauses related to each other in complex chains and patterns. As Halliday argued, each mode is complex, but in different ways. Such work has been taken up by a number of educators (e.g., Gibbons, 2009, 2014; Hammond, 1990; Wells, 1999). They argue that speech and writing play pivotal, but different (although complementary) roles in education; and that the more dynamic, dialogic and flexible nature of speech makes it ideal for mediating initial learning—for introducing and explaining concepts, for trying out ideas, for exploring logic, whereas extended writing encourages consolidation of ideas, clarification of logic and opportunities for reflecting on one's own thinking and learning.

While distinctions between *most spoken* and *most written* language at either end of the mode continuum are generally consistent and clear, there are many instances of language use in middle sections of the continuum where these distinctions are not clear. The lines between spoken and written language are increasingly blurred by the proliferation of information technology—when we produce text messages or emails our language is written (in the sense that we key in letters and numbers) but the resulting texts may have many features that are more typical of casual spoken language (abbreviated vocabulary and sentences; slang); radio announcers speak to their audiences, but may read texts that have been deliberately written to sound as if they are spoken. Similarly, the talk that occurs in interactions between teachers and students frequently blurs the boundaries between spoken and written language. And it is here that the notion of literate talk becomes particularly relevant.

To explore implications that can be drawn from both mode and literate talk for program planning and implementation I turn now to the research that my colleagues and I undertook into teaching and learning practices designed to address the needs of EAL students in mainstream Australian classrooms (Gibbons, 2008; Hammond & Gibbons, 2005; Hammond, 2008; Hammond, 2014a).

The research involved working with teachers in schools where 60 percent or more of the student population were EAL students. Our focus was on students who were beyond the initial (and obvious) stages of learning English and who were located in mainstream classes. We invited experienced classroom and specialist EAL teachers in six schools, who were team teaching in the middle years of schooling (Years 5–8), to work with us to plan and implement programs that aimed to ensure EAL students had access to the full school curriculum, and that they also had access to the high levels of support necessary to enable them to engage with that curriculum. The research was informed by Vygotskian theories of learning (Mercer, 1994; Vygotsky, 1978; Wells, 1999) and the assumption that learning occurs primarily in collaborative social interactions between learners and more knowledgeable others. It was also informed both by the work of Alexander and others with their emphasis on the importance of dialogic interaction in learning, and by systemic functional linguistics, including an understanding of the mode continuum. The research itself involved cycles of professional and theoretical input, collaborative program planning, documentation and analysis of the impact of programs and shared reflection on teaching practices. Documentation of programs involved video recording of lessons, collection of students' written texts and collection of key curriculum and teaching resources.

In the discussion that follows, I focus in particular on one Year 6 Science program from the research to illustrate ways in which participating teachers worked with the notions of mode and of literate talk to assist in their processes of program planning and implementation.

The Mode Continuum and the Place of Literate Talk in a Year 6 Science Program

In many ways, the Year 6 Science program under focus here was typical of other junior Science programs in Australian schools. In line with mandatory curriculum guidelines, the program was designed around the topic of Vision. Many of the classroom tasks that students engaged in throughout the program were similar to those undertaken in other Australian schools. The program differed from some others, however, not in the nature of individual classroom tasks, but in the relationship between tasks, and in the way they were sequenced to support students' learning both of scientific concepts and of the language that would enable them to talk, read and write about those concepts.

While planning the Science program, the teacher identified the following as priority student needs:

- To extend students' understanding of scientific processes and thinking and, related to this:
  - To extend students' use of scientific vocabulary

- To develop students' understanding of scientific explanations (both spoken and written), including their ability to understand and use cause/effect sentences
- To develop students' abilities in scientific writing

The process of identifying priorities assisted the teacher in taking account of students' existing knowledge and abilities, and in planning sequences of lessons and tasks that addressed their needs. In addition, as part of their program planning processes, this teacher, along with others who participated in our research project, was encouraged to plan and locate sequences of classroom tasks in relation to the mode continuum. That is, teachers were encouraged to use the continuum from *most spoken/language accompanying action* to *most written/language as reflection* as a planning device to assist them in developing "a conceptual map of what was to be taught" (Alexander, 2008a, p. 50). To illustrate, tasks selected for the Year 6 Science unit included (for brevity not all unit tasks are included here):

- Hands-on experiments and simulations of visual impairments
- Oral reconstruction of procedures and outcomes from experiments
- Library research about specific visual impairments
- Preparation for oral explanations of visual impairment
- Presentations of oral explanations
- Negotiation to prepare questions for forthcoming visiting speaker
- Review of structure and language features of genre of explanation
- Drafting of written explanation of specific visual impairment
- Completion of written explanation

The teacher located these in relation to the mode continuum as illustrated in Figure 8.2.

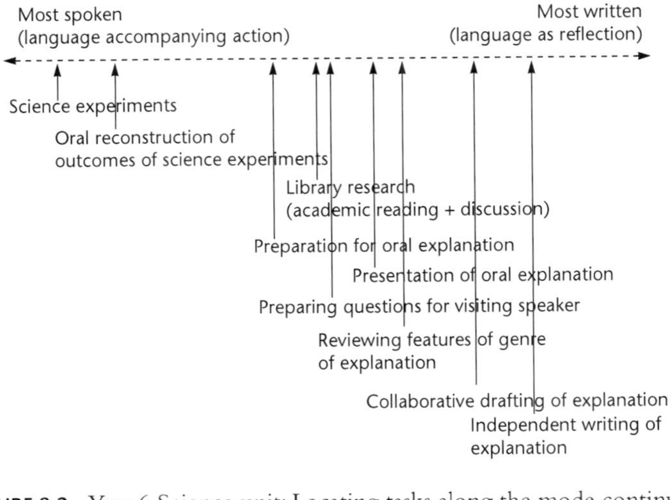

FIGURE 8.2 Year 6 Science unit: Locating tasks along the mode continuum

The value within the research of locating tasks in relation to the mode continuum lay not in the precise location of each task, but, rather, in the discussions that were generated amongst participating teachers regarding the specific cognitive as well as linguistic demands that each task placed on students. The research exercise also generated considerable reflection regarding the selection and sequencing of tasks within programs to ensure that steps between tasks were appropriate to the students' cognitive and linguistic abilities (with subsequent adjusting of sequences of tasks, and inclusion of additional tasks as deemed necessary). The aim of the exercise was to ensure programs included sequential tasks that challenged students, but were not so far beyond their current abilities that students were unable to engage with the task. In Vygotskian (1978) terms, the aim was to push students to work at the outer limits of the zone of proximal development, but not to lose them.

As indicated, while individual tasks within the Science program were not unusual, their sequencing was important. The inclusion of hands-on science experiments early in the unit on Vision introduced key scientific concepts—of transparent, translucent and opaque materials; convex and concave lens; and simulations of various visual impairments—concepts that were central to the unit. The experiments thus established a basis of shared scientific knowledge and talk that was built upon in subsequent tasks. While final tasks required students to engage in extended and independent scientific writing, prior tasks provided a basis for consolidating and extending students' understanding of the concepts and of their abilities to engage in the talk necessary for such engagement. Thus the cluster of tasks located around the middle of the mode continuum played an important role in supporting and consolidating students' engagement with key scientific concepts of the program. At the same time these tasks were designed to introduce students to the relevant vocabulary, grammar and text structures that would enable them to talk, and subsequently write, about these concepts. As Figure 8.3 highlights, the tasks introduced students to the *literate talk* that was pivotal to engagement with the scientific concepts, and that also supported their abilities to write about those concepts.

The differences in language demands between tasks located towards the most-spoken and most-written ends of the mode continuum in the Year 6 Science program were significant. The challenge for the Year 6 Science teacher lay not only in recognizing, but in understanding the more subtle shifts in language demands that occurred in the middle tasks in the program, and in being able to plan and implement those tasks in ways that supported students in sufficiently small steps to build their knowledge both of science and of academic language.

Our research suggested that the process of program planning where teachers located tasks in relation to the mode continuum was very helpful here. Teachers reported that the collaborative exercise of plotting the classroom tasks, and of

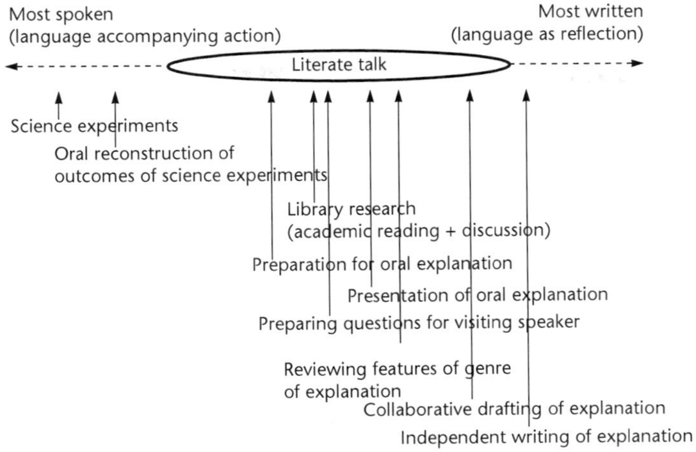

FIGURE 8.3 The place of literate talk in the Year 6 Science program

justifying the location of tasks along the continuum, pushed them to reflect on their students' current language abilities, and on their program goals, in more detail than usual. It also pushed them to analyze specific demands of individual tasks in more detail, and then to draw on this knowledge to sequence tasks with appropriate small steps, and to embed the teaching of relevant aspects of language and literacy within the tasks. Figure 8.4 illustrates how, as part of the process of program planning, and then in program implementation, the Year 6 Science teacher embedded the teaching of language and literacy with Science in her program.

As Figure 8.4 shows, the teaching of language and literacy within the science program occurred both implicitly (reinforcing of scientific vocabulary) and explicitly (teaching of grammar of cause and effect; focusing students' attention on the rhetorical structure of explanations). As they moved from one task to the next, the students learned science and they also increasingly developed control of the literate talk necessary for the "acquisition and development of more complex conceptual structures and cognitive processes" (Wallace, 2002, p. 113). I suggest the sequencing of tasks within this program, with the dual focus within the middle tasks on teaching science and teaching language/literacy, provided a bridge between students' initial everyday ways of talking about vision, and their development of more scientific and academic ways of thinking and talking, and subsequently writing, about key concepts related to vision. That is, the literate talk that was central to those middle tasks—talk that supported students' developing knowledge of scientific vocabulary, of relevant grammatical structures and of text organization—provided a bridge to students' developing control of academic writing.

Classroom task	Teaching of language
Science experiments	Modeling of new scientific vocabulary
Oral reconstruction of what happened in experiments	Modeling of grammar of cause and effect in sentences; subsequent explicit focus on structure of cause and effect sentences
Library research about specific visual impairments	Discussion of research skills of finding specific information; skimming and scanning; reading for detail
Preparing oral explanations of visual impairment	Reminder of grammar of cause and effect and of text structure relevant for oral presentations
Oral explanations of visual impairment	Analysis of strengths and any possible areas for improvement of students' oral presentations: dual focus on curriculum content and use of language
Written questions for forthcoming visiting speaker	Discussion of structure of questions and appropriate level of politeness
Review of written explanation genre	Review of rhetorical structure and specific language features of written explanations
Drafting of written explanation of specific visual impairment	Collaborative writing with teacher support, including discussion of text structure and grammatical features of explanations
Final independent written explanation of visual impairment	Feedback from teacher regarding structure, grammar and vocabulary of written texts

FIGURE 8.4 Embedding of language teaching in the Year 6 Science program

Conclusions

In the introduction to this chapter I argued that, as with other educational metaphors, the value of literate talk lies both in its ability to capture something that is recognizable to teachers, and in the theoretical insights it can offer. In concluding the chapter, I return to this argument.

As indicated previously, there is consistent research evidence in Australia and other English-speaking countries that shows, while teachers recognize the importance of supporting students' development of academic language and literacy, they lack the knowledge and confidence to do so effectively. Discussions with teachers that took place during our research and in subsequent professional development programs confirm that the notion of *literate talk* is useful here. These discussions assisted teachers to get a clearer *handle* on the challenges faced by students in learning academic language and literacy. They also provided a starting point for understanding why and how academic language differs from everyday spoken language, and why it is so much more challenging to learn. Our research confirms that the notion of literate talk is indeed something that resonates with teachers.

I also argued that to draw out the theoretical implications of metaphors such as literate talk, we need to go beyond general descriptions (despite the value of such descriptions in initial discussions about academic language and literacy). In this paper, I have attempted to develop a more robust account of literate talk by drawing both on the work of Alexander and others who have emphasized the role of talk in educational learning, and on the work of systemic linguists, especially those who have focused on mode. As indicated, within our research we worked with the notion of mode continuum as a way of teasing out the academic language and literacy demands that were placed on second-language learners as they engaged with mainstream curricula. We also drew on this notion to provide theoretical support for programs designed to enable students to move between the domains of everyday conversations and common-sense knowledge and more educational domains of specialized and reflexive ways of thinking and talking about curriculum knowledge (Macken-Horarik, 1996). Our focus on mode enabled us to articulate the nature and role of literate talk in educational programs, and to explain, for example, why it is problematic simply to *talk* in general terms about a concept before asking students to write about that concept. It also enabled us to highlight the need for teachers to plan for, sequence and embed the implicit and explicit teaching of language and literacy within curriculum programs.

Finally, I return more directly to the issue of academic writing. As indicated earlier, my particular interest is with the education of school students who are learning English as an additional language while participating in mainstream classes. Perhaps more obviously than in some other contexts, academic writing development for such students is necessarily embedded in their engagement with key curriculum constructs, and thus cannot occur in isolation from their developing abilities to talk about such constructs. While support for students' academic writing remains a major priority for teachers across all curriculum subjects, such support is likely to be more effective when it occurs within educational programs that challenge students intellectually; that provide them with opportunities to engage in deep learning; and that include opportunities for in-depth and sustained talk about that learning. To teach academic writing effectively, teachers therefore need to have substantial knowledge of their curriculum discipline as well as sufficient knowledge about language and literacy to be able to provide students with embedded, targeted support for development of the spoken and written language that will enable them to talk, read and also write about key curriculum constructs. I would argue that such knowledge of language and literacy is equally relevant to those concerned with academic writing in adult EAL and EFL educational contexts. I would further argue that the notion of literate talk provides a useful way to begin to clarify and elaborate the nature of such knowledge.

References

Alexander, R. J. (2001). *Culture and pedagogy: International comparisons in primary education.* Oxford, UK, and Malden, MA: Blackwell.

Alexander, R. (2008a). *Toward dialogic teaching: Rethinking classroom talk* (4th ed.). York: Dialogos, Thirsk, UK Ltd.

Alexander, R. (2008b). *Essays on pedagogy*. London: Routledge.
Baynham, M. (1993). Literacy in TESOL and ABE: Exploring common themes. *Open Letter, 2*(2), 4–16.
Christie, F., & Martin, J. (2007). *Language, knowledge and pedagogy: Functional linguistic and sociological perspectives*. London: Continuum.
Cummins, J. (2000). *Language, power and pedagogy: Bilingual children in the cross-fire*. Clevedon: Multilingual Matters.
Cummins, J. (2008). BICS and CALP: Empirical and theoretical status of the distinction. In B. Street & N. H. Hornberger (Eds.), *Encyclopedia of language and education* (2nd ed.), *Literacy: Vol. 2*. (pp. 71–83). New York: Springer Science & Business Media LLC.
Eggins, S. (1994). *An introduction to systemic functional linguistics*. London: Pinter.
Gibbons, P. (2008). 'It was taught good and I learned a lot': Intellectual practices and ESL learners in the middle years. *Australian Journal of Language and Literacy, 31*(2), 155–173.
Gibbons, P. (2009). *Challenging expectations: Literacy, intellectual quality and English language learners in the middle years*. Portsmouth, NH: Heinemann.
Gibbons, P. (2014). *Scaffolding language, scaffolding learners: Teaching English language learners in the mainstream classroom* (2nd ed.). Portsmouth, NH: Heinemann.
Halliday, M. A. K. (1978). *Language as social semiotic: The social interpretation of language and meaning*. London: Edward Arnold.
Halliday, M. A. K. (1989). *Spoken and written language*. New York: Oxford University Press.
Halliday, M. A. K. (1993). Towards a language based theory of learning. *Linguistics and Education, 5*, 93–116.
Halliday, M. A. K. (2008). Three aspects of children's language: Learning language, learning through language, learning about language (1980). In J. Webster (Ed.), *The language of early childhood – M. A. K. Halliday* (pp. 308–326). New York: Continuum.
Halliday, M. A. K., & Hasan, R. (1989). *Language, context and text: Aspects of language in as social-semiotic perspective*. Oxford: Oxford University Press.
Halliday, M. A. K., & Matthiessen, C. M. I. M. (2014). *Halliday's introduction to functional grammar* (4th ed.). London and New York: Routledge.
Hammond, J. (1990). Is learning to read and write the same as learning to speak? In F. Christie (Ed.), *Literacy for a changing world* (pp. 26–53). Melbourne: ACER.
Hammond, J. (2008). Intellectual challenge and ESL students: Implications of quality teaching initiatives. *Australian Journal of Language and Literacy, 31*(2), 128–154.
Hammond, J. (2014a). An Australian perspective on standards-based education, teacher knowledge and English as an additional language students. *TESOL Quarterly, 48*(3), 507–532.
Hammond, J. (2014b). *The transition of refugee students from intensive English centres to mainstream high schools: Current practices and future possibilities* (Final Report). Retrieved from NSW Department of Education and Communities.
Hammond, J. (2016). Dialogic space: Intersections between dialogic teaching and systemic functional linguistics. *Research Papers in Education, 16*(1), 5–22.
Hammond, J., & Gibbons, P. (2005). Putting scaffolding to work: The contribution of scaffolding in articulating ESL education. *Prospect, 20*(1), 6–30.
Hammond, J., & Macken-Horarik, M. (2001). Teachers' voices, teachers' practices: Insider perspectives on literacy education, *Australian Journal of Language and Literacy, 24*(2), 112–132.
Hyland, K. (2017). Learning to write for academic purposes: Specificity and second language writing. In J. Bitchener, N. Storch, & R. Wette (Eds.), *Teaching writing for academic purposes to multilingual students: Instructional approaches* (pp. 24–41). New York: Routledge.
Jones, P., & Chen, H. (2012). Teachers' knowledge about language: Issues of pedagogy and expertise. *Australian Journal of Language and Literacy, 35*(2), 147–168.

Luk, J., & Lin, A. (2015). Voices without words: Doing critical literate talk in English as a second language. *TESOL Quarterly*, *49*(1), 67–91.

Macken-Horarik, M. (1996). Literacy and learning across the curriculum: Towards a model of register of secondary school teachers. In R. Hasan & G. Williams (Eds.), *Literacy in society* (pp. 232–278). New York: Addison Wesley Longman.

Macken-Horarik, M, Love, K., & Unsworth, L. (2011). Grammatics good enough for school English in the 21st century, *Australian Journal of Language and Literacy*, *34*(1), 9–23.

Manchón, R. (Ed.). (2011). *Learning to write and writing to learn in an additional language*. Amsterdam: John Benjamins Publishing Company.

Manchón, R. M. (2017). The multifaceted and situated nature of the interaction between language and writing in academic settings: Advancing research agendas. In J. Bitchener, N. Storch, & R. Wette (Eds.), *Teaching writing for academic purposes to multilingual students: Instructional approaches* (pp. 183–200). New York: Routledge.

Mercer, N. (1994). Neo-Vygotskian theory and classroom education. In B. Stierer & J. Maybin (Eds.), *Language, literacy, and learning in educational practice: A reader* (pp. 92–110). Multilingual Matters LTD in association with The Open University.

Mercer, N. (2002). Developing dialogues. In G. Wells & G. Claxton (Eds.), *Learning for life in the 21st century: Sociocultural perspectives on the future of education* (pp. 141–153). Great Britain: Blackwell Publishers Ltd.

Mercer, N., & Littleton, K. (2007). *Dialogue and the development of children's thinking: A sociocultural approach*. London: Routledge.

Mercer, N., Dawes, L., & Kleine Staarman, J. (2009). Dialogic teaching in the primary classroom. *Language and Education*, *23*(4), 353–369.

Myhill, D. (2006). Talk, talk, talk: Teaching and learning in whole class discourse. *Research Papers in Education*, *21*(1), 19–41.

Paltridge, B. (2017). Context and the teaching of academic writing: Bringing together theory and practice. In J. Bitchener, N. Storch, & R. Wette (Eds.), *Teaching writing for academic purposes to multilingual students: Instructional approaches* (pp. 9–23). New York: Routledge.

Skidmore, D. (2006). Pedagogy and dialogue. *Cambridge Journal of Education*, *36*(4), 503–514.

Tardy, C. M. (2017). The challenge of genre in the academic writing classroom: Implications for L2 writing teacher education. In J. Bitchener, N. Storch, & R. Wette (Eds.), *Teaching writing for academic purposes to multilingual students: Instructional approaches* (pp. 69–83). New York: Routledge.

Thomas, W. P., & Collier, V. P. (1997). *School effectiveness for language minority students*. Washington, DC: George Washington University, The National Clearinghouse for Bilingual Education.

Vygotsky, L. (1978). *Mind in society: The development of higher psychological processes* (M. Cole, V. John-Steiner, S. Scribner, & E. Souberman, Eds.). Cambridge, MA: Harvard University Press.

Wallace, C. (2002). Local literacies and global literacy. In D. Block & D. Cameron (Eds.), *Globalization and language teaching* (pp. 101–114). London: Routledge.

Watkins, M., Learn, G., Noble, G., & Dunn, K. (2013). *Rethinking multiculturalism reassessing multicultural education* (Project Report No. 1). University of Western Sydney: NSW Department of Education and Communities and NSW Institute of Teachers.

Wells, G. (1999). *Dialogic inquiry: Towards a sociocultural practice and theory of education*. Cambridge: Cambridge University Press.

Wells, G., & Chang-Wells, G. L. (1992). *Constructing knowledge together: Classroom as centres of inquiry and literacy*. Portsmouth, NH: Heinemann.

9

IMPLEMENTING AND ASSESSING COLLABORATIVE WRITING ACTIVITIES IN EAP CLASSES

Neomy Storch

Introduction

One of the issues facing EAP writing teachers is the choice of classroom activities that will prepare students for their future writing needs and at the same time encourage learners to focus on language use—on how to express their ideas clearly, appropriately and accurately. A writing activity that may fulfill these twin goals is collaborative writing, simply defined as the co-authoring of a single text by two or more writers (for a more elaborate definition see Storch, 2013).

Collaborative writing is prevalent in the workplace and in mainstream classes across all levels of education. In the workplace it is often referred to as team writing; in education it is known as group assignments. Investigations of workplace writing have shown that various types of reports are often composed by teams, drawing on the expertise of many professionals (e.g., Ede & Lunsford, 1990; Knoch, May, Macqueen, Pill, & Storch, 2016; Mirel & Spilka, 2002). This research has shown not only that team writing is prevalent but that the ability to contribute and manage such team writing projects are skills that employers value in new graduates.

Collaborative group assignments are common forms of assessment in Western universities (e.g., Davies, 2009; Strauss & U, 2007). They are said to confer a number of benefits on the participants: exposing learners to a range of ideas, engaging them critically with different ideas and enabling them to practice their negotiation skills and teamwork. However, group assignments have also been shown to pose challenges for second language writers (Leki, 2001, 2007; Yang, 2014) when they need to collaborate with native speaker peers. Second language writers often defer to the native speaker members of the group, and contribute very little to the writing activity.

It should be noted at the outset that workplace team writing and group assignments are strictly speaking cooperative writing tasks rather than collaborative writing tasks. The main distinction between cooperative and collaborative writing is that in cooperative writing the task is generally divided into subtasks (e.g., gathering information, writing the first draft, editing) or into separate sections, with each author having responsibility for one subtask or one section of the written document. In collaborative writing, all co-authors are involved in all stages of the writing, and thus share responsibility for the creation of the entire text. Nevertheless, I believe that the inclusion of collaborative writing activities in EAP classes prepares students for cooperative writing; that is, collaborative writing affords learners the opportunity for *learning to write* (Manchón, 2011).

Furthermore, research on collaborative writing tasks implemented in a range of EAP contexts (e.g., Storch, 2002; Storch & Aldosari, 2013; Storch & Wigglesworth, 2007; Wigglesworth & Storch, 2009) has shown that collaborative writing tasks provide learners with opportunities for language learning. This research has shown that collaborative writing activities encourage learners to engage in deliberations and negotiations about how best to express their intended meaning. During these vocalized deliberations, termed *languaging* by Swain (2010), learners give and receive immediate peer feedback, both positive (reassuring) and corrective. They are also exposed to alternative ways of expressing ideas. The deliberations often also encourage students to pool their linguistic resources (see Storch, 2002; Wigglesworth & Storch, 2009), in a process termed *collective scaffolding*. Thus collaborative writing activities provide language learners, and particularly intermediate and advanced proficiency learners, with opportunities to learn to write for professional and academic purposes and to further develop their language abilities (Storch, 2013).

However, simply assigning students to produce a text jointly will not necessarily promote L2 learning nor provide students with training in collaborative writing. In this chapter I focus on three key design and implementation decisions: (i) the choice of writing task, (ii) the optimal grouping of students and (iii) whether and how these activities should be assessed. These decisions are relevant for the implementation of collaborative and cooperative writing activities regardless of whether these activities are implemented in the face to face or computer mediated environment (e.g., using wikis or Google Docs). They pertain to implementation of such tasks in all L2 writing classes, although my main focus in this chapter is on EAP classes, with intermediate or relatively proficient L2 writers.

My discussion of these decisions draws on available research on L2 collaborative writing and on my own extensive experience of implementing collaborative writing activities in the suite of EAP subjects we offer for credit at my university. I argue that in making these decisions teachers need to take into consideration not only their learners' L2 proficiency but also the pedagogical goals of the classes, and whether the predominate goal is to promote language learning or learning to write for professional and academic purposes. I conclude with some final reflections on the implementation of collaborative writing tasks in EAP classes.

Choice of Tasks for Collaborative Writing Activities

When determining what kind of tasks are best suited for collaborative writing activities in L2 writing classes, including EAP classes, it is helpful to distinguish between meaning-focused and language-focused tasks. In what follows I explain and exemplify the difference between these two kinds of tasks, briefly review research that has investigated learners' engagement with these task types and then conclude with some guidelines on task choice.

Meaning-Focused vs. Language-Focused Collaborative Tasks

Meaning-focused writing tasks require students to compose a text and attention to language in such tasks is incidental; that is, it occurs when the co-authors encounter a difficulty in the process of composing their text. In this sense, it is difficult for teachers to predetermine not only how much attention to language the tasks will generate but also which structures are likely to draw learners' attention. Examples of such meaning-focused tasks that we have employed in our EAP classes (with intermediate and advanced ESL learners) include a data commentary report, a summary of a section of a text or of a research article and a short argumentative essay. The data commentary report requires learners to describe or discuss a graphic prompt (e.g., a graph depicting a country's economic growth or a figure depicting a process).

In contrast, language-focused tasks generally require students to amend a given text or to reconstruct a text from notes or key words, rather than compose a new text. The main aim of these tasks is to draw learners' attention to language forms, which are often predetermined. An example of such tasks is the editing task, where students are asked to improve a passage by correcting errors in grammar and word choice. The passage may be one that was written by a previous student, or one created by the teacher and that contains the kind of errors commonly found in the writing of a particular group of students (see Storch, 2009). Another version of an editing task that I have used in my classes is peer editing, where learners work in pairs providing corrective feedback on texts written by other pairs. Other language-focused tasks that have been used in research on collaborative writing include the dictogloss and the text reconstruction task. In the dictogloss, learners listen to a short dictation and take notes, which are then used to reconstruct an acceptable version of the originally dictated text (e.g., see Leeser, 2004). The dictated text can be on a topic discussed in class so that it includes familiar vocabulary. The text can also include many examples of grammatical structures that the teacher wants to draw learners' attention to (e.g., past tense). In a text reconstruction, students are given content words and are required to produce a text based on the given words, inserting all the necessary function words (e.g., prepositions, articles) and inflecting words (e.g., for tense, number) to produce a coherent and grammatically accurate text (e.g., see Storch, 2009).

Research on Collaborative Tasks

Researchers who have compared learners' attention to language generated by meaning and language-focused tasks (e.g., Alegría de la Colina & García Mayo, 2007; Storch, 2001) have shown, perhaps not surprisingly, that language-focused tasks tend to generate more attention to language forms (e.g., choice of verb tense) whereas meaning-focused tasks tend to generate more attention to lexis (word choice and word meaning). The unit of analysis in these studies is the Language Related Episode (LRE)—instances in the interaction when learners deliberate about language.

The dictogloss task has been used in a number of studies, with both adult (e.g., Alegría de la Colina & García Mayo, 2007) and adolescent learners (e.g., Kim & McDonough, 2008). This research suggests that the dictogloss task is quite challenging, particularly for lower proficiency learners (Alegría de la Colina & García Mayo, 2007; Leeser, 2004). Research conducted with lower proficiency learners (e.g., Alegría de la Colina & García Mayo, 2007; Nassaji & Tian, 2010) has also shown that in language-focused tasks, the pre-selected forms may be beyond the learners' linguistic repertoire. This may explain why learners have been observed in these studies to engage in superficial deliberations about language, which are reflected in very short LREs or they may abandon or resolve LREs incorrectly.

In meaning-focused tasks, the choice of forms that learners deliberate about is driven by their own needs. Thus the forms are more likely to be within the learners' knowledge range. Learners may also choose not to pay attention to grammatical forms. In our study with very proficient EAP learners completing an argumentative essay and a data commentary report (Wigglesworth & Storch, 2009), we found that these learners paid attention predominantly to lexical choices rather than grammar because they already had a high level of grammatical accuracy in their writing. Instead they focused not only on lexical choices, but also on how to structure their argumentative essay (e.g., what information to include in an introduction).

Choosing Appropriate Tasks

Thus the choice of task when implementing collaborative writing activities in EAP classes depends on the L2 proficiency of the learners and the pedagogic goal of the class. With lower proficiency learners, if the goal is to direct learners' attention to the use of particular grammatical structures, then language-focused tasks with carefully pre-selected grammatical structures may be more suitable than meaning-focused tasks. With more advanced EAP learners, authentic meaning-focused tasks, such as summaries of texts that students are required to read, data commentary tasks that students are required to produce in certain disciplines (e.g., commerce, engineering) and small research projects may be more suitable for a collaborative writing activity. In the case of small research projects, given that such tasks tend to require more extensive writing and time investment, they may be best implemented using online collaborative writing platforms such as wikis and Google Docs (see an example of such a project with EAP students in Kessler, Bikowski, & Boggs, 2012).

In my EAP classes, I deploy both meaning- and language-focused tasks. When implemented in the class, the tasks tend to be quite short (250–300 words). I allocate about 30–40 minutes for task completion. These tasks are often not formally assessed (see the "Assessing Collaborative Writing" section later in the chapter). Longer meaning-focused tasks (e.g., a summary of an academic article from the students' field of study) are set as assessed homework tasks. These longer tasks (about 500 words long) can be completed using Google Docs.

I should also note that I no longer use argumentative essays as a collaborative writing activity in my EAP classes. This decision is based on empirical evidence and my own observations. In interviews we conducted with students in a large-scale study that compared learners' engagement with data commentary reports and argumentative essays (Wigglesworth & Storch, 2009), the students claimed that they found the argumentative essay difficult to complete because of the need to reach consensus about the arguments to include in their essay. Although engagement in arguments and negotiations is a constructive learning activity, these findings confirmed my observations of students composing argumentative essays collaboratively in my EAP classes. I observed that negotiations between students on content related issues often took a large proportion of the time assigned to produce a joint text and seemed to frustrate the students.

Grouping Learners: Size, Composition and Selection

Another important decision that teachers need to make when implementing collaborative writing activities is how best to group students. This decision in fact entails three related considerations: the size of the group working on the collaborative writing task, the proficiency of members of the group and whether students are allowed to self-select their group. I discuss each of these considerations separately.

Size of Group

Collaborative writing groups can range in size from pairs to large teams, the latter made possible by the use of online collaborative writing platforms such as wikis or Google Docs. For example, Kessler (2009) had his entire class of 40 EFL learners completing a wiki project. The project required the learners to produce a collective definition of the key construct (culture) discussed in the course the students attended (teacher education). However, having such large groups working on one collaborative writing task may not be pedagogically sound. Kessler and Bikowski (2010) analyzed the data that had been collected by Kessler (2009), focusing on learners' contribution to the class project. The researchers found that the majority of the learners (22 out of 40) made minimal contributions to the class wiki. Furthermore, when the contributions were made, they were often posted late in the life of the project, which meant that other members of the group had little opportunity to engage with the postings. The researchers suggest that large groups may discourage learners' contributions because of a diffused sense of responsibility to the project. The literature on cooperative learning has in fact discussed quite extensively the problem of a lack of personal responsibility to the group, a phenomenon termed *social loafing* (e.g., Johnson & Johnson, 2009; Brickner, Harkins, & Ostrom, 1986). Such loafing is said to increase as the size of the group increases. Thus one way of addressing this problem is to reduce the group size. A number of researchers recommend using smaller groups, with the ideal group size being three to four members (see review in Pfaff & Huddlestone, 2003).

In L2 contexts, most researchers promote even smaller group sizes, with pairs being viewed as best even in the online environment (e.g., Elola & Oskoz, 2010; Kost, 2011), which can technically handle larger group sizes. The main advantage of pair work is that by its very nature it requires both learners to contribute to the task (although that depends of course on the relationship the pair forms, see Storch, 2002, 2013). In group work the task can be completed with little input from some members of the group (e.g., Fernández Dobao, 2012; Foster, 1998). The need to contribute in pair work also means that learners have more opportunities to practice using the L2 for a range of functions (e.g., explaining, providing counter-suggestions, offering feedback).

However, some researchers suggest that small groups may be more conducive to language learning than pairs. For example, Fernández Dobao (2012), who compared the performance of small groups (composed of four students) and of pairs on a collaborative task, found more deliberations about language and more correctly resolved deliberations in groups than in pairs. The researcher suggests that small groups of L2 learners are superior to pairs because they have more linguistic resources at their disposal (i.e., they can draw on the linguistic knowledge of four students rather than two). In a subsequent study, Fernández Dobao (2016) reported that even the less active members of small groups benefitted from the collaborative writing activity.

I must admit that despite these findings, in my own EAP classes (and research) I favor the use of pairs over small groups, particularly for in-class collaborative writing activities. Pair work, as mentioned above, may encourage greater learner involvement in the decision-making processes in collaborative writing activities and also provide each learner with more L2 speaking practice. I also monitor the interaction of pairs to ensure that the relationships they form are conducive to language learning.

In an early study on collaborative writing (Storch, 2002), I discovered that the relationships learners establish when working on collaborative writing tasks are quite distinct and that not all relationships are conducive to language learning.

Whereas collaborative and expert/novice relationships were found to provide learners with plentiful opportunities to engage in deliberations about language and show evidence of language gains, this was not the case when learners established dominant/passive relationships. In a dominant/passive relationship, one student dominates the interaction and the other contributes very little. Such relationships afford very few opportunities for language learning for the passive participant. Importantly, the study also found that once learners establish a relationship, the relationship tends to persist regardless of the passage of time or task type. Thus when implementing collaborative writing tasks in my EAP classes, I encourage students to work with different class members over the semester in different collaborative writing activities.

Proficiency Grouping

In any one L2 writing class (including EAP), students may vary in terms of their L2 proficiency. Thus the pertinent questions that need to be considered when implementing collaborative writing activities are: Is it best to have students of similar or different levels of L2 proficiency work together? Which proficiency grouping will optimize the language learning opportunities for all students, the lower as well as the higher proficiency learner?

Despite the importance of this decision, it is surprisingly an under-researched issue. Leeser's (2004) study is one of the few that investigated the impact of proficiency pairing on learners' interaction, focusing on the impact the pairing has on learners' attention to form. Leeser compared the performance of three groups of Spanish L2 learners paired according to their L2 proficiency when completing a dictogloss task. One group was composed of relatively high proficiency pairs (high-high), another was composed of relatively low proficiency pairs (low-low) and the third group was composed of mixed proficiency pairs (high-low). The study found that L2 proficiency pairing affected the quantity and quality of attention to form, that is, the quantity of LREs, what the LREs dealt with and how the LREs were resolved. The study found that pairs composed of high-high proficiency learners produced the largest number of LREs, mostly dealing with grammar, and that the majority of the LREs were resolved correctly. The low-low pairs paid generated the smallest number of LREs and many of these LREs were abandoned because the learners had insufficient linguistic resources to draw on to resolve their deliberations. The performance of mixed proficiency pairs was similar to that of low-low pairs, suggesting that pairing high proficiency learners with low proficiency learners bears no advantage for the low proficiency learner and disadvantages the high proficiency learners.

A longitudinal study conducted with EFL learners in a university in Saudi Arabia (Storch & Aldosari, 2013), where learners were also paired according to their English proficiency (high-high, low-low and high-low) to complete a range of collaborative writing tasks, produced similar findings to those reported by Leeser. However, in our study we found that mixed proficiency pairs generated more LREs than low-low pairs (but fewer than high-high pairs). We also analyzed the relationship all the pairs established and found that whereas similar proficiency pairs tended to collaborate, two (out of the five) mixed proficiency pairs formed a dominant/passive relationship. In this pattern of interaction, the more proficient learner dominated the interaction, producing long monologues but paying relatively little attention to language, and the low proficiency learner contributed little to the task talk. However, the other three pairs in the mixed proficiency group formed relationships more conducive to language learning. One pair worked collaboratively and the other two established an expert/novice relationship where the more proficient learner took on the role of an expert and assisted the low proficiency learner by providing word meaning (often in the L1) and explanations of grammatical conventions. Both learners in such expert/novice relationships benefitted from the interaction. For the more proficient learner, the act of explaining may help consolidate language knowledge. For the low proficiency learner, the benefit is in terms of the availability of immediate and accessible feedback (often in the shared L1) and exposure to more advanced vocabulary and structures. Low-low pairs generated fewer LREs than high-low pairs, but low-low pairs tended to work collaboratively with both members of such pairs actively engaging in the activity and using their L2 (English) in relatively long turns.

These findings underscore the importance of monitoring the relationships learners establish when completing collaborative writing tasks (Storch, 2002, 2013). However, they also highlight the importance of taking into consideration the goal of the activity when making decisions about proficiency pairing. If the goal is to provide learners with opportunities to use their L2 and engage in the collaborative writing task, then relatively lower proficiency learners in the class may be best paired with learners of a similar proficiency. However, if the goal is to focus on form, then mixed proficiency pairing may work for the benefit of both low and high proficiency learners, but only if they form an expert/novice type of relationship. It is interesting to note, however, that when asked, learners overwhelmingly prefer to work with more proficient partners (e.g., Kim & McDonough, 2008; Storch & Aldosari, 2013).

How to Form Groups: Teacher Allocation vs. Self-Selection

One final issue to consider when arranging students to work on collaborative writing tasks is whether to allow students the option of self-selecting their partners or whether the teacher should allocate students into groups (or pairs). This issue of what the best strategy to use is when forming groups has received much attention in the general education literature. A number of studies have reported on the impact of group selection methods on group dynamics and learning outcomes (e.g., Chapman, Meuter, Toy, & Write, 2006) as well as on students' attitude to the group activity (e.g., Hilton & Philips, 2008; Myers, 2011). A review of this literature suggests some disagreement about whether it is best to allow students to self-select or to leave the decision in the hands of the teacher.

One of the greatest advantages of allowing students to self-select their partners is that they will select to work with learners with whom they are already familiar and this tends to be associated with best group experiences. Surveys conducted with students who participated in group work in a range of university subjects (e.g., Hilton & Philips, 2008; Myers, 2011; Russell, 2010), including EFL creative writing classes (e.g., Hassaskhah & Mozaffari, 2015), have reported that students express a strong preference for the self-selection approach to group formation because it enables them to choose to work with peers with whom they are familiar. Students admit to being more willing to share ideas and to being more comfortable about challenging each other and accepting criticism (including corrective feedback) when working with familiar peers. These findings suggest that familiarity may be conducive to collaboration. At the same time, however, self-selected groups have been observed to engage in more off-task talk than teacher-assigned groups (Price, 2006).

The advantage of having the teacher allocate students to pairs/small groups is that it enables the teacher to determine the group composition according to the goals of the task or the profile of the students in the class. Criteria for allocation may be L1 background, L2 proficiency or certain personality traits. For example, in second language contexts where learners come from diverse L1 backgrounds, allocating students based on L1 background may help prevent the formation of shared L1 groups where the inclination to use the L1 excessively is perhaps more likely. Teachers may also allocate students on the basis of L2 proficiency, in line with the pedagogical goals of the collaborative writing activity as discussed above.

Shehadeh (2011) recommends allowing students to self-select their groups but at the same time instructing them to change partners on a regular basis. In his study, L2 learners working over a semester on a range of collaborative writing and grammar tasks were required to change partners every two to three weeks. In interviews conducted at the end of the semester most students said that they like working with different partners. In my own EAP classes, I adopt an eclectic approach. I tend to allow students to self-select their partners when I first introduce collaborative writing activities. However, in subsequent collaborative writing activities during the semester, I encourage the students to change partners.

Assessing Collaborative Writing

Another decision that teachers need to make is about whether to grade the text produced collaboratively, and if so how. A rationale for grading the text is that it may encourage learners' engagement and contribution to the activity. However, a number of classroom-based studies have shown that students seem to engage in the collaborative writing activity even if it is ungraded (e.g., Ewald, 2005; Storch, 2002).

Grading collaboratively produced texts may be more relevant for group assignments, especially since such texts tend to be more extensive. When assessing any group assignments, there are two assessable elements: the jointly written text (product) and the interaction (process). In assessing the product, one of the contentious issues is whether all members of the group should receive the same grade. The advantage of awarding the same grade is that it may promote a sense of accountability to the group effort (Johnson & Johnson, 2009). A disadvantage of such a grading practice is that it may be perceived as unfair because it rewards those who may have contributed little to the activity, the so called "free riders." Another argument against awarding the same grade to all group members is that the grade may not reflect the true competence of individual learners. This may be an issue in learning environments with a strong exam culture and when the stakes are high.

The alternative approach is to award individual grades that take into consideration the learner's contribution to the collaborative composition process. There are a number of strategies that can be adopted to monitor learners' contribution including peer and individual reflective diaries and teacher observations. The use of online collaborative writing platforms makes monitoring and assessing learners' contribution to the collaborative writing task easier because these platforms have a log of all contributions. Assessment rubrics that reward contributions need to take into account not only the quantity (i.e., the number of postings) but also the quality of contributions and the level of engagement with the contributions made by other members of the group. Thus the overall assessment of a collaborative writing activity is a composite grade that includes an overall text grade (the same for all members of the group) and an individual component that captures each student's contribution to the activity (see for example MacDonald, 2003).

As I mentioned previously, in my own EAP classes I include short language- and meaning-focused tasks as regular classroom activities, and these are not formally assessed. However, I also encourage students to work on one of the assessment tasks collaboratively. To date I have assessed these tasks on the basis of the product rather than the process because of the difficulties in capturing students' quality of contributions. However, as more and more students complete these collaboratively assigned tasks using Google Docs, I am now considering including an individual mark for contribution as part of the overall grade for the collaborative writing assignment.

Some Final Reflections

I have noted over the years a growing interest in investigating and implementing collaborative writing activities in a diverse range of contexts. More recent research has focused on the nature of collaboration when students engage in online collaborative writing, using wikis or Google Docs. The proliferation of these collaborative writing platforms suggests that we are likely to see an even greater need to prepare EAP students for collaborative writing.

This growing body of research and my own observations suggests that collaborative writing activities are more likely to achieve their pedagogical goals if they are preceded by careful planning, including the choice of an appropriate task, determining in advance how best to group students and whether and how to assess the activity. Such decisions need to be made on the basis of local factors, not the least being the proficiency of the learners in the class. Once implemented, such activities need to be carefully monitored. Furthermore, collaborative writing activities need to be implemented on more than one occasion, to enable learners to become familiar with this mode of composing texts, particularly given that most writing at university (and school) tends to be done individually.

Despite the documented advantages that collaborative writing activities afford students both in terms of language learning and learning to write (see review in Storch, 2013), I would like to emphasize that I am not suggesting that all writing tasks in the EAP class should be collaborative, nor that all students should be compelled to work collaboratively. In my EAP classes I implement collaborative writing activities on several occasions during the teaching semester, integrating them into regular class work and assessment tasks. I give my students a choice of whether to work collaboratively or not on both the assessed and non-assessed tasks. However, and most importantly, the implementation of collaborative writing activities is preceded by a brief explanation about the potential benefits of the activity for learning to write and for language learning. I have found over the years that most (but by no means all) of my EAP students enjoy the activity, and most prefer to work collaboratively rather than individually when given the choice.

References

Alegría de la Colina, A., & García Mayo, M. P. (2007). Attention to form across collaborative tasks by low-proficiency learners in an EFL setting. In M. P. García Mayo (Ed.), *Investigating tasks in foreign language learning* (pp. 91–116). Clevedon: Multilingual Matters.

Brickner, M., Harkins, S., & Ostrom, T. (1986). Effects of personal involvement: Thought-provoking implications for social loafing. *Journal of Personality and Social Psychology, 51*, 763–770.

Chapman, K. J., Meuter, M., Toy, D., & Write, L. (2006). Can't we pick our own group? The influence of group selection method on group dynamics and outcomes. *Journal of Management Education, 30*, 557–569.

Davies, W. M. (2009). Group work as a form of assessment: Common problems and recommended solutions. *Higher Education, 58*, 563–584.

Ede, L., & Lunsford, A. (1990). *Singular texts/plural authors*. Carbondale: Southern Illinois University Press.

Elola, I., & Oskoz, A. (2010). Collaborative writing: Fostering foreign language and writing conventions development. *Language Learning and Technology, 14*, 51–71.

Ewald, J. D. (2005). Language-related episodes in an assessment context: A "small group quiz." *The Canadian Modern Language Review, 6*, 565–586.

Fernández Dobao, A. (2012). Collaborative writing tasks in the L2 classroom: Comparing group, pair, and individual work. *Journal of Second Language Writing, 21*, 40–58.

Fernández Dobao, A. (2016). Peer interaction and learning: A focus on the silent learner. In S. Ballinger & M. Sato (Eds.), *Peer interaction and second language learning* (pp. 22–62). Amsterdam/Philadelphia: John Benjamins.

Foster, P. (1998). A classroom perspective on the negotiation of meaning. *Applied Linguistics, 19*, 1–23.

Hassaskhah, J., & Mozaffari, H. (2015). The impact of group formation method (student selected vs. teacher-assigned) on group dynamics and group outcomes in EFL creative writing. *Journal of Language Teaching and Research, 6*, 147–156.

Hilton, S., & Philips, F. (2008). Instructor-assigned and student-selected groups: A view from inside. *Issues in Accounting Education, 25*, 15–33.

Johnson, D. W., & Johnson, R. T. (2009). An educational psychology success story: Social interdependence theory and cooperative learning. *Educational Researcher, 38*, 365–379.

Kessler, G. (2009). Student-initiated attention to form in wiki-based collaborative writing. *Language Learning and Technology, 13*, 79–95.

Kessler, G., & Bikowski, D. (2010). Developing collaborative autonomous learning abilities in computer mediated language learning: attention to meaning among students in wiki space. *Computer Assisted Language Learning, 23*, 41–58.

Kessler, G., Bikowski, D., & Boggs, J. (2012). Collaborative writing among second language learners in academic web-based projects. *Language Learning and Technology, 16*, 91–109.

Kim, Y., & McDonough, K. (2008). The effect of interlocutor proficiency on the collaborative dialogue between Korean as a second language learners. *Language Teaching Research, 12*, 211–234.

Knoch, U., May, L., Macqueen, S., Pill, J., & Storch, N. (2016). Transitioning from university to the workplace: Stakeholder perceptions of academic and professional writing demands. *IELTS Research Reports Online Series, 1*, 1–37.

Kost, C. (2011). Investigating writing strategies and revision behaviour in collaborative writing projects. *CALICO Journal, 28*, 606–620.

Leeser, M. J. (2004). Learner proficiency and focus on form during collaborative dialogue. *Language Teaching Research, 8*, 55–81.

Leki, I. (2001). "A narrow thinking system": Nonnative-English-speaking students in group projects across the curriculum. *TESOL Quarterly, 35*, 39–68.

Leki, I. (2007). *Undergraduates in a second language: Challenges and complexities of academic literacy development*. New York: Erlbaum Associates.

MacDonald, J. (2003). Assessing online collaborative learning: Process and product. *Computers and Education, 40*, 377–391.

Manchón, R. (2011). Writing to learn the language: Issues in theory and research. In R. Manchón (Ed.), *Learning-to-write and writing-to-learn in an additional language* (pp. 61–84). Amsterdam/Philadelphia: John Benjamins.

Mirel, B., & Spilka, R. (Eds.). (2002). *Reshaping technical communication: New directions and challenges for the 21st century*. Mahwah, NJ: Lawrence Erlbaum.

Myers, S. A. (2011). Students' perceptions of classroom group work as a function of group member selection. *Communication Teacher, 26*, 50–64.

Nassaji, H., & Tian, J. (2010). Collaborative and individual output tasks and their effects on learning English phrasal verbs. *Language Teaching Research, 14*, 397–419.

Pfaff, E., & Huddleston, P. (2003). Does it matter if I hate teamwork? What impacts student attitudes toward teamwork. *Journal of Marketing Education, 25*, 37–45.

Price, P. (2006). Group work. In W. Buskist & S. F. Davis (Eds.), *Handbook for the teaching of psychology* (pp. 265–269). Malden, MA: Blackwell Publishing.

Russell, M. (2010). The formation of effective work groups within an FE classroom. *Research in Post-Compulsory Education, 205*, 205–221.

Shehadeh, A. (2011). Effects and student perceptions of collaborative writing in L2. *Journal of Second Language Writing, 20*, 286–305.

Storch, N. (2001). Comparing ESL learners' attention to grammar on three different collaborative tasks. *RELC Journal, 32*, 104–124.

Storch, N. (2002). Patterns of interaction in ESL pair work. *Language Learning, 52*, 119–158.

Storch, N. (2009). *The nature of pair interaction. Learners' interaction in an ESL class: Its nature and impact on grammatical development*. Saarbrücken, Germany: VDM Verlag.

Storch, N. (2013). *Collaborative writing in L2 classrooms*. Bristol, UK: Multilingual Matters.

Storch, N., & Aldosari, A. (2013). Pairing learners in pair work activity. *Language Teaching Research, 17*, 31–48.

Storch, N., & Wigglesworth, G. (2007). Writing tasks: Comparing individual and collaborative writing. In M. P. García Mayo (Ed.), *Investigating tasks in formal language learning* (pp. 157–177). London: Multilingual Matters.

Strauss, P., & U, A. (2007). Group assessments: Dilemmas facing lecturers in multicultural tertiary classrooms. *Higher Education Research and Development, 26*, 147–161.

Swain, M. (2010). Talking-it-through: Languaging as a source of learning. In R. Batestone (Ed.), *Sociocognitive perspectives on language use and language learning* (pp. 112–130). Oxford: Oxford University Press.

Wigglesworth, G., & Storch, N. (2009). Pairs versus individual writing: Effects on fluency, complexity and accuracy. *Language Testing, 26*, 445–466.

Yang, L. (2014). Examining the mediational means in collaborative writing: Case studies of undergraduate ESL students in business courses. *Journal of Second Language Writing, 23*, 74–89.

Approaches to Academic Language Development

10

FACILITATING L2 WRITERS' ACADEMIC LANGUAGE DEVELOPMENT

Dana Ferris

Introduction

Researchers and teacher educators who focus on the *language* aspect of second language (L2) writing tend to place heavy emphasis on the problem of *error* in student writing and whether/how best to *treat* it pedagogically (see, e.g., Ferris, 2011). The issue of corrective feedback (CF) in L2 writing has been highly controversial over its history and has been extensively researched over the past 20 years in particular. This body of recent work has yielded valuable new insights on the "big question" (Ferris, 2004, p. 50)—whether or not teachers should provide CF to student writers—and especially about specific ways to approach CF (for reviews, see van Beuningen, de Jong, & Kuiken, 2012; Bitchener, 2008; Bitchener & Ferris, 2012; Bitchener & Storch, 2016; Ferris, 2010).

Nonetheless, it could be argued that the study of CF, while useful, has not gone far enough in promoting linguistic competence for L2 writers, especially for those writing in demanding academic contexts. The *treatment of error* is in essence *reactive*: it addresses what students can (or cannot) already produce accurately in their L2 writing. However, even if L2 writers can progress to the point of producing texts that are close to error-free (or at least devoid of serious errors that impede reader comprehension), studies have shown that texts of L2 writers may be lexically and syntactically underdeveloped (too simple) compared to the writing of their L1 peers in English for Academic Purposes (EAP) contexts, often unfairly portraying them to academic readers as lacking in sophistication or strong thinking skills (see, e.g., Hinkel, 2002; Hyland, 2002; Silva, 1993).

What is needed, therefore, in addition to helping L2 writers develop strategies to cope with error, is a *proactive* approach to helping students acquire complex language suitable for writing for academic and professional purposes. Such advanced linguistic competence should help them meet the expectations of varying audiences (see Paltridge, this volume) and appropriately write in different genres and registers to fulfill their own rhetorical and communicative goals. This chapter focuses on the *what* and the *how* of academic language development for L2 writers in EAP courses. Building on insights from research on academic genres and findings from corpus linguistics, it discusses principles that teachers can use to select lexical and syntactic structures on which to focus with their students. It further examines ways that teachers can effectively teach those structures, going beyond lists or decontextualized formal grammar lessons to present academic language for both receptive and productive purposes. The goal of this chapter is to provide teachers with practical strategies for addressing language with their EAP students in ways that are authentic and fully integrated with other class goals and activities so that students can be prepared to communicate successfully for academic purposes.

Background

Three insights from theory and research in second language acquisition (SLA) and second language writing inform the pedagogical suggestions to follow in this chapter. First, learners best acquire language structures—vocabulary and grammar—through exposure to meaningful content. This principle was articulated early by Krashen in his Input Hypothesis (e.g., Krashen, 1982) but also taken up in various forms by advocates of Content-Based Instruction (see Brinton, Snow, & Wesche, 2003) and English for Specific Purposes (see Hyland, 2007) as pedagogical models of L2 instruction. The benefits of content-based pedagogy have been further argued in specific research examining the effects of extensive reading on SLA (see Day & Bamford, 1998; Hedgcock & Ferris, 2009; Krashen, 2004) and of thematic instruction (Leki, 1991/92; Raimes, 1991) for the development of L2 writing abilities in general and academic writing skills in particular. As this insight relates to the goals of this chapter, EAP instructors wishing to help students further develop their language repertoires should ideally anchor most or all such instruction in the content of the EAP course (i.e., through academic reading and writing tasks already built into the syllabus).

Second, studies have demonstrated that writers (whether composing in L1 or L2) may not successfully apply knowledge from decontextualized formal grammar instruction to their own writing. There is ample research to demonstrate this point dating back over a century (see Bitchener & Ferris, 2012; Connors, 2003; Santa, 2006 for reviews); indeed, the demonstrated futility of such endeavors is used by some L1 compositionists as an argument to dispense with any in-class language development efforts whatsoever (see Hartwell, 1985; MacDonald, 2007). On the L2 side, Frodesen and Holten (2003) noted "Teachers find that even when a grammatical feature has been covered and practiced, students may not use it accurately in their own writing" (p. 142). The suggestions in this chapter therefore emphasize approaches to language development in the EAP class that are carefully and authentically integrated with other writing course goals and activities rather than being stand-alone, disconnected aspects of the syllabus or lesson.

Third, research on transfer in learning and especially in writing/composition instruction clearly suggests that activities that promote metalinguistic awareness and metacognition about writing and language use increase the likelihood that students will transfer and extend knowledge to new learning situations in academic contexts, such as general education and major coursework (Beaufort, 2007; Yancey, Robertson, & Tacsak, 2014). Recent research on CF points to the value of metalinguistic explanation (i.e., providing symbolic or verbal cues or rule reminders) in promoting uptake of error correction (Ellis, Loewen, & Erlam, 2006; Shintani & Ellis, 2013), and research on students' charting their own errors suggests that such charting builds awareness of problem areas and encourages mindfulness in future writing (Ferris, Liu, Sinha, & Senna, 2013; Hartshorn et al., 2010; Lalande, 1982). The specific teaching suggestions in this chapter build on research on facilitating transfer through metacognitive awareness (reflection) and on the value of providing and helping learners apply explicit metalinguistic information (from feedback and instruction) to their own writing so that they can function well not only in the EAP course but also in their future academic and professional endeavors.

Promoting Academic Language Development: The *Why*

Before expounding upon the *what* and *how* of language development in EAP classes, it is useful to remind ourselves of the *why* of doing so. While the answer to this question might seem obvious to some, for instructors trained primarily in L1 composition settings, it is not always self-evident that any focus on language in a writing course is necessary or appropriate. As a result, few writing instructors are formally trained in the structure of the target language (i.e., linguistics and grammar), let alone the pedagogy of presenting it effectively in the context of a writing course (MacDonald, 2007).

While the absolute neglect of language in writing instruction is likely indefensible for any group of student writers regardless of language background, it is especially so for L2 writers, who are simultaneously attempting to acquire a second language along with advanced academic writing skills. Whether researchers and teachers like it or not, L2 writers *do* make errors that are different in quantity and type from those made by L1 writers (see Bitchener & Ferris, 2012, p. 97 for a clear visual on this point), and sometimes those errors *do* matter in academic and professional settings—they can interfere with the successful communication of a message (*global* errors; see Bates, Lane, & Lange, 1993; Burt & Kiparsky, 1972; Hendrickson, 1978), and they can be stigmatizing when intended academic and professional audiences (readers) judge them harshly (Beason, 2001; Hairston, 1981; Janopolous, 1992; Santos, 1988). EAP instructors thus must help their students make progress in remediating troublesome error patterns in their writing over time.

However, as noted at the beginning of this chapter, helping students find, correct and avoid errors in L2 writing does not go far enough. EAP students, still in the long-term process of SLA, need encouragement and support in continuing to build their academic language repertoires so that they have choices—linguistic tools—to accomplish their communicative purposes successfully. They also need strategies to analyze genres and rhetorical situations so that they can deploy their linguistic knowledge most appropriately. In short, they need help with learning and using optimal lexical and syntactic structures that will help them persuade and meet expectations of readers in a wide variety of disciplinary and professional settings. Research in corpus linguistics (e.g., Biber, 2006; Biber, Conrad, Reppen, Byrd, & Helt, 2002; Byrd & Bunting, 2008; Hyland, 2008) and in genre studies (especially Systemic Functional Linguistics, e.g., Schleppegrell, 1998, 2001) has over recent decades begun to provide classroom instructors with specific guidance as to how to identify and select structures for their EAP students to learn and apply to their own language production (Bennett, 2010; Reppen, 2010).

Promoting Academic Language Development: The *What*

A challenge for many instructors when considering language development in their EAP classes is that there are simply too many choices and too little time. Considering vocabulary, for example, the English lexicon is enormous, and even research-based word lists such as the General Service List (West & West, 1953) or the Academic Word List (Coxhead, 2000) include far more items than any student can master or any teacher can discuss. Similarly, corpus-based reference grammars (e.g., Biber, Johannson, Leech, Conrad, & Finegan, 1999) identify a broad range of structures that could be useful for student writers depending upon the task, genre and audience. Further, as noted by Byrd and Bunting (2008): "We do not have one single all-purpose grammar of English [or any language] but several overlapping and interlocking grammars that are characterized by particular subsets of grammar and vocabulary" (p. 62). With these challenges and issues in mind, it is more useful to articulate principles for teacher selection of language forms to teach and discuss than it is to present lists of such structures as if it were possible to identify priorities for every group of learners and every writing context. Figure 10.1 presents several principles that I will discuss further in this section.

1. For whole-class study of vocabulary, choose items that are important within assigned texts (for reading) and/or for required writing tasks.
2. As with vocabulary instruction, build on assigned reading and writing tasks to help students understand grammar in context and apply it to their own writing projects.
3. Choose other points for grammar and mechanics instruction based on a careful study of class needs.

FIGURE 10.1 Principles for selecting vocabulary and grammar topics for a writing class

Principle 1: Study Vocabulary within Assigned Reading/Writing Tasks

As already noted, there is far too much important academic L2 vocabulary for any EAP teacher to cover adequately in one course or even by a program in a series of courses. However, teachers can effectively model both vocabulary-learning strategies (Coxhead, 2006; Folse, 2004; Zimmerman, 2009) and approaches to applying learned vocabulary to students' own written texts. I will discuss the *how* of such activities in the next section, but first it is useful to note that teachers can and should build on already occurring reading and writing tasks in the syllabus to help students understand and practice these strategies.

For example, in a textbook that I recently co-authored (Ferris & Ferrando, 2015) for one of the EAP courses in our program, students had read a lengthy and challenging article on younger generations in China today (contemporary to US Generations Y and Z) and had already discussed its main points and details. As a follow-up vocabulary exercise, they were shown three paragraphs from the text with words from the Academic Word List (AWL) bolded. These words were identified with the online AWL Highlighter tool (www.nottingham.ac.uk/alzsh3/acvocab/awlhighlighter.htm) by running a digital version of the text through the tool. The students were asked to complete a couple of activities with these AWL items (discussed in the next section), but the key point here is that they were (1) chosen from a text that the class had already read and discussed and (2) identified through a systematic analysis using a freely accessible and easy-to-use online tool. Because the students were then required to write a summary-response paper based on that article and later an expository essay that drew upon readings in the textbook unit, the vocabulary study also had direct relevance to ongoing writing assignments as well and modeled both strategies and resources that students could use to select academic vocabulary for their own writing in the future.

Principle 2: Choose Grammar Points from Class Reading and Writing Tasks

Teachers can similarly build upon class reading and writing tasks to select grammar points to highlight. For example, in an earlier article (Brenoff, 2013) in the same teaching unit just described on generational differences (Ferris & Ferrando, 2015), the US-based author shifted between a first-person narrative (an anecdote she told to begin the article) and a broader discussion of how the story illustrated a specific difference between her generation (Baby Boomers) and her younger coworker's generation (Millennials). Because students would later be asked to write a story about their own experience with a generational difference and connect it to broader observations (from subsequent articles) about generations, it was relevant to have students analyze the verb tense shifts made by the article's author and then to connect it to the writing students themselves were doing (see Figure 10.2). For broader EAP goals, working with students on analyzing verb tense shifts is relevant in a range of academic genres in which some form of

Analyzing Language: Grammar. Parts of Brenoff's article are told as a story. Notice how the verb tenses work in these sections.

I just **had** lunch with Anna Almendrala, the 27-year-old associate editor of Huffington Post's Los Angeles page. She **ended** our meal by ordering a cup of coffee to go, and **whipped** out a plastic card to pay for it. I *think* the coffee **cost** $2.75.

It **dawned** on me: Anna *is* part of the generation that *doesn't* carry cash. Never, as in Not Ever. I *find* this kind of fascinating because if I didn't have a wad of cash in my wallet, my inclination would be to drop what I was doing and rush to the nearest ATM. The thing with carrying cash? *It's* a generational thing.

Anna *uses* a debit or credit card for everything, including parking meters. She *uses* plastic to fill up her gas tank, pay for her restaurant meals, make her in-store and online purchases. There *is* not so much as a single fat nickel in her slim wallet, just her credit and debit cards and her driver's license for ID.

She *feels* liberated. The mother in me **wanted** to press a ten-spot into her palm.

Verb Analysis Activities:

1. The verbs in **bold** are in **simple past tense**. The verbs in *italics* are in **simple present tense**. Look at the two sets of verbs. Why is past tense used where it is? What about present tense?
2. Now go back to the article and look at the verbs in the next three paragraphs (starting with "No, it's not just Anna."). Find and mark the verbs that are in simple past tense and the ones that are in simple present tense. Discuss with your teacher and classmates why the two tenses are used when they are.

FIGURE 10.2 Sample grammar analysis activity based upon an assigned reading (Ferris & Ferrando, 2015; original text excerpt is from Brenoff, 2013)

narration and analysis might be required—for literary analysis papers, for writing about history or government, or for writing up case studies in business writing or in health sciences courses.

Similarly, for a later writing assignment, students were asked to write an opinion essay based upon several readings on a topic. A grammar point that related well to this reading/writing task was the use of modal auxiliaries in opinion statements, so students were provided with a brief lesson on this point before writing the essay. In many academic writing genres, students must articulate a strong yet appropriately nuanced thesis, so a focus on the use of modals in expressing opinions is valuable beyond the EAP course.

While there are grammar topics that appear to be relevant across a range of academic writing genres (and disciplines) such as reporting verbs and the use of past or present tense to discuss ideas written by another author, passive voice (preferred in science writing but dispreferred in humanities), and hedging structures (for a summary, see Ferris, 2011, p. 181, Figure 6.6), it is probably most optimal for the teacher to pick and choose from among the many options by looking carefully at structures naturally occurring in assigned class readings and/or structures over which students will need control to complete class writing tasks. In this way, vocabulary and grammar instruction can be authentically integrated with other EAP class activities.

Principle 3: Choose Grammar and Vocabulary Topics Based on Class Needs

It should be self-evident that *all* teaching, including writing and language instruction, should be based on the careful analysis of the needs of a particular group of students. Some EAP classes are quite homogeneous, with most or all of the students coming from similar language and educational backgrounds, but in other settings, students may have a broad range of abilities, experiences and frames of reference. It is thus important for an EAP teacher desiring to provide language development for student writers to make a thoughtful assessment of the knowledge base(s) within each new group. Too often, teachers simply choose grammatical structures out of a textbook or out of their own prior experience with other classes and may thus waste students' time providing formal instruction that they do not need and/or missing key points about which students need more information.

Analyzing diagnostic writing samples. In an EAP class, there are two major ways in which the instructor can assess the language development needs of the students. The first is through systematic analysis of a diagnostic writing sample, which could either be taken from placement examination essays or completed during the first day or two of class. The teacher could analyze these writing samples for language issues (with content and organization being separate matters for the purposes of this discussion) in various ways. See Appendix A for a sample of this type of error analysis activity.

A different approach to diagnostic analysis involves applying a holistic rubric to students' language use in their writing samples. A sample of such a rubric, developed for a classroom research project (Ferris, Eckstein, & DeHond, 2015), is shown in Appendix B. This rubric allows the teacher not only to note error patterns but also to evaluate other aspects of language use, such as facility with vocabulary or underdeveloped sentence style. If the instructor desires to go beyond the simple consideration of error patterns in student writing to broader language development topics important in EAP settings, this type of needs analysis is important.

Student self-evaluation. A second type of needs analysis activity involves asking the students themselves to self-evaluate their own knowledge and confidence levels about different language issues and structures—both their formal knowledge and their ability to apply that knowledge successfully to their own writing. It can also ask them to identify their self-editing strategies when writing and their preferences about receiving error feedback from teachers or peers. Such an activity promotes metacognition about language development processes, elicits prior metalinguistic knowledge and actively encourages student agency and goal-setting, all of which, as noted earlier, are preconditions for transfer of learning to future academic contexts. A sample questionnaire designed for this purpose is shown in Appendix C.

Both types of diagnostic activities—the analysis of the writing sample and the questionnaire—can then be followed up with a student reflection and goal-setting activity (see the last part of Appendix C). Again, this exercise helps the student reflect and take some ownership of his or her own learning, and this reflection can be revisited later in the term so that students can see how/if they have made progress toward better control of the academic language issues they have prioritized. Such reflection and goal-setting can also build motivation and confidence in students who may otherwise feel overwhelmed at the vastness of the language they have yet to master and apply to their reading and writing tasks.

To summarize this section, in a crowded EAP syllabus, teachers should thoughtfully set goals for what they and their students should try to discuss and learn about various language structures. Careful consideration of students' present and future academic needs, together with selection of language forms that naturally occur within course reading materials and writing tasks, can help teachers to narrow the vast universe of language topics to a manageable set of priorities. While such initial analysis and prioritization takes time at the beginning of a term, the results of the process lead to much more satisfying outcomes for teachers and students alike.

Promoting Academic Language Development: The How

Effective language development in the context of an EAP class in most cases involves a judicious combination of approaches that include instruction, strategy training, feedback and guided self-learning. Different groups of students will have a range of backgrounds as to formal instruction on L2 grammar and usage, but even those who have experienced extensive prior L2 teaching can likely benefit from reminders (about terms and rules learned or partially learned years ago) and/or opportunities to practice and strategies to apply what they know in the context of their own writing. Finally, because there tends to be a great deal of variety across individual learners (even in homogenous classes) and especially because there simply is not enough time to cover all important L2 grammar and vocabulary in an EAP classroom setting, it may also be useful to encourage or require students to engage in a program of guided self-learning.

Providing Language Instruction in a Writing Class

An EAP class is not the same as a stand-alone L2 grammar (or vocabulary) class, and language instruction cannot be allowed to crowd out other important course topics (idea development, rhetoric and process, and close reading strategies, for example).

Further, as already discussed, decontextualized grammar teaching is unlikely to help students to improve their language control in writing. Thus, formal language instruction in the EAP class should be *brief, narrowly focused* and *integrated with other class activities* (i.e., reading and writing tasks).

Mini-lessons. I have suggested elsewhere (Ferris, 2011, 2014; Ferris & Hedgcock, 2014) that *mini-lessons* be used to teach language structures and self-editing strategies. Mini-lessons should be brief so that they do not take up too much class time (but could include a preparatory homework assignment or a follow-up activity before the next class) and should not attempt to cover too much ground at one time—so, for example, highlighting three important rules for the use of the English article rather than every nuance related to the article system. A series of related mini-lessons that build on one another is likely the best approach for most EAP classes.

Mini-lessons ideally should include *discovery/analysis* activities, *explanation* (with clear definitions and examples), *practice* and *application* (to students' own writing). These components will necessarily take different forms depending upon the language/usage topic, and they do not always need to be in that particular order. However, considering that many students already have extensive formal knowledge about the L2 but not effective strategies for using that knowledge for demanding academic writing tasks, it could be argued that the application portion of the mini-lesson is the most important. For example, returning to the mini-lesson discussed in the previous section on past and present tense verbs in storytelling (Figure 10.2), students were asked, after analyzing and discussing the use of the verb tenses in the assigned reading, to apply the same analysis to their own recently completed writing (Figure 10.3).

This mini-lesson was reinforced later in the textbook unit when students had to produce a final paper and were specifically reminded in both the assignment prompt and during a peer feedback workshop to check their use of simple past and simple present verb tenses while telling their own stories about generational differences. Again, this language application point is useful not only for the specific EAP course assignment but also for other academic writing students will do in the future.

Applying Grammar to Your Own Writing

Go back to the short paper (discovery draft) in which you wrote a story about a generational difference. Exchange the paper with a partner. Go through and mark present and past tense verbs as you did for Brenoff's article. Are there any places where you're not clear why your partner used present tense instead of past, or past instead of present? Discuss your findings with your partner.

FIGURE 10.3 Mini-lesson application activity (Ferris & Ferrando, 2015)

Integrating language mini-lessons with other class activities. Mini-lessons can be naturally incorporated at several points of a writing class lesson or syllabus. As already discussed, students can analyze the language of a text they have read for content. As an illustration, the previous section described how a portion of an assigned text was analyzed for examples of items from the Academic Word List. Students were asked to complete a chart (see Figure 10.4) in which they first tried to determine what the words meant in context and then to say whether the word was a topic-specific item or a more general one (that could be found in academic texts in other disciplines or on different subject matter). For example, they might have selected *liberation* or *regions* as more topic-specific words and *defined* as a general term.

This activity accomplished three things simultaneously: (1) it allowed students to practice analyzing vocabulary meanings in context; (2) it helped them understand more about *academic* vocabulary as a construct (they had already been introduced to the Academic Word List and to several online text analyzers that will identify AWL words within in a text); and (3) it helped them understand that some AWL words are topic/content-specific while others could be utilized more generally across tasks and disciplines.

Word	**Meaning (your guess)**	**Topic-specific (TS) or general (G) academic vocabulary?**
evidenced	shown, proven	G (general)
cultural		
identified		
regions		
established		
similar		
defined		
tradition		
dominated		
liberation		

FIGURE 10.4 Sample vocabulary analysis activity from course reading (Ferris & Ferrando, 2015)

After this activity, in which AWL items were identified for students, they were asked to run a digital version of the text through the AWL Highlighter tool and to choose ten additional highlighted words (five topic-specific and five general) to add to a vocabulary chart. Later, when writing a paper based upon this source, they were required to choose and correctly incorporate at least one topic-specific item and one general AWL term from the source text into their own papers. This follow-up step modeled for them that they should identify and incorporate both topic-specific and general academic vocabulary into their own texts and some strategies for doing so effectively. In short, language development mini-lessons can be about a wide range of topics and can be created from authentic materials and built naturally into other EAP reading/writing activities. The possibilities are infinite.

Guided self-study for language development. As already noted, the universe of L2 vocabulary and grammar is too vast and complex to be covered in one EAP course or program of study, and students enter courses and programs with different needs for instruction. Therefore, opportunities (or requirements) for students to engage in self-directed study of language can supplement in-class instruction and feedback on writing, allowing students both to learn new language forms on their own and, even more importantly, to practice strategies for doing so that will help them in future academic endeavors.

Guidelines for self-directed language study in EAP courses are similar to those for extensive reading (Day & Bamford, 1998; Hedgcock & Ferris, 2009): teachers should lead students through some initial explanation and goal-setting activities; students should have guidance about which self-study resources to use; and there should be at least some loosely structured deadlines and accountability for completing the work. As already noted, such activities not only meet practical needs (for individualized language study beyond what the EAP classroom or teacher can provide), but they also promote student autonomy and responsibility and foster metacognitive awareness of language development processes and strategies that in turn facilitate knowledge transfer for future academic writing tasks.

Conclusion

Designing and implementing a strategy for students' ongoing L2 development in an EAP class is complex, but it is not impossible. If teachers investigate their students' prior knowledge, preferences and needs, match instruction and feedback to those needs and thoughtfully integrate language-focused activities with other EAP class priorities, they will find such work not only effective but also motivating and engaging for students. Perhaps even more importantly, they will equip students with strategies for ongoing L2 acquisition—a challenging long-term process—after the EAP class ends. Such investigation and integration requires some up-front thought and work by teachers, but done well, it is a great gift to EAP students.

References

Bates, L., Lane, J., & Lange, E. (1993). *Writing clearly: Responding to student writing*. Boston: Heinle.

Beason, L. (2001). Ethos and error: How business people react to errors. *College Composition and Communication, 53*, 33–64.

Beaufort, A. (2007). *College writing and beyond: A new framework for university writing instruction*. Logan, UT: Utah State University Press.

Bennett, G. (2010). *Using corpora in the language learning classroom*. Ann Arbor: University of Michigan Press.

Biber, D. (2006). *University English: A corpus-based study of written and spoken registers*. Amsterdam: John Benjamins.

Biber, D., Conrad, S., Reppen, R., Byrd, P., & Helt, M. (2002). Speaking and writing in the university: A multi-dimensional comparison. *TESOL Quarterly, 36*, 9–48.

Biber, D., Johansson, C., Leech, S., Conrad, S., & Finegan, E. (1999). *The Longman grammar of spoken and written English*. London: Longman.

Bitchener, J. (2008). Evidence in support of written corrective feedback. *Journal of Second Language Writing, 17*, 102–118.

Bitchener, J. & Ferris, D. (2012). *Written corrective feedback in second language acquisition and writing*. New York: Routledge.

Bitchener, J. & Storch, N. (2016). *Written corrective feedback for L2 development*. Bristol, England: Multilingual Matters.

Brenoff, A. (2013). Why Anna doesn't carry cash. Accessed 22 May 2015 from www.huffingtonpost.com/ann-brenoff/generational-differences-caring-cash_b_2442734.html.

Brinton, D., Snow, M. A., & Wesche, M. B. (2003). *Content-based second language instruction*. Ann Arbor: University of Michigan Press.

Burt, M. K., & Kiparsky, C. (1972). *The gooficon: A repair manual for English*. Rowley, MA: Newbury House.

Byrd, P., & Bunting, J. (2008). Myth 3: Where grammar is concerned, one size fits all. In J. Reid (Ed.), *Writing myths: Applying second language research to classroom teaching* (pp. 42–69). Ann Arbor: University of Michigan Press.

Connors, R. (2003). Grammar in American college composition: An historical overview. In L. Ede & A. A. Lunsford (Eds.), *Selected essays of Robert J. Connors* (pp. 117–138). Boston: Bedford/St. Martin's.

Coxhead, A. (2000). A new academic word list. *TESOL Quarterly, 34*(2), 213–238.

Coxhead, A. (2006). *Essentials of teaching academic vocabulary*. Boston: Houghton Mifflin.

Day, R. R., & Bamford, J. (1998). *Extensive reading in the second language classroom*. Cambridge, England: Cambridge University Press.

Ellis, R., Loewen, S., & Erlam, R. (2006). Implicit and explicit corrective feedback and the acquisition of L2 grammar. *Studies in second language acquisition, 28*(2), 339–368.

Ferris, D. R. (2004). The "grammar correction" debate in L2 writing: Where are we, and where do we go from here? (And what do we do in the meantime…?). *Journal of Second Language Writing, 13*, 49–62.

Ferris, D. R. (2010). Second language writing research and written corrective feedback in SLA: Intersections and practical applications. *Studies in Second Language Acquisition, 32*, 181–201.

Ferris, D. R. (2011). *Treatment of error in second language student writing* (2nd ed.). Ann Arbor: University of Michigan Press.

Ferris, D. R. (2014). *Language power: Tutorials for writers*. Boston: Bedford St. Martin's.

Ferris, D., Eckstein, G., & DeHond, G. (2015). *Self-directed language development: A study of first-year college writers.* Manuscript under review for publication.
Ferris, D., & Ferrando, J. (2015). *Exploring generations 1.* Southlake, TX: Fountainhead Press.
Ferris, D., & Hedgcock, J. (2014). *Teaching readers of English: Students, texts, and contexts* (3rd ed.). New York: Routledge.
Ferris, D. R., Liu, H., Sinha, A., & Senna, M. (2013). Written corrective feedback for individual L2 writers. *Journal of Second Language Writing, 22*(3), 307–329.
Ferris, D. R., & Roberts, B. J. (2001). Error feedback in L2 writing classes: How explicit does it need to be? *Journal of Second Language Writing, 10,* 161-184.
Folse, K. (2004). *Vocabulary myths: Applying second language research to classroom teaching.* Ann Arbor: University of Michigan Press.
Frodesen, J. & Holten, C. (2003). Grammar and the ESL writing class. In B. Kroll (Ed.), *Exploring the dynamics of second language writing* (pp. 141–161). Cambridge, England: Cambridge University Press.
Hairston, M. (1981). Not all errors are created equal: Nonacademic readers in the professions respond to lapses in usage. *College English, 43,* 794–806.
Hartshorn, J. K., Evans, N. W., Merrill, P. F., Sudweeks, R. R., Strong-Krause, D., & Anderson, N. J. (2010). The effects of dynamic corrective feedback on ESL writing accuracy. *TESOL Quarterly, 44,* 84–109.
Hartwell, P. (1985). Grammar, grammars, and the teaching of grammar. *College English, 47*(2), 105–127.
Hedgcock, J. & Ferris, D. (2009). *Teaching readers of English: Students, texts, and contexts.* New York: Routledge.
Hendrickson, J. M. (1978). Error correction in foreign language teaching: Recent theory, research, and practice. *Modern Language Journal, 62,* 387–398.
Hinkel, E. (2002). *Second language writers' text: Linguistic and rhetorical features.* Mahwah, NJ: Erlbaum.
Hyland, K. (2002). *Teaching and researching writing.* Harlow, UK: Pearson Education.
Hyland, K. (2007). English for Specific Purposes. In J. Cummins & C. Davison (Eds.), *International handbook of English language teaching* (pp. 391–402). New York: Springer.
Hyland, K. (2008). Myth 4: Make your academic writing assertive and certain. In J. Reid (Ed.), *Writing myths: Applying second language research to classroom teaching* (pp. 70–89). Ann Arbor: University of Michigan Press.
Janopolous, M. (1992). University faculty tolerance of NS and NNS writing errors. *Journal of Second Language Writing, 1,* 109–122.
Krashen, S. D. (1982). *Principles and practices in second language acquisition.* Oxford, England: Pergamon Press.
Krashen, S. D. (2004). *The power of reading: Insights from the research* (2nd ed.). Westport, CT: Libraries Unlimited.
Lalande, J. F. (1982). Reducing composition errors: An experiment. *The Modern Language Journal, 66*(2), 140–149.
Leki, I. (1991/92). Building expertise through sequenced assignments. *TESOL Journal, 1*(2), 19–23.
MacDonald, S. P. (2007). The erasure of language. *College Composition and Communication, 58,* 585–625.
Raimes, A. (1991). Out of the woods: Emerging traditions in the teaching of writing. *TESOL Quarterly, 25*(3), 407–430.

Reppen, R. (2010). *Using corpora in the language classroom*. Cambridge, UK: Cambridge University Press.

Santa, T. (2006). *Dead letters: Errors in composition, 1873–2004*. Creskill, NJ: Hampton Press.

Santos, T. (1988). Professors' reactions to the academic writing of nonnative-speaking students. *TESOL Quarterly, 22*, 66–90.

Schleppegrell, M. (1998). Grammar as resource: Writing a description. *Research in the Teaching of English, 32*, 182–211.

Schleppegrell, M. (2001). Linguistic features of the language of schooling. *Linguistics and Education, 12*, 431–459.

Shintani, N., & Ellis, R. (2013). The comparative effect of direct written corrective feedback and metalinguistic explanation on learners' explicit and implicit knowledge of the English indefinite article. *Journal of Second Language Writing, 22*(3), 286–306.

Silva, T. (1993). Toward an understanding of the distinct nature of L2 writing: The ESL research and its implications. *TESOL Quarterly, 27*, 657–677.

van Beuningen, C., de Jong, N. H., & Kuiken, F. (2012). Evidence on the effectiveness of comprehensive error correction in second language writing. *Language Learning, 62*(1), 1–41.

West, M., & West, M. P. (Eds.). (1953). *A general service list of English words: With semantic frequencies and a supplementary word-list for the writing of popular science and technology*. London: Addison-Wesley.

Yancey, K. B., Robertson, L., & Tacsak, K. (Eds.) (2014). *Writing across contexts: Transfer, composition, and cultures of writing*. Logan: Utah State University Press.

Zimmerman, C. B. (2009). *Word knowledge: A vocabulary teacher's handbook*. New York: Oxford University Press.

Appendix A

Sample Diagnostic Error Analysis Activity

(adapted from Ferris, 2014; Ferris & Ferrando, 2015)

Your teacher has marked errors in the essay you wrote in class last time according to the categories below. Go through your essay and:

1. Number each error your teacher marked
2. Identify which category you think the error is (you can ask classmates and your teacher for help with this)
3. See if you can correct the error. If you can't, just write a "?" for that error.
4. Complete the chart below.

Note: This chart has space for 25 errors. If you have more than 25, just categorize the first 25 your teacher marked.

Error Category Description	*Examples*	*Correct Form*
Verb tense or form is incorrect	I **arrive** in Davis last month. I can **understood** the shows on American TV very well.	**arrived** **understand**
Word form (part of speech) is incorrect	San Francisco is a very **beauty** city.	**beautiful**
Article is missing, unnecessary or incorrect	My parents came to ^ United States 10 years ago. To get around **the** UC Davis, you need **the** bicycle.	**the United States** **UC Davis** **a** bicycle
Noun plural marker is missing, unnecessary or incorrect	There are too many **bicycle** in Davis.	**bicycles**
Subject and verb do not agree in number (singular/plural form)	College students **does** not obey the traffic laws on their bicycles.	**do**
Wrong preposition	I came **at** UC Davis three weeks ago.	**to**
Wrong word (meaning is incorrect for sentence)	The choice was **oblivious.**	**obvious**
Word choice (too formal/ informal or otherwise inappropriate)	I know my major will **pay off** with a good job after college.	**result in/ lead to**

(continued)

(continued)

Error Category Description	*Examples*	*Correct Form*
Run-on sentence (two or more sentences incorrectly joined)	Next year's election for U.S. president will be very **interesting there** are several women in the race.	**interesting. There…** **OR** **interesting; there…** **OR** **Interesting because there…**
Sentence fragment (incomplete sentence)	**If the Giants win the World Series again.**	**If the Giants win the World Series again, I will be very happy.**
Punctuation (missing or incorrect comma, period, semicolon, apostrophe or other)	**Lets eat Grandma!**	**Let's** eat, Grandma!
Mechanics (spelling or capitalization incorrect)	**your an idot.**	**You're** an **idiot**

Error Analysis Chart		
Error #	*Error Category (if not sure, put "?")*	*Correction (if not sure, put "?")*
1		
2		
3		
4		
5		
6		
7		
8		
9		
10		

Error Analysis Chart

Error #	*Error Category (if not sure, put "?")*	*Correction (if not sure, put "?")*
11		
12		
13		
14		
15		
16		
17		
18		
19		
20		
21		
22		
23		
24		
25		

Appendix B

Language Use Holistic Rubric for Needs Analysis

(Ferris, Eckstein, & DeHond, 2015)

Language Use Scoring Rubric		
Score	*General Descriptor*	*Specific Descriptors*
6	**Excellent language use**	• There are very few if any errors of any type (lexical, syntactic, mechanical). • Lexical choices are sophisticated and appropriate. • Sentences are varied and rhetorically effective.
5	**Strong language use**	• Syntactic and lexical errors will occur at this level. They are, however, generally infrequent. Meaning is never obscured by errors. • Vocabulary choices are solid and appropriate. • Sentences are well written and demonstrate strong command of complex sentence patterns.
4	**Competent language use**	• Frequency of local errors keeps this writing from the next level. • There may be some awkward wording, but meaning is not obscured. • Sentence variety and complexity are very good.
3	**Underdeveloped language use**	• Local errors are frequent and sometimes distracting; some global errors may occur at this level. • Vocabulary choices are usually accurate but may be repetitive or simple and/or ineffective (cliché, informal, etc.) • Sentence choices are usually simple and do not show much variety. When the writer attempts more complex structures, the grammar sometimes breaks down.
2	**Weak language use**	• Writing at this level is generally understandable but has many errors. Global errors that obscure meaning may be present but not frequent. • Vocabulary choices may be occasionally inaccurate and even confusing. • Sentences are predominantly simple. If more complex structures are attempted, grammar breaks down consistently or frequently.

Language Use Scoring Rubric		
Score	*General Descriptor*	*Specific Descriptors*
1	**Unacceptable language use**	• Errors of all types are frequent, distracting and obscure meaning. • Lexical errors cause processing difficulties. • Sentences are out of control and very hard to understand.
0	**Unable to score**	• No submission or other problem

Appendix C

Grammar Knowledge Questionnaire & Reflective Goal-Setting

(adapted from Ferris, 2014; Ferris & Ferrando, 2015; Ferris & Roberts, 2001)

Please respond thoughtfully and honestly to the questions below. You will use your answers to help set goals for your language and writing progress during this class.

1. In English classes you have taken before, have you ever learned any English grammar terms or rules (noun, verb, tense, agreement, etc.)?
   a. Yes, often or always
   b. Sometimes
   c. Very little or never
   d. Not sure
2. Overall, how confident do you feel about your current knowledge of English grammar, vocabulary, punctuation and other mechanics (spelling, capitalization)?
   - ☐ Very confident
   - ☐ Confident
   - ☐ Unconfident
   - ☐ Very unconfident
3. In the chart below are several important areas of language knowledge. Please indicate your confidence level with each.

Area of Knowledge	*very confident*	*somewhat confident*	*not confident*	*not sure*
Identifying parts of speech of individual words in a sentence				
Identifying the subject and verb in a sentence				
Identifying different phrase types (prepositional phrase, noun phrase, etc.)				
Distinguishing dependent and independent clauses				

4. In the chart below are listed common problems experienced by college student writers with grammar and mechanics. Please indicate how much you struggle with each of these problems.

Issue/Error	*frequently struggle with*	*sometimes struggle with*	*never struggle with*	*not sure*
Limited vocabulary				
Incorrect word choice				
Word form (for example: using a noun form when you need an adjective, etc.)				
Commas				
Apostrophes				
Other punctuation				
Pronouns				
Verb tenses and other verb forms				
Subject–verb agreement				
Sentence boundaries (run-ons, fragments)				
Noun plurals				
Articles (the/a, etc.)				
Prepositions				
Mechanics (spelling, capitalization)				
Other (specify)				

5. When you write a paper for school, how effective/correct is your English grammar and vocabulary usage?
   - ☐ Very strong or perfect
   - ☐ Fairly strong
   - ☐ Somewhat weak
   - ☐ Very weak

6. Please select one statement that best describes how you feel about your English language knowledge and usage.
   a. My English grammar and vocabulary problems are very serious and really hurt my writing.
   b. Although I don't know much about English grammar (labels and rules), it's not a serious problem for me in writing.
   c. English grammar is not really a serious issue for me. Other writing issues are much more important.
   d. I'm not really sure whether English grammar and vocabulary are a problem for my writing.
7. What self-editing strategies have you used to correct your own writing?

	I always do this	*I sometimes do this*	*I never do this*
Leave time between writing and final editing			
Read paper aloud to catch errors			
Focus on specific known problems			
Use computer/online resources to check errors or research language choices			
Ask someone else to proofread or edit			

8. In your opinion, what is the best way for a teacher to give feedback about language errors in your writing? Please select one statement only.
   a. Don't correct my language errors. Let me try to do this for myself.
   b. Only correct the most serious errors so I know what to focus on first.
   c. Circle or highlight my errors, but don't correct them for me.
   d. Circle my errors and tell me what type of error it is (verb tense, word choice, etc.)
   e. Correct all of my errors for me.

Putting It All Together

Now look back at your questionnaire and your error analysis chart (from the activity in Appendix A). List 3–5 areas of language that you would like to improve in during this class. Be specific. For example, instead of *grammar*, say *verb tense* or *noun plurals*. Instead of *vocabulary*, say *use a greater variety of words in my writing*.

1

2

3

4

5

Write a short paragraph (3–5 sentences) explaining to your teacher what you learned from these activities and what you would like to work on (or would like help with). Write it on a separate piece of paper or Word document) and give it to your teacher.

11

WORKING HARD OR WORKING SMART

Comprehensive versus Focused Written Corrective Feedback in L2 Academic Contexts

Icy Lee

Introduction

Learning to write for academic purposes entails, among other skills, the development of linguistic accuracy in writing. Responding to written errors is therefore an important job for teachers working with multilingual student writers in EAP (English for academic purposes) contexts. In many EAP classrooms, teachers tend to respond to every single error in student writing (Junqueira & Payant, 2015). Such an approach to written corrective feedback (WCF) is comprehensive but unfocused, oftentimes resulting in papers inundated with red ink. Despite the lack of established evidence in support of comprehensive WCF, it remains the most prevalent approach across L2 contexts, particularly EFL contexts (Furneaux, Paran, & Fairfax, 2007). Hairston (1986) refers to teachers adopting comprehensive WCF as composition *slaves*, arguing that an error-focused approach to written feedback is both unproductive and undesirable. When teachers give WCF comprehensively, they easily burn out and have little time left to respond to other important dimensions of writing, such as content and organization. Nonetheless, L2 students welcome detailed feedback on their written errors and think that it is the teacher's responsibility to provide meticulous feedback on errors (Lee, 2005; Leki, 1991). Also, in many classroom contexts, L2 writing teachers opt for comprehensive WCF and consider it to be more authentic and useful than a selective approach to WCF (Hartshorn & Evans, 2015; Van Beuningen, 2010). So should L2 teachers work hard to mark all written errors (i.e., comprehensive WCF), or should they work smart and respond to errors selectively (i.e., focused WCF)?

To address this question, the chapter begins by defining the key terms *comprehensive WCF* and *focused WCF* as used in the chapter. It then reviews relevant literature about these two approaches to WCF, examines their pros and cons and explores their pedagogical implications in L2 academic contexts. Specific ways of implementing focused WCF and a middle position that combines comprehensive and focused WCF are examined. The chapter concludes with suggestions for pedagogical practice and future research.

Defining Terminology

Comprehensive WCF refers to a conventional practice in writing classrooms in which teachers respond to all errors in student writing. Such an approach lacks a focus, and hence it is also referred to as *unfocused WCF* (Ellis, Sheen, Murakami, & Takashima, 2008; Ferris, 2011; Ferris, Liu, Sinha, & Senna, 2013). While comprehensive WCF refers to the "correction of every error" (Van Beuningen, De Jong, & Kuiken 2012, p. 5) in student writing, unfocused WCF is defined in slightly different ways by different researchers. For example, Ellis et al. (2008) refer to *unfocused WCF* as an approach where teachers correct "all (or at least a range of) the errors in learners' written work" (p. 356), which suggests that in giving unfocused WCF, teachers may respond to a range of or all written errors. Ferris (2011), however, defines *unfocused feedback* as feedback on "all problems observed in the text without a preconceived approach in mind" (p. 30). For Ferris (2011) then, unfocused WCF is synonymous with comprehensive WCF where teachers provide feedback on all written errors. Similarly, Bitchener (2012) characterizes *unfocused WCF* as "feedback on a comprehensive range of forms and structures" (p. 856). Although researchers tend to use *unfocused WCF* and *comprehensive WCF* interchangeably (e.g., Ferris et al., 2013; Van Beuningen, 2010), from the above definitions a slight distinction can be made between *comprehensive* and *unfocused* WCF. While comprehensive WCF describes an approach where teachers respond to all written errors, unfocused WCF covers all or a range of errors (see Ellis et al., 2008). To avoid confusion, in this chapter I use the term *comprehensive WCF* to refer to an approach where teachers respond to all errors in student writing.

Focused WCF, on the other hand, is an approach that "selects specific errors to be corrected and ignores other errors" (Ellis et al., 2008, p. 356). While Ferris (2011) refers to *focused feedback* as "feedback that is targeted to specific error types or patterns" (p. 30) without specifying the number of selected error items, Bitchener (2012) characterizes *focused WCF* in his study as an approach that "targets only one or two linguistic forms or structures" (p. 856). Bitchener's (2012) *focused WCF* is, to be exact, a highly/narrowly focused approach that targets only one or two error types. Frear and Chiu (2015) define focused WCF as "the provision of WCF on one or a few *pre-selected* [emphasis added] structures" (p. 24). Due to the nature of the experimental design in recent research on focused WCF, the error categories are pre-selected before feedback is provided (e.g., Ellis et al., 2008; Sheen, Wright, & Moldawa, 2009). Pre-selection of errors, however, need not be a defining characteristic of focused WCF; in real classrooms, it is possible that teachers both pre-select error focuses for feedback, as well as select errors while they are

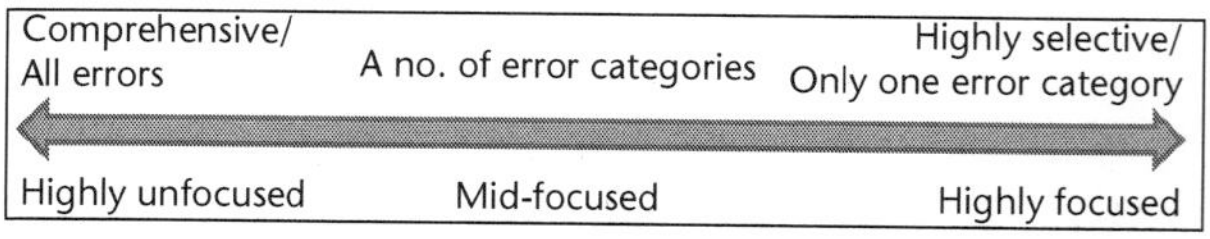

FIGURE 11.1 Comprehensive-focused WCF continuum

responding to student papers (Ferris et al., 2013) e.g., focusing on recurrent error patterns, or errors based on individual student needs. In this chapter, *focused WCF* is used to refer to an approach where teachers select specific error types (one or more) for WCF, whether the errors are pre-selected and/or selected during the feedback process. In this chapter, the term *focused WCF* is used interchangeably with *selective WCF* (e.g., Van Beuningen, 2010).

Figure 11.1 presents a diagrammatic representation of comprehensive and focused WCF as a continuum. To elaborate, when teachers respond to all errors comprehensively, the approach is highly unfocused (i.e., the left end of the continuum in Figure 11.1). Conversely, when teachers respond to only one error category selectively, the WCF is highly/narrowly focused (i.e., the right end of the continuum in Figure 11.1). Between the two ends of the continuum, when a number of error categories is targeted, the WCF can be referred to as mid-focused. Specifically, Liu and Brown (2015) define mid-focused WCF as feedback on two to five categories. To sum up, comprehensive WCF refers to feedback on all errors and it is highly unfocused, whereas focused WCF refers to feedback on one or more selected errors (up to five error types) as highly focused to mid-focused. As the number of the targeted error categories increases (e.g., six, seven, eight and so on), the WCF becomes less and less focused (i.e., leaning towards the left end of the continuum in Figure 11.1). In real classroom contexts, however, teachers opting for focused WCF are unlikely to respond to a very large number of error categories as this renders the WCF less and less focused.

Comparing Comprehensive and Focused WCF: Research Insights

While earlier studies on comprehensive WCF failed to produce evidence about the effectiveness of such an approach over time (Kepner, 1991; Robb, Ross, & Shortreed, 1986; Semke, 1984; Sheppard, 1992), recent research efforts on WCF have concentrated on the effects of focused WCF and demonstrated its benefits (Bitchener, 2008; Bitchener & Knoch, 2008, 2010a, 2010b; Ellis et al., 2008; Sheen, 2007; Sheen et al., 2009). In fact, arguments against comprehensive WCF are mostly commonsensical, and also backed up by research on second language acquisition (SLA) and WCF. One major argument against comprehensive WCF is that it is overwhelming for both teachers and students. For teachers, comprehensive WCF is "unpleasant and time-consuming, problems [*sic*] which are almost certain to result in a lower quality of correction" (Truscott, 2001, p. 93) and easily leads to teacher burnout (Ferris, 2003). Even though teachers may want to capture all errors for students, they are often unable to do so (Ferris & Helt, 2000) due to different reasons, such as fatigue, time pressure or sometimes lack of knowledge. Lee's (2004) study found that only slightly over half of teachers' error corrections were accurate. When teachers are overloaded and have to respond to errors comprehensively, they are likely to make mistakes in their WCF, and poorly done WCF might harm students' written accuracy development. A preponderant focus on errors also relegates language teachers to grammar teachers and distracts them from other meaningful aspects of their work as writing teachers (Zamel, 1982, 1985). For students, comprehensive WCF can lead to "information overload" (Bitchener, 2008, p. 109), "overloading students' attentional capacity" (Sheen et al., 2009, p. 559), and it can be discouraging and demotivating for students to see their papers inundated with the red ink (Hyland & Hyland, 2006; Semke, 1984; Truscott, 2001). More than a decade ago, Truscott argued that "standard thinking is that correction must be used selectively" (p. 93). From the SLA perspective, a primary theoretical reason in support of focused WCF is that learners are more likely to notice and understand the feedback when a limited number of error types is targeted (Ellis et al., 2008), which is crucial for acquisition to take place (Ellis, 2005; Schmidt, 1994). For students, particularly those of lower language proficiency, a selective approach to WCF is more manageable as they can be helped to develop their written accuracy in a focused and incremental manner. The studies by Bitchener (2008, 2012), Bitchener and Knoch (2008, 2009a, 2009b) and Sheen (2007), which involved feedback on two functional uses of the article system, demonstrated the effectiveness of focused WCF in improving students' written accuracy of the targeted structure. Just as oral corrective feedback is most effective when it is focused, addressing a specific linguistic item in a repeated manner (Ellis, Loewen, & Erlam, 2006; Lyster, 2004), it is argued that WCF is also most effective when it is *focused and intensive* (Sheen et al., 2009), addressing patterns of errors rather than loads of unrelated errors (Ferris, 2002).

To gather further evidence for the benefits of focused WFC, researchers compared the effects of focused WCF and unfocused WCF. Ellis et al. (2008) examined the relative effectiveness of these two approaches to WCF, with focused WCF delivered to two functional uses of the English article (*a* and *the*), and unfocused WCF to a variety of linguistic errors including articles, past tense, preposition and vocabulary. The results of the study showed that focused and unfocused WCF could be equally effective, with some evidence suggesting the efficacy of focused WCF for a longer term. Since the efficacy of WCF in the study was measured with regard to the use of articles only, the results failed to show if focused WCF had any effect on the accuracy of error categories other than articles. To address such a limitation, Sheen et al. (2009) compared the effects of focused and unfocused WCF on articles, as well as three other grammatical structures including copula *be*, regular and irregular past tense, and prepositions (temporal and locative—e.g., at, in, on). The findings of their study showed that focused WCF was more effective than unfocused WCF in improving students' written accuracy. Worthy of note in these two studies is that *unfocused WCF*, as defined by the researchers, covered four grammatical items while the focused WCF was highly focused as it targeted only one linguistic domain. Viewed on the WCF continuum in Figure 11.1, the unfocused WCF in these studies was still relatively focused as it covered four linguistic items, i.e., mid-focused according to Liu and Brown (2015), though not as narrowly focused as in the focused WCF that targeted only one error category. In fact, the definition of unfocused WCF provided by Ellis et al. (2008), that is, "teachers correct all (or at least a range of) the errors in learners' written work" (p. 356) is ambiguous, especially since *all errors* and *a range of errors* could in fact denote a comprehensive and a selective/focused approach to WCF respectively. Ellis et al. (2008) themselves admit that the distinction between focused and unfocused WCF in their study "may not have been successfully operationalized" (p. 368), and that "it might be better to characterize the differences between the two types of CF in this study as 'focused' versus 'less focused' rather than 'focused' versus 'unfocused'" (p. 367). In other words, instead of showing the benefits of focused WCF over comprehensive WCF, the studies by Ellis et al. (2008) and Sheen et al. (2009) suggested that a narrowly focused approach to WCF was more beneficial than mid-focused WCF in improving written accuracy.

While the two experimental studies by Ellis et al. (2008) and Sheen et al. (2009) have confirmed findings from oral corrective feedback research that demonstrates the benefits of focused, intensive and repeated corrective feedback, the practical application of such research in L2 academic writing contexts is limited (Evans, Hartshorn, & Strong-Krause, 2011). In real classrooms, L2 students have to pay attention to a large number of error categories in order to produce grammatically accurate writing (Hartshorn & Evans, 2015; Van Beuningen, 2010), and it is not at all practical to target only one linguistic item. After all, L2 students hope to improve accuracy in general, rather than accuracy of a small number of items. Opponents of focused WCF argue that it fails to meet the needs of students who want to know all the errors they have made in writing, thus calling for a more authentic approach to WCF that focuses on "the accuracy of all aspects of writing, simultaneously" (Hartshorn, Evans, Merrill, Sudweeks, Strong-Krause, & Anderson, 2010, p. 89). Some recent research has demonstrated the efficacy of comprehensive WCF (Van Beuningen, De Jong, & Kuiken, 2008, 2012), showing that students who received comprehensive WCF improved their written accuracy, compared with students who engaged in writing practice without WCF and in self-editing without WCF. Hartshorn and Evans (2015) found that dynamic WCF (meaningful, manageable, timely and constant feedback) that involved comprehensive WCF on 10-minute paragraph writing over a 30-week period led to improvements in linguistic accuracy. Overall, however, studies that demonstrate the benefits of comprehensive WCF are relatively sparse, and research findings that show the advantages of comprehensive WCF over focused WCF are unavailable.

In the absence of conclusive research evidence, teachers should decide on the amount of WCF according to the proficiency level of students, as well as the complexity of the target grammar structures (Bitchener & Ferris, 2012). For low-proficiency L2 learners who make a large number of errors in writing, focused WCF is generally more manageable than comprehensive WCF. For advanced L2 learners who make few errors in writing, and for "the most competent and motivated student writers" in particular (Ferris, 2011, p. 31), comprehensive WCF may be more desirable than focused WCF.

Focused WCF: Principles for Error Selection

In contexts where teachers decide to adopt focused WCF, the chief question to ask is how focused WCF should be implemented. It is important that teachers use a principled approach taking account of a number of important considerations, as examined in the following.

Number of Error Types

There are no hard and fast rules for the number of error types that should be targeted for WCF; the major principle is whether the total number is manageable for students. Depending on the needs of the students, the number of error types can vary during the course/academic year. For instance, to begin with focused WCF can be given to two to three different error types, and increased to four to five as the course progresses—i.e., from highly focused to mid-focused.

What Error Types to Select

The error types targeted for focused WCF could be items that are specific to the genres that students are learning to write. For instance, if the target genre is argumentative writing in typical EAP contexts, the error types selected for focused WCF may include verb tense and logical connectives. Another consideration is to select errors that tie in with pre-writing grammar instruction, if any. Such instruction can relate directly to the genre that students are learning to write. For example, if students are learning how to write a narrative, the pre-writing instruction may involve a focus on the past tense, dialogue, connectives (to sequence events and signal cause and effect) and adjective/adverbs to describe setting and characters. In other instructional contexts where grammar instruction figures prominently (as in some EFL contexts), focused WCF can be aligned with the grammar syllabus itself. Teachers can select grammar items from the syllabus for focused WCF in a systematic manner, making sure that they sequence the grammar items according to student needs and recycle them where appropriate.

Also worthy of attention in the choice of errors is the nature of the error type in terms of correctability (Truscott, 2001), and hence simplicity and discreteness should be considered important criteria for error selection. Lexical errors, for example, are simpler and more discrete (and hence more correctable) than syntactic errors and could be selected for WCF. Teachers can also make a distinction between mistakes (such as spelling mistakes), which are easily self-corrected, and those that need to be pointed out by the teacher (i.e., not amenable to self-correction) (Bitchener & Ferris, 2012)—e.g., collocation errors. Another approach to error selection is to distinguish between local and global errors—the former referring to errors that do not impede communication (e.g., morphological errors), while the latter are those that result in communication breakdown (e.g., syntax and lexical errors). In general, it can be argued that global errors deserve more attention than local errors (Burt, 1975); however, global errors are harder to correct for students of low language proficiency, and teachers should target error types according to student needs. Ferris (1999, 2002) has made a distinction between treatable (rule-governed) and untreatable errors (non rule-governed), suggesting that WCF is most effective for treatable errors (e.g., *articles*). While there is no rigid rule about error selection, it is important to take into account students' needs, their proficiency level, as well as the nature of the error types. For instance, more advanced L2 learners may benefit from WCF on more complex linguistic items.

A final consideration regarding error types is whether teachers should go for smaller categories like *verb tense* and *verb form* or larger categories like *verbs* (Ferris & Hedgcock, 2014). In general, it is less confusing both for teachers and students if larger categories are used because sometimes it is even difficult for teachers themselves to pin down the error type. In *I gone to school*, for example, is the error a verb tense or verb form error?

When to Select Errors

As defined earlier, focused WCF involves feedback on both pre-selected errors and those selected while teachers are responding to student writing. For the latter, teachers can focus on high-frequency and/or stigmatizing errors in students' own specific contexts—i.e., errors that are likely to label students as less proficient writers. An example of a stigmatizing error for Hong Kong learners is the erroneous structure *there has*, which is common in Cantonese learners' writing (Chan, 2010).

Who Should Select Errors

While teachers are expected to select errors for students, it is possible to empower students and help them develop a sense of ownership by asking them to select errors for themselves. In addition to the teacher-selected errors, students can make special requests of the errors or error types they want to get feedback on. They can write those on a cover sheet, or highlight certain expressions that they are not sure of in their own texts, so that teachers can give specific WCF to those student-selected errors that cater to individual needs.

Error Selection That Caters to Student Needs

Above all, in considering the number of error types, what error types should be targeted for focused WCF, etc., a fundamental principle is whether WCF is geared towards individual student needs—that is, whether it is meaningful and manageable for students, referred to as *dynamic WCF* by Evans et al. (2011). To facilitate dynamic WCF, teachers can respond to the most frequent or the most severe error patterns in student writing, based on needs analysis conducted at the beginning of the course, and vary their focused WCF according to individual student needs. When selecting errors for feedback, teachers have to take account of learner characteristics such as age, proficiency level and motivation. In general, younger/less proficient learners merit a different approach to focused WCF than older/more proficient learners, in terms of both the error types and the number of error categories that should be selected for feedback. Student motivation is another crucial factor. When learners are not motivated in the writing classroom, they are less likely to engage with teacher feedback, and therefore a more focused approach that targets a smaller number of error categories may help. Overall, error selection should be based on a student-centered approach so that WCF is more likely to lead to student uptake.

A Middle Position: Combining Comprehensive and Focused WCF

Instead of seeing comprehensive and focused WCF as a dichotomy, teachers can adopt a *middle* position (Ferris, 2010) that combines both approaches. For example, teachers can give comprehensive WCF to a few paragraphs and focused WCF to the rest of the writing, or comprehensive WCF to paragraph writing but focused WCF to essay writing (Evans et al., 2010; Hartshorn & Evans, 2015), or comprehensive WCF to shorter essays but focused WCF to more extended essays. They can give focused WCF to interim drafts, and lead students through comprehensive self-editing in the penultimate or final draft, helping them fix as many errors as they can so as to produce a relatively accurate text in the final stage of writing (Bitchener & Ferris, 2012). Whether teachers adopt comprehensive or focused WCF, or a combined approach, they have to factor their students' needs and proficiency levels into their decision-making (Bitchener & Ferris, 2012).

A combination of focused and comprehensive WCF can be used for diagnostic purposes, too. Teachers can give focused WCF to the majority of the writing tasks but comprehensive WCF to two or three pieces of diagnostic writing tasks administered at different points of the course/academic year (e.g., beginning, middle and end) in order to track students' accuracy development. Through the comprehensive WCF provided to the first piece of writing at the beginning of the course/academic year, teachers can analyze the errors students make (see Table 11.1 for a sample error analysis sheet, adapted from Ferris, 2002), work out the error ratio

TABLE 11.1 An Error Ratio Analysis Sheet

	Error type	*Code*	*Number of errors made*	*Error ratio**	*Error gravity ranking ***
1	Verb (tense & form)	V	3	0.1	4
2	Articles	Art	2	0.07	5
3	Pronoun	Pron	1	0.03	6
4	Word choice	Wc	5	0.17	3
5	Number	Num	7	0.23	1
6	Spelling	Sp	3	0.1	4
7	Prepositions	Prep	6	0.2	2
8	Word form	Wf	1	0.03	6
9	Subject–verb agreement	Agr	2	0.07	5
	Total number of errors		30		

Adapted from Appendix C in Ferris (2002).
*Error ratio = Divide the number of errors in each category by the total errors (i.e., the larger the ratio, the more serious the error).
**Mark "1" for the most serious error type (the largest error ratio), then "2" (the second largest error ratio), "3" (the third largest error ratio) and so on.

(by dividing the number of errors in each error category by the total number of errors) and error gravity for each error type (the higher the error ratio, the more severe the error is), and let students understand their strengths and weaknesses so that they can use such information to monitor their own written accuracy development. The results of error analysis based on the first essay could also be used to guide the focused WCF in subsequent pieces of student writing, both for individual students and the whole class, and can inform grammar instruction as well (e.g., the severest error patterns from the results of error analysis will be prioritized for instruction). Comprehensive WCF provided to the second and/or third diagnostic writing task (at other points of the course/academic year—e.g., middle and end), as well as analysis of student errors (see Table 11.1), will provide further information to help students identify their improvement, if any, and weaknesses for further improvement. One caveat is that since the errors students make in writing may be genre-specific, the error analysis results based on the above diagnostic writing tasks (which may involve different genres) is unlikely to provide a complete picture of students' written accuracy development. Nonetheless, through combining comprehensive and focused WCF, and through using WCF for diagnostic purposes, teachers can integrate assessment with instruction and allow learners to become more aware of their own strengths and weaknesses in written accuracy so that they can better monitor their own writing accuracy development.

Concluding Remarks

For L2 students of lower language proficiency who commit a large number of errors in writing, comprehensive WCF, being extensive and highly unfocused, is not manageable for both teachers and students. Instead of working very hard and responding to errors comprehensively, as in a large number of EAP contexts, it is advisable for teachers to work smarter to incorporate a more focused approach to WCF, and perhaps to combine comprehensive and focused WCF, where appropriate, to benefit student learning. Dynamic WCF as proposed by Evans et al. (2010) and Hartshorn and Evans (2015), in which comprehensive WCF is given to paragraph writing on a regular basis, could be used in addition to focused WCF for longer pieces of writing. Ultimately, the aims of WCF are to maximize students' learning, facilitate uptake and develop them into independent writers capable of self-editing. How these can be achieved through WCF, comprehensive and/or focused, and used with different WCF strategies (e.g., direct, coded, supported by metalinguistic explanation) merits further research attention. Research on focused and unfocused WCF has mainly used the direct WCF strategy, i.e., with correct answers provided for errors, except for the recent study by Frear and Chiu (2015), who explored the effects of focused WCF and unfocused indirect WCF. Findings about the merits of direct and indirect WCF remain inconclusive. Although the benefits of indirect WCF have been recognized by a number of researchers (e.g., Bitchener & Knoch 2010a, 2010b; Ferris 2006; Lalande 1982), recent research has found that direct WCF may be more effective in the long term (Van Beuningen et al., 2008, 2012; Bitchener & Knoch, 2010b), and "preferable if learners are unable to correct their own errors" (Shintani, Ellis, & Watura, 2014, p. 105). While indirect WCF can guide the learners to self-correct the errors, thereby fostering reflection upon their existing knowledge (Bitchener & Ferris, 2012), direct WCF is "more immediate" (Bitchener & Ferris, 2012, p. 65), and provides more explicit information about the errors made. Without conclusive evidence about what WCF strategies should be used with focused and comprehensive WCF, teachers should choose the WCF strategies judiciously and flexibly according to error types and student needs.

In terms of research focus, studies that address focused vis-à-vis comprehensive WCF are worthy of attention. Recent WCF research that demonstrates the benefits of focused WCF has compared a narrowly focused approach to WCF (i.e., one linguistic item) with a more focused approach (i.e., a few linguistic items) (see Ellis et al., 2008; Sheen et al., 2009). Since teachers in many L2 contexts respond to errors comprehensively, what is urgently needed is research that compares the effectiveness of comprehensive and focused WCF, particularly in real classroom contexts.

If such research finds that focused WCF is more effective than comprehensive WCF, or that it produces similar results as comprehensive WCF, then evidence is available to support a selective approach to WCF. However, if research shows that comprehensive WCF is more effective than focused WCF, teachers should continue to embrace this conventional approach. As regards research methodology, with the preponderance of the experimental design in existing WCF research there is a need to broaden our research perspectives to incorporate a focus on naturalistic classroom contexts. Also, ethnographic case study research can be conducted to explore the implementation of focused WCF (e.g., WCF that targets a number of error types, ties in with grammar instruction and caters to student needs) and to investigate how WCF can be implemented systematically over time to benefit student learning in real classroom contexts, as well as what variables influence the efficacy of focused WCF. To produce findings with practical value for L2 learners, more classroom-based research that specifically explores teachers' and students' needs in authentic classroom contexts is needed to answer the host of questions that have hitherto remained unanswered in existing WCF research.

References

Bitchener, J. (2008). Evidence in support of written corrective feedback. *Journal of Second Language Writing, 17*(2), 102–118.

Bitchener, J. (2012). Written corrective feedback for L2 development: Current knowledge and future research. *TESOL Quarterly, 46*(4), 855–860.

Bitchener, J., & Ferris, D. R. (2012). *Written corrective feedback in second language acquisition and writing*. New York: Routledge.

Bitchener, J., & Knoch, U. (2008). The value of written corrective feedback for migrant and international students. *Language Teaching Research, 12*, 409–431.

Bitchener, J., & Knoch, U. (2009a). The relative effectiveness of different types of direct written corrective feedback. *System, 37*(2), 322–329.

Bitchener, J., & Knoch, U. (2009b). The value of a focused approach to written corrective feedback. *ELT Journal, 63*(3), 204–211.

Bitchener, J., & Knoch, U. (2010a). Raising the linguistic accuracy level of advanced L2 writers with written corrective feedback. *Journal of Second Language Writing, 19*(4), 207–217.

Bitchener, J., & Knoch, U. (2010b). The contribution of written corrective feedback to language development: A ten-month investigation. *Applied Linguistics, 31*(2), 193–214.

Burt, M. K. (1975). Error analysis in the adult EFL classroom. *TESOL Quarterly, 9*(1), 53–63.

Chan, A. Y. W. (2010). Toward a taxonomy of written errors: Investigation into the written errors of Hong Kong Cantonese ESL learners. *TESOL Quarterly, 44*(2), 295–319.

Ellis, R. (2005). Principles of instructed language learning. *System, 33*(2), 209–224.

Ellis, R., Loewen, S., & Erlam, R. (2006). Implicit and explicit corrective feedback and the acquisition of L2 grammar. *Studies in Second Language Acquisition, 28*(2), 339–368.

Ellis, R., Sheen, Y., Murakami, M., & Takashima, H. (2008). The effects of focused and unfocused written corrective feedback in an English as a foreign language context. *System, 36*(3), 353–371.

Evans, N. W., Hartshorn, K. J., McCollum, R. M., & Wolfersberger, M. (2010). Contextualizing corrective feedback in second language writing pedagogy. *Language Teaching Research, 14*(4), 445–463.

Evans, N.W., Hartshorn, K.J., & Strong-Krause, D. (2011). The efficacy of dynamic written corrective feedback for university-matriculated ESL learners. *System, 39*, 229–239.

Ferris, D. R. (1999). The case for grammar correction in L2 writing classes: A response to Truscott (1996). *Journal of Second Language Writing, 8*(1), 1–10.

Ferris, D. R. (2002). *Treatment of error in second language student writing*. Ann Arbor: The University of Michigan Press.

Ferris, D. R. (2003). *Response to student writing: Implications for second language students*. Mahwah, NJ: Lawrence Erlbaum Associates.

Ferris, D. R. (2006). Does error feedback help student writers? New evidence on the short- and long-term effects of written error correction. In K. Hyland & F. Hyland (Eds.), *Feedback in second language writing: Contexts and issues* (pp. 81–104). New York: Cambridge University Press.

Ferris, D. R. (2010). Second language writing research and written corrective feedback in SLA: Intersections and practical applications. *Studies in Second Language Acquisition, 32*(2), 181–201.

Ferris, D. R. (2011). *Treatment of error in second language student writing* (2nd ed.). Ann Arbor: The University of Michigan Press.

Ferris, D. R., & Hedgcock, J. (2014). *Teaching L2 composition: Purpose, process, and practice* (3rd ed.). New York: Routledge.

Ferris, D. R., & Helt, M. (2000, March). *Was Truscott right? New evidence on the effects of error correction in L2 writing classes?* Paper presented at the American Association of Applied Linguistics Conference, Vancouver, British Columbia, Canada.

Ferris, D. R., Liu, H., Sinha, A., & Senna, M. (2013). Written corrective feedback for individual L2 writers. *Journal of Second Language Writing, 22*(3), 307–329.

Frear, D., & Chiu, Y. H. (2015). The effect of focused and unfocused indirect written corrective feedback on EFL learners' accuracy in new pieces of writing. *System, 53*(10), 24–34.

Furneaux, C., Paran, A., & Fairfax, B. (2007). Teacher stance as reflected in feedback on student writing: An empirical study of secondary school teachers in five countries. *International Review of Applied Linguistics in Language Teaching, 45*, 69–94.

Hairston, M. (1986). On not being a composition slave. In C.W. Bridges (Ed.), *Training the new teacher of college composition* (pp. 117–124). Urbana, IL: NCTE.

Hartshorn, K.J., & Evans, N.W. (2015). The effects of dynamic written corrective feedback: A 30-week study. *Journal of Response to Writing, 1*(2), 6–34.

Hartshorn, K. J., Evans, N. W., Merrill, P. F., Sudweeks, R. R., Strong-Krause, D., & Anderson, N.J. (2010). Effects of dynamic corrective feedback on ESL writing accuracy. *TESOL Quarterly, 44*(1), 84–109.

Hyland, K., & Hyland, F. (2006). Contexts and issues in feedback on L2 writing: An introduction. In K. Hyland & F. Hyland (Eds.), *Feedback in second language writing: Contexts and issues* (pp. 1–22). New York: Cambridge University Press.

Junqueira, L., & Payant, C. (2015). "I just want to do it right, but it's so hard": A novice teacher's written feedback beliefs and practice. *Journal of Second Language Writing, 27*, 19–36.

Kepner, C. G. (1991). An experiment in the relationship of types of written feedback to the development of second-language writing skills. *The Modern Language Journal, 75*, 305–313.

Lalande, J. F. (1982). Reducing composition errors: An experiment. *The Modern Language Journal, 66*(2), 140–149.
Lee, I. (2004). Error correction in L2 secondary writing classrooms: The case of Hong Kong. *Journal of Second Language Writing, 13*(4), 285–312.
Lee, I. (2005). Error correction in the writing classroom: What do students think? *TESL Canada Journal, 22*(2), 1–16.
Leki, I. (1991). "You cannot ignore": Graduate L2 students' experience of and response to written feedback practices within their disciplines. In K. Hyland & F. Hyland (Eds.), *Feedback in ESL writing: Contexts and issues* (p. 266–285). Cambridge: Cambridge University Press.
Liu, Q., & Brown, D. (2015). A methodological synthesis of research on corrective feedback in L2 writing. *Journal of Second Language Writing, 30*, 66–81.
Lyster, R. (2004). Differential effects of prompts and recasts in form-focused instruction. *Studies in Second Language Acquisition, 26*, 399–432.
Robb, T., Ross, S., & Shortreed, I. (1986). Salience of feedback on error and its effect on EFL writing quality. *TESOL Quarterly, 20*(1), 83–96.
Schmidt, R. (1994), Deconstructing consciousness in search of useful definitions for applied linguistics. *Aila Review, 11*, 11–26.
Semke, H. D. (1984). Effects of the red pen. *Foreign Language Annals, 17*, 195–202.
Sheen, Y. (2007). The effect of focused written corrective feedback and language aptitude on ESL Learners' acquisition of articles. *TESOL Quarterly, 41*(2), 255–283.
Sheen, Y., Wright, D., & Moldawa, A. (2009). Differential effects of focused and unfocused written correction on the accurate use of grammatical forms by adult ESL learners. *System, 37*(4), 556–569.
Sheppard, K. (1992). Two feedback types: Do they make a difference? *RELC Journal, 23*, 103–110.
Shintani, N., Ellis, R., & Suzuki, W. (2014). Effects of written feedback and revision on learners' accuracy in using two English grammatical structures. *Language Learning, 64*(1), 103–131.
Truscott, J. (2001). Selecting errors for selective error correction. *Concentric: Studies in English Literature and Linguistics, 27*(2), 93–108.
Van Beuningen, C. G. (2010). Corrective feedback in L2 writing: Theoretical perspectives, empirical insights, and future directions. *International Journal of English Studies, 10*(2), 1–27.
Van Beuningen, C. G., De Jong, N. H., & Kuiken, F. (2008). The effect of direct and indirect corrective feedback on L2 learner's written accuracy. *International Journal of Applied Linguistics, 156*, 279–296.
Van Beuningen, C. G., De Jong, N. H., & Kuiken, F. (2012). Evidence on the effectiveness of comprehensive error correction in second language writing. *Language Learning, 62*, 1–41.
Zamel, V. (1982). Writing: The process of discovering meaning. *TESOL Quarterly, 16*, 195–209.
Zamel, V. (1985). Responding to student writing. *TESOL Quarterly, 19*(1), 79–101.

PART III

Future Research in EAP

12

THE MULTIFACETED AND SITUATED NATURE OF THE INTERACTION BETWEEN LANGUAGE AND WRITING IN ACADEMIC SETTINGS

Advancing Research Agendas

Rosa M. Manchón

Introduction

This chapter will explore several dimensions of the interaction between language and writing in academic settings through both a retrospective and a forward-looking lens. As such, it builds on and expands the discussion in Manchón (2016), although the present chapter is centrally concerned with the consideration of the multifaceted and situated nature of such interaction, a multidimensional phenomenon with important psycholinguistic, pedagogical, ethical, ideological and socio-political components.

The chapter is structured as follows. I will start with a brief reference to the way in which the linguistic component of L2 academic literacies has featured in recent disciplinary discussions. I will then present a synthesis of key strands of research that have applied diverse lenses to the analysis of the role of language in the learning and teaching of writing in an additional language (L2) in diverse academic contexts (mainly English for academic purposes—EAP henceforth), establishing a basic distinction between research that has focused on texts and research that is concerned with writers. This overview will be followed by a more detailed analysis of significant scholarly contributions centered on writers. This discussion will take stock of past achievements and, as announced in the title of the chapter, will also advance potential avenues to be explored in future research agendas. Although this is not a primarily pedagogically oriented chapter, the concluding section—in line with the general focus and aims of the book—will synthesize the main points covered in the chapter and will highlight the pedagogical implications that may derive from the issues raised and the prospective theoretical and empirical research avenues suggested.

The Linguistic Component of L2 Academic Literacies in Current Disciplinary Discussions

It is widely accepted by all concerned with learning, teaching and researching academic writing, in general, and EAP, in particular, that language is a crucial building block in the acquisition of academic literacies although, as we are also continuously reminded, language is not everything when it comes to developing academic competences in an L2. Certainly, there are many other components that are equally important, as evidenced in different contributions to this collection. However, as I hope to be able to show in the ensuing discussion, these additional components are in one way or another closely linked to language-related considerations. This can help explain why the exploration of the diverse facets of the linguistic component of academic literacies has occupied and still occupies center stage in diverse, and at times disconnected, strands of research on academic writing, in addition to being a most relevant pedagogical preoccupation.

Focusing just on developments taking place in the last few years, there has been a proliferation of collective volumes in the form of edited books and special issues in flagship journals that collectively attest to this disciplinary interest, evidencing at the same time the multidimensional and situated nature of the phenomenon in focus. Some of these dimensions are closely linked to language policy considerations, as explored in a substantial number of papers and special issues in various journals. For instance, Cots, Llurda and Garrett's (2014) guest-edited monograph on *Language Policies and Practices in the Internationalisation of Higher Education on the European Margins* contains a number of contributions that collectively look into language policies and practices as connected with *internationalization*, a most relevant concern in many parts of the world, and certainly in the European context: across Europe we are immersed in intense and demanding processes of internationalization of research, institutions, evaluation procedures in research-funding programs and, importantly, internationalization of people's academic profiles. This internationalization movement—ever present in our professional lives and practices in the Spanish context as well—systematically brings with it important language-related implications and challenges for policy makers, institutions and peoples.

One of these implications, and one that has occupied many pages in scholarly debates and publications, is the focus of Maria Kuteeva and Anna Mauranen's (2014) recent guest-edited issue on writing for publication in multilingual contexts. This collective work contains a number of most illuminating, critical, thought-provoking and ideologically committed papers on language use (interestingly, including both English and other languages) in the research and publishing practices of scholars working outside the English-speaking world, mostly in Europe.

The challenges faced by scholars taking part in these internationalization movements, in general, and in publishing in an additional language, in particular, have also received book-length treatments. Two recent representative examples are Ramona Tang's (2012a) edited collection, *Academic Writing in a Second or Foreign Language: Issues and Challenges Facing ESL/EFL Academic Writers in Higher Education Contexts*, and Lucia Thesen and Linda Cooper's (2014) edited book with the very telling title of *Risk in Academic Writing: Postgraduate Students, Their Teachers and the Making of Knowledge*. One of the risks, or causes of risks, discussed in Thesen and Cooper's book is language-related because, as the editors state, the internationalization of higher education brings with it issues of language choice and language use, with concomitant implications for issues of writer's agency and identity. In effect, these language, agency and identity considerations are relevant not only in the case of students undertaking language for academic purposes courses (the population in focus in this book), but also in the case of more seasoned academics, a facet of the interaction between language and L2 writing that has been also critically scrutinized in Hyland's (2015) recent book *Academic Publishing: Issues and Challenges in the Construction of Knowledge*, which I shall revisit towards the end of the chapter.

Other publications have shifted the lens from these relevant policy-related, educational, ideological and socio-political dimensions of the interaction between language and writing. As examples, two recent special issues published in the *Journal of Second Language Writing* have taken a more linguistic orientation, in this case looking into the linguistic component of academic literacies from the perspective of text analysis, evaluation and assessment (Connor-Linton & Polio, 2014; Vyatkina, 2015).

Finally, language-related concerns are also focused on in a body of publications that have adopted a completely different perspective, this time reverting the direction of the relationship; instead of reflecting on how language affects writers and writing in an L2, the spotlight is directed at the manner in which writing itself may have an effect on language, which means looking into the way in which writing may contribute to L2 learning. This is a more psycholinguistic, second language acquisition (SLA)-oriented strand, well represented in a special issue published in the *JSLW* in 2012 on SLA-L2 writing interfaces in which leading SLA-oriented L2 writing specialists collectively reflected on the theoretical foundations of and provided empirical evidence on the language learning potential of the very act of writing and of feedback processing. Along the same lines, a number of books that have seen the light of day in the last few years attest to this growing scholarly interest in what I have termed the writing-to-learn-language (WLL) dimension of L2 writing (Manchón, 2011a, 2014 and elsewhere). These publications include books on feedback (Bitchener & Ferris, 2012; Bitchener & Storch, 2016), collaborative writing (Storch, 2013), writing development (Manchón, 2012) and tasks and writing (Byrnes & Manchón, 2014a). Although a rather recent addition to disciplinary debates, there are clear indications that analyses and explorations of the WLL dimension of L2 writing in diverse instructional settings have become central to the field.

Notably, these various examples of recent publications provide convincing evidence that the interaction between language and writing is a timely issue and it is indeed a multifaceted phenomenon that has been and should continue being explored from a myriad of angles to be able to account satisfactorily for its linguistic, psycholinguistic, pedagogical, ethical, ideological and socio-political components. However, and rather crucially, not all these facets and dimensions are equally relevant or manifest themselves in identical manner across academic contexts, geographical locations, writers and genres, hence the need to adopt a socially situated stance in theoretical and empirical research.

Key Issues of Debate: Research on Texts and Writers

In Manchón (2016) I reviewed several well-established strands of research that have applied diverse lenses to the analysis of the role of language in the learning and teaching of EAP by both international students (mostly in university contexts) and multilingual scholars from a wide range of disciplines. Collectively considered, as shown in Figure 12.1, research efforts can be conveniently grouped into those that have centered on texts and those that have looked at writers.

Text-oriented scholarship has applied different lenses to the study of the characteristics of L2 writers' texts and their development (Manchón, 2012; Polio & Park, 2016; and several other contributions to Manchón & Matsuda, 2016), while it has also heavily engaged in linguistic explorations of academic discourses and research genres (cf. Gray, 2015; Hyland, 2005, 2009, 2012; Murata, 2015; Plo Alastrué & Pérez-Llantada, 2015 for representative recent examples). As noted in Manchón (2016), the research in the area is rich in the theoretical perspectives informing it, including, but not limited to, Systemic Functional Linguistics (cf. Byrnes, 2013; Hood, 2016), intercultural rhetoric (Connor, Ene, & Traversa, 2016), genre analysis (Shaw, 2016), theories of multicompetence (cf. Kobayashi & Rinnert, 2012;

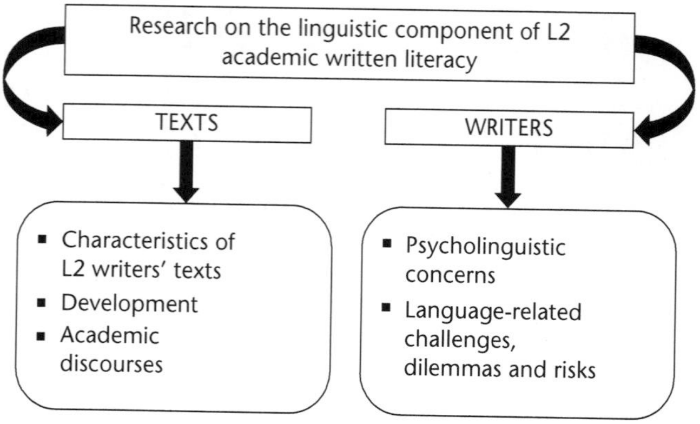

FIGURE 12.1 Key dimensions of research on the linguistic component of L2 academic written literacy

Rinnert & Kobayashi, 2016), multimodal approaches (O'Halloran, Tan, & Smith, 2016) or Complex Dynamics Systems (cf. Polio & Park, 2016). Importantly for the advancement of research agendas, these diverse theoretical and empirical works on L2 writers' texts and their development, genres and academic discourses have been complemented with critical methodological reflections and proposals on how to best measure linguistic performance and progress in writing (see Polio & Freedman, 2017, for the most comprehensive treatment of methodological considerations in L2 writing research to date). This is a research preoccupation that was initiated with the publication of Wolfe-Quintero, Inagaki and Kim's (1998) seminal book, and one that continues to raise abundant interest at both global and specific levels. One example of the former would be Norris and Manchón's (2012) critical account of methodological considerations of research on diverse facets of writing development. Representative examples of the latter would include Laif's (2009) analysis of fluency, Polio and Shea's (2014) and Evans, Hartshorn, Cox and de Jel's (2014) reflections on linguistic accuracy, Biber, Gray and Poonpon (2011) and Lu (2011) on grammatical complexity, and Vyatkina's (2015) guest-edited volume on complexity. Readers are referred to these publications for a wealth of well-founded principles that ought to guide future research endeavors.

The study of the connection language and writing has also been undertaken from the perspective of writers. Such connection has been explored from two main perspectives: one is psycholinguistic in its foundation and orientation, and the other is more socio-political and ideological in nature. As shown in Figure 12.2, several influential research strands can be identified in each of these two broad research domains. Thus, psycholinguistic approaches have resulted in cognitively oriented theoretical and empirical analyses of (i) the interplay

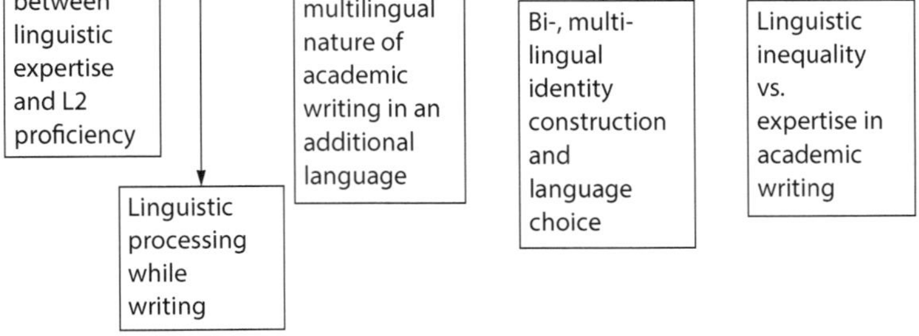

FIGURE 12.2 Research on the linguistic component of L2 academic written literacy (focus on writers)

between writing expertise and language proficiency (a perennial preoccupation in L2 writing studies) and (ii) the linguistic processing that takes place while writing and while making use of feedback (a line of research to be further elaborated below), together with (iii) the multilingual nature of the act of writing in an additional language (see Manchón, 2013; Roca de Larios, Coyle & Nicolás-Conesa, 2016 for syntheses of research in these three domains). Also focusing on writers are various lines of inquiry that have collective explored language-related challenges, dilemmas and risks faced by L2 academic writers. A particularly important research preoccupation in this domain concerns issues of identity and ideology experienced by multilingual writers when exercising their language choices. Another relevant direction in this research domain is represented by the ongoing debates on the once denounced linguistic inequality/disadvantage of additional language writers, especially publishing academics, recently referred to by Hyland as the *linguistic advantage orthodoxy* (Hyland, 2015, 2016). I shall return to this *orthodoxy* shortly.

The next section offers further elaboration of some areas of interest in these broad research domains. The choice is partly motivated by the fact that debates in these areas are closely bound to my own research interests and trajectory, as well as to my professional practices, experiences and concerns. Importantly, however, the chosen areas for the analysis cover a whole range of profiles of L2 writers/learners/users, and certainly those identified in the following description (Mauranen, Hynninen, & Ranta, 2016):

> Higher education across the world is being permeated by English, but a very small share falls onto its native speakers. The overwhelming majority of the world's students are speakers of other languages, but ever larger proportions among them will carry out some or all their university studies in English. If we think of those who read textbooks, listen to lectures, present in seminars, pass examinations and write their theses and dissertations in English, it may seem natural to perceive them as learners of English while they are also learners of academic skills. But if we turn to those who participate in conferences, lecture at universities, review papers, examine doctorates, review promotions and appoint professors, it becomes much harder to assign the role of permanent language learners to them. (p. 52)

The psycholinguistic-oriented research strand included in Figure 12.2 has shed light mainly, although not solely, on the former group, namely, those acquiring concurrently language and academic skills in instructional setting. Incidentally, this group of academic writers have also featured in numerous other lines of research (see Ferris, 2016), including educational and policy-oriented lines of inquiry. As we will see next, central questions in research agendas in the psycholinguistic domain inquire about whether or not there is a synergy between language and writing in the sense of whether or not the process of learning to write and engaging in academic writing and feedback processing results in tangible language learning outcomes. In contrast, discussions of language challenges, risks and dilemmas (the second main research direction in Figure 12.2) are more centered on the latter group, that is, on those L2 users who, by choice and/or as a result of institutional/professional requirements, routinely develop their professional careers and engage in disciplinary practices in an additional language. These practices include meeting their publishing institutional requirements, and it is precisely here where Hyland's already mentioned native speaker linguistic advantage orthodoxy becomes relevant in the analysis.

Psycholinguistic Accounts of the Interaction between Language and Writing: Past Achievements and Future Directions

An important psycholinguistically oriented research preoccupation on the interaction between language and writing with a long tradition in L2 writing studies is the inquiry into the linguistic processing that takes place during writing and the range of potentially mediating writer-internal and writer-external variables. Research interests in this domain have evolved considerably over the years. Initial preoccupations in this domain were heavily influenced by research on writing processes in L1 writing (see review in Roca de Larios et al., 2016) and had a strong theoretical orientation. In essence, their ultimate aim was to shed light on the distinctive nature of cognitive activity in the act of writing in an additional language. An important preoccupation was to ascertain the architecture of the process of formulation, the central composing process concerned with transforming ideational concerns into language. The abundant body of empirical knowledge on writing process accumulated over the years (see reviews in Manchón, 2013; Roca de Larios et al., 2016) did represent a contribution both to writing studies and, indirectly, to language cognitive processing and processes more generally (although this was not readily evident to the research community until some time later). Importantly for our present purposes, early studies of writing processes provided robust empirical evidence of the intense linguistic activity that characterizes writing in an additional language and, accordingly, of the theoretical and applied relevance of examining the allocation of attentional resources to language-related concerns (see Manchón, Roca de Larios, & Murphy, 2009; Schoonen, Snellings, Stevenson, & Van Gelderen, 2009).

L2 writing and SLA interests have only recently converged in a new research avenue, centrally concerned with how and why this empirically documented intense linguistic processing that takes place while writing (more recently expanded to include both the act of writing itself and the processing of feedback) may lead to L2 learning. Research efforts in this area have progressed in two main directions. On the one hand, there exist (i) comprehensive treatments of the theoretical foundations of the language learning potential that may derive from the linguistic processing associated with writing and feedback, and (ii) thorough reviews of the empirical research to date, often coupled with critical proposals on how to move research in the area forward (Bitchener, 2012; Bitchener & Storch, 2016; Byrnes & Manchón, 2014b; Gilabert, Manchón & Vasylets, 2016; Manchón, 2011a, 2014; Manchón & Roca de Larios, 2007; Manchón & Williams, 2016; Ortega, 2012; Polio, 2012; Roca de Larios, 2013; Williams, 2012).

On the other hand, a growing body of SLA-oriented studies have gradually expanded knowledge within this research domain with empirical evidence on how L2 writing may lead to language learning. Research preoccupations have gradually diversified to include explorations of writing from the perspective of (i) language processing in different conditions (individual and collaborative writing) and environments (pen-and-paper and computer-mediated writing) and (ii) task-related issues, including task complexity, task repetition and task modality effects (see Manchón, 2011a, 2014; Manchón & Williams, 2016 for state-of-the-art accounts of this global research). The second main direction undertaken in empirical research, and one that is expanding at an incredible speed, is centrally concerned with feedback processing, as recently and thoroughly reviewed by Bitchener and Storch (2016).

Progress has certainly been made although there are important avenues worth exploring in future research agendas, all of them somewhat permeated by two research preoccupations (see Bitchener & Storch, 2016; Manchón & Williams, 2016). One relates to a central concern in SLA research: the development, expansion, consolidation and use of explicit and implicit knowledge in the domain of writing. The other research preoccupation concerns the nature of cognitive processes and processing both while writing and while engaged in feedback processing. The potential contribution of feedback to language learning represents a line of inquiry into *feedback for acquisition*, which contrasts with the traditional interest in *feedback for accuracy* in L2 writing studies (Manchón, 2011b). Key empirical questions here relate to the very nature of the processing itself (with concerns about noticing processes being central in the inquiry), the nature and extent of the potential short-term and longer-term language learning effects, and, importantly, the influence of feedback-related and learner-related variables in such processing and potential learning outcomes. These future avenues are thoroughly examined in Bitchener and Storch (2016), who succinctly summarize central concerns in future cognitively oriented research agendas as follows:

> Until recently, little attention has been given to investigations of the information processing that occurs from written CF [corrective feedback] input to modified output […]. It is this line of inquiry that will reveal at which points along the information processing continuum from input to output a learner's conscious processing and hypothesizing successfully moves from one stage to another or breaks down at one of the stages. (p. 66)

And they add something crucially important from both theoretical and applied perspectives:

> While the research to date has shown that written CF, as explicit input, has the potential, under certain conditions at least, to help learners develop their L2 explicit knowledge through consciously attending to the information it supplied and use it accurately on subsequent occasions, less is known empirically about why learners are able to progress (or fail to progress) from one stage of processing to another and how individual and contextual factors may moderate the processing of written CF input. (p. 66)

Hence, their recommendation for feedback research to explore, *inter alia*, (i) the theoretically and pedagogically relevant issue of the "moderating effect on both cognitive and non-cognitive factors/variables on a leaner's response to cognitive processing of and use of written CF in revised and new pieces of writing" (p. 128), and (ii) the theoretically motivated, although less pedagogically relevant, question of the use of explicit and/or implicit knowledge when producing *accurate output* after processing feedback, as well as the role that providing and processing written corrective feedback may have in converting explicit knowledge into implicit knowledge.

Language-Related Challenges, Dilemmas and Risks Experienced by L2 Writers in Academic Settings: Past Achievements and Future Directions

The last stream of research to be covered in the chapter is concerned with the language-related challenges, dilemmas and risks experienced by L2 writers in EAP settings. Two areas intensively scrutinized in EAP theory and research have been chosen for further analysis: language choice, ideology and identity construction, on the one hand, and linguistic inequality, on the other. Together, they serve to exemplify additional facets of interaction between language and writing.

Language Choice, Ideology and Identity Construction

A growing number of studies have delved into aspects of multilinguals' ideology and identity construction as multi-competent language users and how this applies to linguistic choices and language practices. This research has provided rich accounts of the way in which multilingual users exert their agency when balancing demands for using and/or publishing in the various languages that form their linguistic repertoire, as well as the multiple forces that shape their language choice and language practices.

A most illuminating study in this direction is Gentil and Séror's (2014) personal reflection of their *biliteracy development* and *bilingual publication practices*.

Particularly revealing are their observations about what motivates and has motivated their "individual language choices as scholars" (p. 19) and, very importantly, their gradual "commitment to academic biliteracy" (p. 22) and to the dissemination of knowledge in their various languages as a question of "identity and linguistic loyalty" (p. 26). Importantly for our purposes, the choices and bilingual practices and commitments to academic biliteracy reported in the paper occurred in a context in which there has been "continued governmental support in creating enabling contexts for biliteracy" (p. 17). This situation is in sharp contrast with what is the norm in many other contexts and geographical locales, where research shows that language choice by multilingual scholars is much more pragmatically than ideologically determined (Bocanegra-Valle, 2014; McGrath, 2014); hence the need to consider the socially situated nature of the motivations behind multilingual users' building of their professional identities and they way in which they balance their language choices. In fact, what more evidently appears to be the result of an ideological stance is not so much whether or not to publish in an additional language (overwhelmingly English), but rather whether or not to publish in one's local language, as evidenced, for example, in McGrath's (2014) study of Swedish academics in the fields of history, anthropology and linguistics.

Disciplinary and generational considerations also come into play. Discipline-specific idiosyncrasies are very relevant, at least in the European context, and certainly extremely relevant in the Spanish context. For instance, regarding research funding policies, strong criticisms have been raised against guiding funding policies solely on a kind of *research imperialism*, whereby research output and trajectories by academics in all disciplines in the humanities and social sciences are assessed uniformly, thus disregarding knowledge construction policies across disciplines and fields of study. Perhaps future research agendas ought to make room for critical explorations of how those in leading and gatekeeping positions in funding agencies envisage and negotiate the interaction between language and academic writing, a very important dimension of the language component of academic literacies. Certainly in our context we would welcome governmental and institutional support in enabling those *contexts for biliteracy* mentioned by Gentil and Séror (2014). This support is a central component of the Declaration on a Nordic Language Policy with its promotion of parallel language use of English and the main Nordic languages of Europe.

Generational issues are no less important worldwide and certainly in our context as a result of the structure of professional networks. In a nutshell, progressively, research in the humanities has moved from being an individual enterprise to being a question of teamwork. In Spain, research teams carry out their research within the framework of publicly funded research projects, with funding being based on a peer review assessment of the research proposal itself, as well as the research team's trajectory and achievements. Of special relevance are the merits of the head researcher, who is extremely limited in the choices he or she can make in the professional options to take, directions to follow in his/her research career and languages to use in his/her publications. In essence, it means publish, publish and publish, and do it in English. Head researchers therefore feel the responsibility towards the junior and less experienced members of their team, and language choice for them is in part motivated by a professional, mentoring commitment to others. Needless to say, as publishing scholars their language choices are also pragmatically determined. Young scholars in research teams have even less of a choice as their promotion heavily depends on their building of an *international* research track record. In short, language choice and identity construction are seriously constrained in many disciplinary settings and locations. This explains why Hyland (2015) concludes that "attitudes and practices are more complex and multidimensional than the literature might suggest" (p. 52). How and why this is so should continue featuring as a prominent direction in future research explorations of the linguistic component of academic literacies.

Multilingual Writers' Linguistic Challenges and Risks: The Native Speaker Advantage Orthodoxy

As mentioned at the beginning of the chapter, research on academic writing has resulted in intense debates and abundant empirical studies focused on (i) the challenges and risks faced by L2 writers in their attempts to become part of given communities of practice, and (ii) how and why language-related concerns help or hinder L2 users' academic and/or professional success. Importantly, recent debates have helped to challenge the one almost legitimized *deficit* view of EAP writers. Two important developments have been influential in disrupting some ways of categorizing multilingual writers that have dominated past discourses. One is concerned with ascertaining the linguistic and cultural capital that multilingual writers bring with them to their literacy experiences in an additional language (see Chang & Kanno, 2010; Tang, 2012b; see also treatment in Hyland, 2015), and the other important development is the relevance accorded to *expertise*, rather than *nativeness* (Flowerdew, 2013), when considering multilingual writers' literacy acquisition and practices.

The issue of expertise vs. nativeness is central in Hyland's criticism of the *linguistic advantage orthodoxy* announced in earlier sections (Hyland, 2015, 2016). The essence of his position is that "writing for publication is a specialized competence which both Native and non-Native speakers must acquire, a fact that is obscured by two key assumptions of the linguistic disadvantage orthodoxy" (Hyland, 2016, p. 61). These two assumptions are the native–non-native speaker (NS-NNS) divide, on the one hand, and the primacy of language, on the other. As for the NS-NNS divide, Hyland reminds us that

> Academic writing is no one's first language. In fact, "native-speakerhood" refers more accurately to the acquisition of syntactic and phonological knowledge as a result of early childhood socialization and not to the

> acquisition of writing, which requires prolonged formal education. (Hyland, 2015, p. 57).

Hence, Hyland goes on to argue, being a native speaker per se (i.e., without the necessary investment, training and experience), does not guarantee possession of the "necessary know-how and experience to produce publishable papers" (Hyland, 2016, pp. 61–62), whereas experience and training can potentially make L2 users "academically bilingual" (p. 62). Accordingly, he concludes that

> framing publication problems as a crude Native vs. non-Native polarization not only draws on an outmoded respect for "Native speaker" competence but serves to demoralizes EAL writers and marginalize the difficulties experienced by novice L1 English academics. (Hyland, 2016, p. 63)

As he claims, "it seems fairly clear that native-speakerhood confers few advantages when submitting a paper for publication" (2015, p. 63).

As for the *primacy of language*, his main argument is that publication success is closely dependent on a whole range of interacting individual and social factors, and so "degree of training and experience in scientific writing, geographical location, or even number and type of collaborators [...] may be more powerful determinants of publication success regardless of linguistic background" (Hyland, 2015, p. 58). Publishing opportunities may also be constrained by lack of access to professional networks (Lillis & Curry, 2010), or limited access to resources and rhetorical models (Hyland, 2016).

Concluding Remarks

This chapter has attempted a general overview of research strands collectively concerned with diverse facets of the interaction between language and writing in academic settings. It is hoped that the preceding review provides convincing evidence of the multidimensional and socially situated intrinsic character of the linguistic component of academic literacy, such multidimensionality including psycholinguistic, pedagogical, ethical, ideological and socio-political components.

Explorations of language and writing from the psycholinguistic perspective of the language learning potential of writing and feedback processing have gained momentum and they are likely to represent a key development in future explorations of the linguistic component of academic literacies. The research agenda in this domain is rich in empirical questions awaiting an answer, especially those concerned with the connection between language processing and language development in the domain of writing. Interest in the analysis of this connection in relation to feedback processing has grown exponentially in the last few years and this trend is likely to continue in the years to come.

An important pedagogical implication of past and future research in the area relates to decision-making processes by writing instructors as to when to prioritize and how to balance the writing-to-learn language and/or the learning-to-write dimension in the academic writing classroom. In this respect, I feel the distinction between promoting and providing *feedback for accuracy* or *feedback for acquisition* is still a pedagogically valid and relevant one. Equally relevant from a pedagogical angle are questions related to the way in which language abilities influence writing practices. In this sense, Manchón and Williams (2016) suggest:

> Basically, the question for future studies is the following: even if there were clear conclusions about the effect of proficiency on text quality and writing processes, what would the implications for pedagogy be? For example, if writers can focus more on higher-order thinking skills once they have achieved a higher level of linguistic proficiency, does that mean that we should withhold writing instruction until they reach this level of proficiency? Additionally, it is also pedagogically relevant to know when learners of different levels might benefit from different types of writing activities. Importantly too, future basic and applied SLA-oriented L2 writing research needs to explore how L2 proficiency and L2 writing expertise develop and interact in those contexts in which instructed learners (especially pre-university L2 users in foreign language settings) are simultaneously developing writing abilities in all the languages of their educational program (i.e. their L1 and all the L2s that may form part of their school curriculum) and their L2 general proficiency. (p. 580)

From a completely different angle, the research reviewed in this chapter makes evident that the interaction between language and writing possesses important additional ideological, socio-political, pedagogical and ethical dimensions. Future research needs to shed much further light on the range of factors that govern linguistic choices by diverse groups of academic writers, at different stages in the career trajectories, in different disciplines, in monolingual and bilingual settings and in different geographical locations. Future research agendas will surely maintain a crucial interest in the way in which multilingual writers balance their language demands and choices and purposefully invest in developing their expertise in their professional practices within disciplinary communities characterized by an increasing transnational character.

The applied implications of past and future research efforts in this domain are varied. One that I find particularly important is the need to balance pragmatic issues and socio-political issues when planning and implementing academic writing instructional policies and practices in ecologically valid ways. In this respect, and admittedly being very much influenced by my own biography, teaching history and professional practices (including those of head researcher of a research team, past journal and book series editor, and member of editorial boards,

PhD committees and evaluation committees in governmental research funding agencies), I would suggest that it is highly questionable whether it is legitimate to prioritize challenging or resisting hegemonic discourses in certain contexts. An important pedagogical implication would therefore be to take principled and socially sensitive decisions as to whether to prioritize and/or balance the acquisition of functional literacies rather than/in addition to ideological literacies in diverse and distinct EAP contexts.

References

Biber, D., Gray, B., & Poonpon, K. (2011). Should we use characteristics of conversation to measure grammatical complexity in L2 writing development? *TESOL Quarterly, 45*, 5–35.

Bitchener, J. (2012). A reflection on "the language learning potential" of written CF. *Journal of Second Language Writing, 22*, 348–363.

Bitchener, J., & Ferris, D. (2012). *Written corrective feedback in second language acquisition and writing*. New York: Routledge/Taylor & Francis.

Bitchener, J., & Storch N. (2016). *Written corrective feedback for L2 development*. Bristol, UK: Multilingual Matters.

Bocanegra-Valle, A. (2014). "English is my default language": Vices from LSP scholars publishing in a multilingual journal. *Journal of English for Academic Purposes, 13*, 65–77.

Byrnes, H. (2013). Positioning writing as meaning-making in writing research: An introduction. *Journal of Second Language Writing, 2*(22), 95–106.

Byrnes, H., & Manchón, R. M. (Eds.) (2014a). *Task-based language learning—insights from and for L2 writing*. Amsterdam: John Benjamins.

Byrnes, H., & Manchón, R. M. (2014b). Task, task performance, and writing development: Advancing the constructs and the research agenda. In H. Byrnes & R. M. Manchón (Eds.), *Task-based language learning—insights from and for L2 writing* (pp. 267–299). Amsterdam: John Benjamins.

Chang, Y-J., & Kanno, Y. (2010). NNES doctoral students in English-speaking academe: The nexus between language and discipline. *Applied Linguistics, 31*, 671–692.

Connor, U., Ene. E., & Traversa, A. (2016). Intercultural rhetoric. In K. Hyland & P. Shaw (Eds.), *The Routledge handbook of English for academic purposes* (pp. 270–282). New York: Routledge.

Connor-Linton, J., & Polio, C. (2014). Comparing perspectives on L2 writing: Multiple analyses of a common corpus. *Journal of Second Language Writing, 26*, 1–9.

Cots, J. M., Llurda, E., & Garrett, P. (Eds.) (2014). Language policies and practices in the internationalisation of higher education on the European margins: An introduction. *Journal of Multilingual and Multicultural Development, 35*(4), 311–317.

Evans, N. W., Hartshorn, K. J., Cox, T. L., & de Jel, T. M. (2014). Measuring written linguistic accuracy with weighted clause ratios: A question of validity. *Journal of Second Language Writing, 24*, 33–50.

Ferris, D. (2016). Writers in higher education. In R. M. Manchón & P. K. Matsuda (eds.), *The handbook of second and foreign language writing* (pp. 141–160). Boston/Berlin: de Gruyter.

Flowerdew, J. (2013). English for research publication purposes. In B. Paltridge & S. Starfield (Eds.), *The handbook of English for specific purposes* (pp. 301–321). Malden, MA: Wiley-Blackwell.

Gentil, G., & Séror, J. (2014). Canada has two official languages—Or does it? Case studies of Canadian scholars' language choices and practices in disseminating knowledge. *Journal of English for Academic Purposes, 13*, 17–30.

Gilabert, R., Manchón, R. M., & Vasylets, O. (2016). Mode in theoretical and empirical TBLT research: Advancing research agendas. *Annual Review of Applied Linguistics, 36*, 117–135.

Gray, B. (2015). *Linguistic variation in research articles.* Amsterdam: John Benjamins.

Hood, S. (2016). Systemic functional linguistics and EAP. In K. Hyland & P. Shaw (Eds.), *The Routledge handbook of English for academic purposes* (pp. 193–205). New York: Routledge.

Hyland, K. (2005). *Metadiscourse: Exploring interaction in writing.* London: Continuum.

Hyland, K. (2009). *Academic discourse.* London: Continuum.

Hyland, K. (2012). *Disciplinary identities: Individuality and community in academic discourse.* Cambridge: CUP.

Hyland, K. (2015). *Academic publishing: Issues and challenges in the construction of knowledge.* Oxford: OUP.

Hyland, K. (2016). Academic publishing and the myth of linguistic injustice. *Journal of Second Language Writing, 31*, 58–69.

Kobayashi, H., & Rinnert, C. (2012). Understanding L2 writing development from a multicompetence perspective: Dynamic repertoires of knowledge and text construction. In R. M. Manchón (Ed.), *L2 writing development: multiple perspectives* (pp. 101–134). Berlin: De Gruyter Mouton.

Kuteeva, M., & Mauranen, A. (2014). Writing for publication in multilingual contexts. *Journal of English for Academic Purposes, 13*, 1–4.

Laif, M. (2009). Toward a new process-based indicator for measuring writing fluency: Evidence from L2 writers' think-aloud protocols. *The Canadian Modern Language Review, 65*, 531–558.

Lillis, T., & Curry, M. J. (2010). *Academic writing in a global context: The politics and practices of publishing in English.* New York: Routledge.

Lu, X. (2011). A corpus-based evaluation of syntactic complexity measures as indices of college-level ESL writers' language development. *TESOL Quarterly, 45*, 36–62.

Manchón, R. M. (ed.) (2011a). *Learning-to-write and writing-to-learn in an additional language.* Amsterdam/Philadelphia: John Benjamins.

Manchón, R. M. (2011b). The language learning potential of writing in foreign language contexts. In Me. Reichelt & T. Chimasko (Eds.), *Foreign language writing: Research insights* (pp. 44–64). West Lafayette, IN: Parlor Press.

Manchón, R. M. (Ed.) (2012). *L2 writing development: multiple perspectives.* Berlin/Boston: De Gruyter Mouton.

Manchón, R. M. (2013). Writing. In F. Grosjean & L. Ping (Eds.), *The psycholinguistics of bilingualism* (pp. 100–115). Malden, MA: Wiley-Blackwell.

Manchón, R. M. (2014). The internal dimension of tasks: The interaction between task factors and learner factors in bringing about learning through writing. In H. Byrnes & R. M. Manchón (Eds.), *Task-based language learning: Insights from and for L2 writing* (pp. 27–53). Amsterdam: John Benjamins.

Manchón, R. M. (2016). Language and L2 writing: Learning to write and writing to learn in academic contexts. In K. Hyland & P. Shaw (Eds.), *The Routledge handbook of English for academic purposes* (pp. 139–151). New York: Routledge.

Manchón, R. M. & Matsuda, P. K. (Eds.) (2016). *The handbook of second and foreign language writing.* Berlin/Boston: De Gruyter Mouton.

Manchón, R. M., & Roca de Larios, J. (2007). Writing-to-learn in instructed language contexts. In E. Alcón & P. Safont (Eds.), *The intercultural speaker: Using and acquiring English in instructed language contexts* (pp. 101–121). Dordrecht: Springer-Verlag.

Manchón, R. M., Roca de Larios, J., & Murphy, L. (2009). The temporal dimension and problem-solving nature of foreign language composing processes. In R. M. Manchón (Ed.), *Writing in foreign language contexts: Learning, teaching, and research* (pp. 102–129). Bristol, UK: Multilingual Matters.

Manchón, R. M., & Williams, J. (2016). L2 writing and SLA studies. In R. M. Manchón & P. K. Matsuda (Eds.), *The handbook of second and foreign language writing* (pp. 567–586). Boston/Berlin: de Gruyter.

Mauranen, A., Hynninen, N., & Ranta, E. (2016). English as the academic Lingua Franca. In K. Hyland & P. Shaw (Eds.), *The Routledge handbook of English for academic purposes* (pp. 44–55). New York: Routledge.

McGrath, L. (2014). Parallel language use in academic and outreach publication: A case study of policy and practice. *Journal of English for Academic Purposes, 13*, 5–16.

Murata, K. (Ed.) (2015). *Exploring EFL in Japanese academic and business contexts: Conceptualization, research and pedagogical Implications*. New York: Routledge.

Norris, J., & Manchón, R. M. (2012). Investigating L2 writing development from multiple perspectives: Issues in theory and research. In R. M. Manchón (Ed.), *L2 writing development: Multiple perspectives* (pp. 221–244). Boston: de Gruyter Mouton.

O'Halloran, K., Tan, S., & Smith, B. A. (2016). Multimodal approaches to English for academic purposes. In K. Hyland & P. Shaw (Eds.), *The Routledge handbook of English for academic purposes* (pp. 256–269). New York: Routledge.

Ortega, L. (2012). Epilogue: Exploring L2 writing–SLA interfaces. *Journal of Second Language Writing, 21*, 404–415.

Plo Alastrué, R., & Pérez-Llantada, C. (Eds.) (2015). *English as a scientific and research language*. Berlin: De Gruyter Mouton.

Polio, C. (2012). The relevance of second language acquisition theory to the written error correction controversy. *Journal of Second Language Writing, 21*, 375–389.

Polio, C., & Freedman, D. (2017). *Understanding, evaluating and conducting second language writing research*. New York: Routledge/Taylor & Francis.

Polio, C., & Park, J.-H. (2016). Language development in second language writing. In R. M. Manchón & P. K. Matsuda (Eds.), *The handbook of second and foreign language writing*. (pp. 287–306). Berlin: De Gruyter Mouton.

Polio, C., & Shea, M. (2014). An investigation into current measures of linguistic accuracy in second language writing research. *Journal of Second Language Writing, 26*(4), 10–27.

Rinnert, C., & Kobayashi, H. (2016). Multicompetence and multilingual writing. In R. M. Manchón & P. K. Matsuda (Eds.), *The handbook of second and foreign language writing* (pp. 365–386). Berlin: De Gruyter Mouton.

Roca de Larios, J. (2013). Second language writing as a psycholinguistic locus for L2 production and learning. *Journal of Second Language Writing, 22*(4), 444–445.

Roca de Larios, J., Coyle, Y., & Nicolás-Conesa, F. (2016). Focus on writers: Processes and strategies. In R. M. Manchón & P. K. Matsuda (Eds.), *The handbook of second and foreign language writing*. (pp. 267–286). Berlin: De Gruyter Mouton.

Schoonen, R., Snellings, P., Stevenson, M., & Van Gelderen, A. (2009). Towards a blueprint of the foreign language writer: The linguistic and cognitive demands of foreign language writing. In R. M. Manchón (Ed.), *Writing in foreign language contexts: Learning, teaching, and research* (pp. 77–101). Clevedon, UK: Multilingual Matters.

Shaw, P. (2016). Genre analysis. In K. Hyland & P. Shaw (eds.), *The Routledge handbook of English for academic purposes* (pp. 243–255). New York: Routledge.

Storch, N. (2013). *Collaborative writing in L2 classrooms*. Bristol: Multilingual Matters.

Tang, R. (Ed.) (2012a). *Academic writing in a second or foreign language: Issues and challenges facing ESL/EFL academic writers in higher education contexts*. London: Continuum.

Tang, R. (2012b). Two sides of the same coin: Challenges and opportunities for scholars from EFL backgrounds. In R. Tang (Ed.), *Academic writing in a second or foreign language: Issues and challenges facing ESL/EFL academic writers in higher education Contexts* (pp. 204–232). London: Continuum.

Thesen, L., & Cooper, L. (Eds.) (2014). *Risk in academic writing: Postgraduate students, their teachers and the making of knowledge*. Bristol, UK: Multilingual Matters.

Vyatkina, N. (2015). New developments in the study of L2 writing complexity: An editorial. *Journal of Second Language Writing, 29*, 1–2.

Williams, J. (2012). The potential role(s) of writing in second language development. *Journal of Second Language Writing, 21*, 321–331.

Wolfe-Quintero, K., Inagaki, S., & Kim, H.-L. (1998). *Second language development in writing: Measures of fluency, accuracy, and complexity*. Honolulu, HI: University of Hawai'i, Second Language Teaching and Curriculum Center.

PART IV

Epilogue

13
EPILOGUE

Christine Pearson Casanave

Introduction

The motivation for this edited collection is clear: worldwide, populations of L2 and multilingual students who wish or need to learn to write in English for academic and professional purposes, from secondary to doctoral levels, are soaring. For better or for worse, English has become the global language of spoken and written international communication within disciplines and professions. Specialized writing of different kinds is central to the success of such students, given that some kind of writing is often the only or the main form of assessment. Some programs and instructors seem ready for this influx, and have well-developed support systems in place for students who need to learn more about the norms and discourses of academic English as they enter and then pursue specialized work in their subject-matter areas. Others have been caught off guard, either because the demand for English language support services and writing instruction has increased too rapidly for schools and universities to respond quickly, or because of underdeveloped perceptions and assumptions about what it means to learn the norms, values and specialized languages of the disciplines and the professions. Hence the need for this very practically oriented book on EAP practices in different parts of the world.

Specialized academic writing is an unusual and unfamiliar kind of literacy for novice writers, and does not come naturally to any of them, whether they are first or additional users of English. All the authors in this volume are therefore committed to some form of instruction rather than mere immersion in specialized academic discourses. Yes, many of us acquired the specialized discourses and values of academia without taking a single course in academic literacy practices, but given the burgeoning populations of L2 students, particularly in universities, it seems only just to assist students as best we can to find their way as efficiently as possible into the odd (yes, odd!) worlds of academic discourse practices.

However, no one can learn to write in a disciplinary (sub)field or a profession in a one-semester general or specialized writing course. No one can easily understand how to shape academic writing according to different genres without awareness and guidance and then ongoing practice for years, even if they are experts in content areas. No one can comprehend how to write from sources or learn how to avoid plagiarism just from a handout or a university anti-plagiarism policy statement, no matter how explicit the *rules* seem to be. Moreover, being a proficient test-taker of English on one of the major corporate sponsored tests of English does not guarantee that students will succeed in writing English for academic purposes in specific courses. Nor does being a native speaker of English guarantee such success. Learning to read and write in academia is simply too complex and too unlike other kinds of more commonplace literacy practices. Additionally, being a native user of English, or having a graduate degree in education or TESOL or applied linguistics does not automatically equip instructors to teach academic writing, or any kind of writing for that matter. Successful EAP writing teachers have studied about writing, language and genre, and, one would hope, have themselves written academic works in their first or additional languages. Finally, institutions and programs cannot design effective support systems without the help and leadership of faculty and administrators who understand the challenges of academic writing for secondary, undergraduate and graduate students and for writers in the professions. Let's hope that some of those in leadership positions will read this book.

Unlike the approaches to EAP writing that characterize textbooks such as Swales and Feak (2012) and Hyland (2016a), *Learning to Write for Academic Purposes* features detailed descriptions and cases from the authors' own settings and experiences in different geographical areas of the world. A message throughout this book is that in the world of EAP, all academic writing is characterized by various kinds of specific purposes and practices, and so cannot be taught outside the particular contexts in which it will be used. So the authors tell us the following: this is how we do things at my university or in my department or in my classes. We teach academic writing these ways, for these kinds of students, and follow particular instructional approaches for theoretical and practical reasons that we can articulate. Importantly, we have all had many years of experience learning how to do this, monitoring our own practices, shifting and adjusting as needed according to what seems to benefit particular populations of students, many of whom are multilingual emerging writers. The growing numbers of students we serve deserve the best we have to offer from a strong knowledge base of theory and practice. These stances are reflected throughout the chapters in this book, and await perceptive readers to connect the insights and strategies to their own settings. In what follows, I comment on some of the themes and issues that struck me as I read the chapters. The themes cut across and through the themes that are reflected in the different sections of the book rather than following the thematic choices of the editors. I conclude the chapter with some thoughts about directions that EAP pedagogy and research might take in the future.

Thematic Reflections

Explicit Instruction to Fit Local Needs

A message in all the chapters in this book is that EAP instruction for novice L2 writers benefits from being explicit and systematic, and designed to fit local contexts where needs and knowledge are both *situated* and *distributed*, as has been explained in some of the literature on education, learning and literacies (e.g., Barton, Hamilton, & Ivanič, 2000; Brown, Collins, & Duguid, 1989; Kirshner & Whitson, 1997; Lave & Wenger, 1991; Simpson & Matsuda, 2008; Zhang & Patel, 2006). Explicit instruction is described by many authors as needed by students at all levels who are new to academic values and practices in order to understand and then meet the language-related expectations of the writing and speaking that characterizes their particular fields, departments and courses.

At the secondary school level, explicit instruction in a science course in Australia, as described by Hammond, helps young students move from informal conversation about science concepts, to *literate talk*, and then to written language. Her sequence of tasks also serves as explicit instruction for teachers who might not yet be familiar with ways to embed literate concepts into teaching and learning activities. Explicit instruction not only benefits younger students. Undergraduate students too can be alerted to the specific uses of academic discourses in the disciplines through explicit instruction in features of different kinds of academic discourse, such as those that have been widely studied by Hyland. These include features such as nominalizations, impersonal stances, styles of citation and use of metadiscourse, and the specifics of their use that differ by discipline. Hyland describes how important it is in a university that has EAP courses for there to be a smooth and cooperative working relationship with faculty in the disciplines so that the very local and explicit needs of students in their subject matter courses align with their EAP instruction. Establishing this cooperation can be tricky given the widespread lack of interest by some subject matter faculty in writing instruction and the equally widespread belief that the writing teacher (writing program, writing center) should take care of fixing students' writing problems. This unfortunate view disregards the kinds of specificity by discipline, genre and local expectations and requirements that students need to learn. In his chapter, Paltridge gives examples from three different courses of the explicit instruction he offers to undergraduates, master's students and doctoral dissertation writers at his university in Australia. These courses feature focused reflection on specific academic literacy practices through explicit analyses of published work, interviews with local disciplinary faculty, and considerations of reader/writer roles, author purposes, underlying values in discipline-specific writing and specific uses of language suited to the needs of students at his university.

We might expect such explicit instruction at the high school and undergraduate levels. However, as Bitchener points out and Paltridge also demonstrates, we cannot assume that doctoral students understand the particular demands of writing a thesis or dissertation, particularly the more intellectually challenging part-genres such as the arguments needed in a dissertation literature review. Expectations in Bitchener's local context for well-articulated arguments and logical reasoning in this part-genre will sound familiar to anyone who has written, or helped others to write, a conventional Western-oriented doctoral dissertation. Epistemological values in this part-genre are particular to a Western *scientific* way of thinking that novice L2 graduate students, and even L1 students, might not understand well. Explicit, scaffolded instruction can guide students, we hope, more efficiently and less painlessly into this very high stakes writing project than would otherwise be the case. In all these cases of explicit instruction, it works best if it is aligned closely with what students and instructors need in a specific curriculum or class.

Steps, Stages, Sequences and Trajectories

Several of the chapters in this book feature discussions of the steps, stages and sequences of explicit instructional procedures in undergraduate and graduate EAP classes, or of the trajectories that EAP students follow as they develop proficiency and expertise. A step- or stage-like sequence of instructional tasks and student development assumes that students follow a more or less linear progression of increasing proficiency over time in language and content knowledge. Even if debatable, this idea is very compelling, and the clarity it provides to how we approach instruction and understand student change solves many of the otherwise messy issues of what it means to learn something as complex as academic literacy. In his historical look at the development of EAP writing support at his university, Silva, for example, describes a multidisciplinary course for first-year composition in which a carefully thought out sequence of assignments begins with a writer's autobiography, and moves through a proposal, a synthesis paper, an interview task and an argumentative essay, all accompanied by readings students must do. Teachers are left to carry out the sequence as they see fit, but the sequence remains. Bitchener presents a seven-stage scaffolded approach to teaching students to construct an argument in their dissertation literature review, an approach that can be applied to other part-genres in academic writing. The steps consist of selecting appropriate sources, identifying the focuses of the sources and grouping them under key headings, working out the relationships of ideas in the literature that has been selected such as by means of headings and subheadings as in an outline, and writing an overview and then a complete argument in sections or as a whole text.

In her contribution, Wette focuses on the challenge that all students have of learning to write from sources, and proposes a trajectory of skill development, from most novice to fully proficient. All of us will recognize these stages of development, but Wette's chapter contributes greatly to the practical focus of this book by specifying tasks and activities that can be used with students at each stage. Stages of instruction in source use reveal how complex the skill of writing from sources is; teachers who read Wette's lists of everything that students and teachers need to be aware of at each stage might be overwhelmed. But the lists realistically cover what it is that expert writers have learned over years of practice of writing from sources and lay out for instructors' specific skills that can be taught and practiced. Novices need to begin to learn to select sources, but then will probably copy or paraphrase inadequately, with little control of citation conventions. Students at subsequent stages become better at selecting sources and at evaluating them, and improve their ability to paraphrase, summarize and cite even though there is still excessive use of quoted or copied material. Proficient students can integrate source material with their own writing, cite multiple sources appropriately and develop a sense of identity as a confident author with ideas to contribute to disciplinary conversations. Another kind of sequencing concerns mode. At the secondary level, Hammond describes a *mode continuum*, from oral to literate use of language, in which at the early oral stages, young students use language to accompany actions, such as in a science class experiment, and at later stages use written language for reflection and explanation. In short, sequences and stages concern how EAP educators perceive student development and so influence the tasks and activities they assign.

EAP Tasks, Activities and Projects

Although *Learning to Write for Academic Purposes* is not a how-to textbook with instruction and exercises for students in the style of the Swales and Feak publications for graduate students (e.g., 2012), some chapters provide practical and detailed descriptions of tasks and projects that the authors have used successfully with their EAP students. EAP instructors can thus get a clear sense of the kinds of activities that might be used with different kinds of L2 students who are novices to the oddities, conventions and expectations of EAP writing. The detail—specific and localized to the authors' own contexts—allows readers in other contexts to make connections and adapt as needed to their own settings and for their own purposes. One of the advantages of these descriptions is that the activities generally form networks or systems of tasks rather than consisting of isolated exercises. In conjunction with approaches that focus on sequences and trajectories, the tasks, activities and projects take on a holistic sense of purpose that allow us to envision what might happen during an entire term in the EAP class. Wette's chapter is a good example of this—she has specific examples of skills and tasks that can be addressed at the four ability levels she has identified for students who are learning to write from sources. Paltridge's descriptions of tasks he uses in his three courses at different levels (undergraduate, master's, doctoral) also show how systematic activities support a trajectory of EAP development.

Tasks and activities in discipline-specific EAP classes in the university, such as the EAP course for Clinical Pharmacy described by Hyland, are best designed in collaboration with disciplinary faculty, if such cooperative relationships can be established. Initial tasks in such a course help pairs of students acquire the drug information and related genres they will need, such as learning medical vocabulary and citation conventions, practicing ways to synthesize drug information and responding to questions about different drugs from stakeholders. A second set of tasks asks students to prepare a comparative drug evaluation using appropriate sources for a report in a hospital bulletin, with feedback from Pharmacy and English instructors. Hammond, too, in her description of sequences of tasks used in a Year 6 Science class, shows how activities work together to help students successfully complete a project that is discipline specific and carried out over time.

As is the case in Hammond's science class, collaboration features prominently in other kinds of tasks as well, as is common in EAP classes, through student group work. Designing collaborative group work is more difficult than it might seem. A challenge to novice EAP instructors is to first structure groups in ways that will ensure cooperation among students as they work on projects that aim to improve language development or to feed into other academic classes or into the work place. This is a topic that Storch covers in some detail. Her set of tasks aims to help teachers design activities that will suit particular kinds of students with particular goals. Choice and timing of tasks comes first—will tasks focus on language or meaning and how successful are such tasks likely to be when students are working together? Second, teachers need to decide how to group students—by number of students, language group, language proficiency, dominant or passive personalities and so on. Third, teachers need to decide how to assess students who work together in groups—will there be a group grade and/or individual grades?

Other kinds of tasks and activities aim to provide L2 students with specific lexico-grammatical resources they might need for academic and professional purposes. As is evident in the research reviewed by Manchón, writing for the purpose of language learning has become a growing interest in the EAP field. Ferris, for example, asks teachers to use sets of practical strategies for choosing how and what to teach, such as using authentic content, selecting samples of vocabulary and syntax from it, helping students develop metalinguistic awareness and teaching students how to analyze writing samples by means of rubrics and questionnaires. Mini-lessons on various language features help students discover specific features in writing samples, practice them in their own writing and organize and further their understandings by means of charts and questionnaires. Ferris's activities above all help students develop language learning strategies from reading and writing that they can eventually use on their own.

What all of these chapters embody is a fundamental principle of effective EAP instruction: tasks, activities and projects need to fit particular purposes and disciplinary contexts, be built up and practiced over time and avoid being presented as isolated exercises.

Challenges Facing Teachers

Usually when we think about work in EAP, we consider what students need to learn and how they might best learn it. I found it refreshing to read the two chapters in this volume that concentrated on the challenges faced by *teachers* who are charged with teaching academic writing. The implications for writing teacher education are significant. The challenges the authors discuss are quite different but widespread throughout the world, documented here for a case in the United States (Tardy) and one in Hong Kong (Lee). They involve L2 writing teachers' knowledge (or lack of knowledge) of how to teach the genres their students might need to use outside their writing classes in a US university, and the sometimes inhuman workload of some teachers of English in Hong Kong (and elsewhere) who are expected to correct all the errors on the writing of possibly hundreds of students.

In the case of genre approaches, Tardy recounts the challenges confronting L2 writing teachers who are teaching first-year composition to undergraduates in a US university as part of their teaching assistantships or as part-timers who may be unsure what students' needs are outside the first-year writing class. The needs are quite staggering. The problem of the multiplicity of genres across the curriculum in undergraduate education was documented long ago as an especially fraught dilemma for writing teachers who wish to help students transfer newly acquired academic writing skills to subject matter courses (e.g., Herrington, 1985; McCarthy, 1987). The challenge remains today, inspiring educators like Tardy to recommend that pre-service teacher education programs help novice L1 and L2 writing teachers expand their knowledge of language, genre, genre theories, instructional tools and strategies for teaching genre, and ways to integrate specific forms and functions of language into genre-based writing activities. As Tardy discovered, analyzing genre for the purposes of teaching does not come easily or naturally to novice teachers. Both time and support must somehow be provided.

The secondary teachers in Hong Kong that Lee has worked with and documented in much of her work (e.g., Lee, 2003, 2008, 2011) are pressured by time and by expectations from institutions, departments, students and parents that writing teachers will correct all of the errors in students' writing. In spite of the ongoing debates about the value of error correction in improving students' grammar, beginning with Truscott's (1996) article claiming that correction does not help students improve grammar, teachers and students alike have not been able to let go of the deeply held belief that writing needs to be corrected in order to improve. Although she does not review the debate itself, Lee reviews some of the literature that supports a position she takes in her chapter, that selective and focused corrective feedback, rather than comprehensive feedback, might indeed help students improve new pieces of writing and preserve writing teachers' sanity. The problem is to convince teachers, students and administrators that such a selective approach to correction makes sense. Teachers are caught in the middle, between research that finds that correcting all errors on single draft writings is probably a waste of time that can only lead to burnout, and pressures and intuitions from schools and students themselves to correct every error. A *smart* approach, Lee believes, would have teachers judiciously assessing what students need (not just what they want), what kinds of errors might be more serious than others as well as treatable, and what teachers themselves can manage given their workloads.

I was struck in both of these chapters about writing teachers that solutions to some of the challenges facing them require convincing less-invested others that change of some kind is needed, justified and logistically possible. Just as it is difficult for writing specialists to convince disciplinary faculty to work closely with them (as pointed out in Hyland's chapter), so it is difficult to convince departments, curriculum designers, teacher education programs and administrators to support the kinds of research-based practices that EAP writing instructors need to best do their jobs.

Future Directions

In her final chapter in this volume, Manchón reviews research that has been done and that can be done in the future on the connections between language learning and learning to write. Like the other chapters, the focus of this chapter is on the language needs and language development of students who need EAP support. Certainly language concerns are central to the work of EAP specialists, and this volume covers a wide range of these concerns. Nevertheless, in the concluding section of my chapter I hope to focus on other areas that are less frequently covered by EAP scholars in the hope that future work can broaden the discussions about EAP pedagogy and scholarship. I discuss the need for more attention to topic knowledge, to transfer and follow-up studies of students from their EAP classes to other contexts, and to the tensions between convention and risk, and to the need for more reflections by EAP scholars—L1 and L2, and novice and expert—on their own experiences learning EAP. It is possible that some readers will find that these concerns move beyond EAP. However, EAP specialists will benefit from visions of how their work can move beyond the narrow linguistic preoccupations of applied linguistics.

Topic Knowledge

Fundamental to successful EAP writing is writers' control of their content knowledge. As anyone who has tried to write anything knows, it is quite impossible to write well or fluently or effectively if we do not know much about our topics. In EAP, topics go beyond the infamous personal narratives of yore and by definition deal with subject matter in academic settings. This dilemma has not been fully explored in EAP scholarship, and in fact is rarely mentioned. Both pedagogical and research-oriented literature and guidebooks usually assume that a topic is already there, waiting to be written about, and so begin with the language, discourse and rhetorical structures that might be needed in academic and professional contexts. Many studies, including some of those in this book, ask students to read and analyze authentic material in their fields, but most often as a way to mine a reading for its specialized uses of language and its ways of organizing the presentation of ideas and knowledge. How can EAP contribute more effectively to pedagogy and research that explores what is involved in developing, organizing and expanding topic knowledge before or in conjunction with writing instruction? Novice L1 and L2 writers at all levels, and experienced scholars and writers as well, are continuously learning the subject matter and associated values of their fields and developing a sense of the networks of scholars who contribute to their interests. EAP pedagogy is incomplete if we don't address writers' development of topic knowledge as a fundamental precursor to knowing how and what to write, particularly at postgraduate levels (Casanave, 2014).

Transfer

If EAP instruction is provided to students in collaborative courses with subject matter classes and faculty, as some of the chapters in the volume have described and recommended, perhaps the issue of transfer from a reading-writing class to other classes is not so relevant. However, my sense is that much EAP pedagogy is still practiced in writing classes designed either from general principles of academic writing or from local needs analysis within a school or university, apart from collaborations with subject matter faculty. Once EAP students escape from our clutches in a writing class, we cannot be certain what happens in their other academic work or in their professional workplaces without careful follow-up studies. Ideally such studies would be longitudinal and qualitative so that the details of transfer, change and development would become clear. Some studies from the past found that students sometimes did not do much writing at all in their subject matter classes, or that what they learned in their EAP-ESL classes was only marginally relevant to what they needed elsewhere (see, for example, Leki, 2007; Leki & Carson, 1994, 1997). Likewise, more cross-disciplinary collaborations of the type described by Hyland would help EAP specialists expand their knowledge of writing in the disciplines and the efficacy, or not, of transfer (see also the edited volume by Deane & O'Neill, 2011). Collaborative discussions are needed if for no other reason than to have subject matter faculty share their views of the roles of writing and transfer of writing skills with writing specialists.

As Zhu (2004) found, views differ widely, with some faculty holding that general writing skills can be transferred to their subject matter classes, and others that writing skills and instruction need to be discipline and subject matter specific. Such differences reveal that subject matter faculty and writing specialists are likely to view their responsibilities differently. A central question that remains only partially answered for EAP scholars is whether writing instruction outside a subject matter course really matters.

Convention, Agency and Risk

Implicit in much of the EAP literature, particularly that with a pedagogical intent, is the need for novice students and scholars to become familiar with the expectations of their academic audiences, the forms and functions of its conventional texts and genres, and the stances that particular academic audiences expect from authors. In following conventions, novice authors, both L1 and especially L2, presumably can benefit from an efficient and comprehensible route to success in contexts where trial and error or excessive creativity could work against them. I think it is not an exaggeration to say that the entire EAP enterprise is based on an ethic of helping novice writers succeed at what they need to do in academic contexts. To this end, EAP scholars identify as best they can the rhetorical and grammatical structures, styles and stances, lexical items, and source-use conventions typical of the genres in different fields and workplaces and convert those features into samples, lessons and guidebooks. As has been pointed out by scholars of genre and disciplinary and academic discourse (e.g., Hyland, 2000, 2004, 2009; Paltridge, 1997; Paltridge & Starfield, 2007, 2016; Swales, 1990, 2004; Tardy, 2009), conventions do not necessarily have to restrain the agency of writers in the way a static template would. Rather, they allow novice writers to participate in academic communities where, once in, they can begin to add their voices as agents of their own ideas. Agency, in this view, comes within the frameworks provided by convention. Pragmatically, then, as Manchón concludes in her chapter in this book, it might not be wise to ask novice L2 writers to challenge or resist the hegemonic discourses they are trying to acquire.

This push to follow convention is not a dilemma for EAP educators who see their job as one of helping students fit into existing discourses and meet expectations so as not to create obstacles for students. However, future pedagogy and scholarship in EAP will increasingly need to consider what the role is of challenging, resisting and innovating in response to conventional academic discourses, i.e., the role of *risk* in academic writing (Thesen & Cooper, 2014), and how or whether to move beyond the hegemony of established genre conventions (Tardy, 2016). Increasing numbers of educators, particularly those who reside outside the *center* or are sympathetic with peripheral scholarship (Braine, 2003; Canagarajah, 1999, 2002, 2003; Thesen, 2014) wish to help themselves and their students escape the dominance of traditional Anglophone approaches to scholarship. As the authors in the Thesen and Cooper volume document, local knowledge, values and discourse forms and styles are lost when *northern* scientific conventions dominate academic writing. But the dangers of resisting are many and the journey of resistance can be long and stressful (Cadman, 2014); and even the most passionate of resisters would not want to risk the success of their students. Change, it seems, must come from the top, not from students. All EAP educators therefore need to ask: What is EAP supposed to be doing? How can it achieve its goals without causing harm to novice scholars but still help them develop agency and voice? How can it describe not only what has been done and what is being done, but also what might be done?

Reflections by EAP Scholars

Finally, novice EAP writers and writing instructors would benefit from knowing more about how established EAP scholars found their own ways into academic writing in their disciplines and how emerging L2 writing scholars are doing the same. I wondered as I read these chapters by mainly white scholars under the influence of Anglophone traditions of scholarly writing whether and how they struggled to get where they are today. Studies would be equally interesting by L2 scholars on how they manage to learn to situate themselves and their writing in acceptable ways within their fields. In both cases, more autoethnographic or autobiographical writing is called for (e.g., Canagarajah, 2012) that goes *beyond convention* (Tardy, 2016), as I mentioned in the previous section. Stereotypes persist that native English speakers do not have the difficulties with high level academic writing such as writing for publication that L2 speakers do, a stance that Hyland (2016b) and I (Casanave, 2008) contest. Some difficulties may differ, but others confront all of us. Academic writing is no one's first language.

Of course, writing such potentially confessional pieces may cause discomfort for some established scholars, but perhaps especially for emerging scholars, who need to build and maintain an aura of expertise. Still, I believe all of us would benefit from such reflections—students, scholars and instructors of EAP writing alike. I am convinced that we would come to appreciate more than we do now the very individual pathways we all take to becoming accomplished EAP writers. With such evidence, we can go back to our EAP pedagogy and ask how controlled and conforming it needs to be and how much innovation and risk educators and their students can safely undertake. If paths to expertise vary greatly by individuals, how do we take such variability into account as we design tasks, activities and projects in our EAP classes? And as experts, how do established EAP educators help themselves, their colleagues and their students decide whether risks are worthwhile? There is a lot to think about in future EAP work.

References

Barton, D., Hamilton, M., & Ivanič, R. (Eds.). (2000). *Situated literacies: Reading and writing in context.* London: Routledge.

Braine, G. (2003). Negotiating the gatekeepers: The journey of an academic article. In C. P. Casanave & S. Vandrick (Eds.), *Writing for scholarly publication: Behind the scenes in language education* (pp. 73–90). Mahwah, NJ: Lawrence Erlbaum Associates.

Brown, J. S., Collins, A., & Duguid, P. (1989). Situated cognition and the culture of learning. *Educational Researcher, 18*(1), 32–42.

Cadman, K. (2014). Of house and home: Reflections on writing and knowing for a "Southern" postgraduate pedagogy. In L. Thesen & L. Cooper (Eds.), *Risk in academic writing: Postgraduate students, their teachers and the making of knowledge* (pp. 166–200). Bristol, UK: Multilingual Matters.

Canagarajah, A. S. (1999). *Resisting linguistic imperialism in English teaching.* Oxford, UK: Oxford University Press.

Canagarajah, A. S. (2002). *A geopolitics of academic writing.* Pittsburgh: University of Pittsburgh Press.

Canagarajah, A. S. (2003). A somewhat legitimate and very peripheral participation. In C. P. Casanave & S. Vandrick (Eds.). *Writing for scholarly publication: Behind the scenes in language education* (pp. 197–210). Mahwah, NJ: Lawrence Erlbaum Associates.

Canagarajah, A. S. (2012). Autoethnography in the study of multilingual writers. In L. Nickoson & M. P. Sheridan (Eds.), *Writing studies research in practice: Methods and methodologies* (pp. 113–124). Carbondale, IL: Southern Illinois University Press.

Casanave, C. P. (2008). The stigmatizing effect of Goffman's stigma label: A response to John Flowerdew. *Journal of English for Academic Purposes*, 7(4), 264–267.

Casanave, C. P. (2014). *Before the dissertation: A textual mentor for doctoral students at early stages of a research project.* Ann Arbor: University of Michigan Press.

Deane, M., & O'Neill, P. (Eds.). (2011). *Writing in the disciplines.* New York: Palgrave Macmillan.

Herrington, A. (1985). Writing in academic settings: A study of the contexts for writing in two college chemical engineering courses. *Research in the Teaching of English, 19*, 331–361.

Hyland, K. (2000). *Disciplinary discourses: Social interactions in academic writing.* London: Longman.

Hyland, K. (2004). *Genre and second language writing.* Ann Arbor: University of Michigan Press.

Hyland, K. (2009). *Academic discourse.* London: Continuum.

Hyland, K. (2016a). *Teaching and researching writing* (3rd ed.). New York: Routledge.

Hyland, K. (2016b). Academic publishing and the myth of linguistic injustice. *Journal of Second Language Writing, 31*, 58–69.

Kirshner, D., & Whitson, J. A. (Eds.). (1997). *Situated cognition: Social, semiotic, and psychological perspectives.* Mahwah, NJ: Lawrence Erlbaum Associates.

Lave, J., & Wenger, E. (1991). *Situated learning: Legitimate peripheral participation.* Cambridge, England: Cambridge University Press.

Lee, I. (2003). L2 writing teachers' perspectives, practices and problems regarding error feedback. *Assessing Writing, 8*, 216–237.

Lee, I. (2008). Understanding teachers' feedback practices in Hong Kong secondary classrooms. *Journal of Second Language Writing, 17*(1), 69–85.

Lee, I. (2011). Working smarter, not working harder: Revisiting teacher feedback in the L2 writing classroom. *The Canadian Modern Language Review, 67*(3), 377–399.

Leki, I. (2007). *Undergraduates in a second language: Challenges and complexities of academic literacy development*. Mahwah, NJ: Lawrence Erlbaum Associates.

Leki, I., & Carson, J. G. (1994). Students' perceptions of EAP writing instruction and writing needs across the disciplines. *TESOL Quarterly, 29*(1), 81–101.

Leki, I., & Carson, J. (1997). "Completely different worlds": EAP and the writing experiences of ESL students in university courses. *TESOL Quarterly, 31*, 39–69.

McCarthy, L. P. (1987). A stranger in strange lands: A college student writing across the curriculum. *Research in the Teaching of English, 21*, 233–265.

Paltridge, B. (1997). *Genre, frames, and writing in research settings*. Amsterdam: John Benjamins.

Paltridge, B., & Starfield, S. (2007). *Thesis and dissertation writing in a second language: A handbook for supervisors*. New York: Routledge.

Paltridge, B., & Starfield, S. (2016). *Getting published in academic journals: Navigating the publication process*. Ann Arbor: University of Michigan Press.

Simpson, S., & Matsuda, P. K. (2008). Mentoring as a long-term relationship: Situated learning in a doctoral program. In C. P. Casanave & X. Li (Eds.), *Learning the literacy practices of graduate school: Insiders' reflections on academic enculturation* (pp. 90–104). Ann Arbor: University of Michigan Press.

Swales, J. M. (1990). *Genre analysis: English in academic and research settings*. New York: Cambridge University Press.

Swales, J. M. (2004). *Research genres: Explorations and applications*. Cambridge: Cambridge University Press.

Swales, J. M., & Feak, C. B. (2012). *Academic writing for graduate students: Essential tasks and skills* (3rd ed.). Ann Arbor: University of Michigan Press.

Tardy, C. (2009). *Building genre knowledge*. West Lafayette, IN: Parlor Press.

Tardy, C. M. (2016). *Beyond convention: Genre innovation in academic writing*. Ann Arbor: University of Michigan Press.

Thesen, L. (2014). Risk as productive: Working with dilemmas in the writing of research. In L. Thesen & L. Cooper (Eds.), *Risk in academic writing: Postgraduate students, their teachers and the making of knowledge* (pp. 1–24). Bristol, UK: Multilingual Matters.

Thesen, L., & Cooper, L. (Eds.). (2014). *Risk in academic writing: Postgraduate students, their teachers and the making of knowledge*. Bristol, UK: Multilingual Matters.

Truscott, J. (1996). The case against grammar correction in L2 writing classes. *Language Learning, 46*, 327–369.

Zhang, J., & Patel, V. L. (2006). Distributed cognition, representation, and affordance. *Pragmatics and Cognition, 14*(2), 333–341.

Zhu, W. (2004). Faculty views on the importance of writing, the nature of academic writing, and teaching and responding to writing in the disciplines. *Journal of Second Language Writing, 13*(1), 29–48.

INDEX